PROPERTY

STEVEN L. EMANUEL

Harvard Law School
J.D. 1976

The CrunchTime Series

Aspen Law & Business
A Division of Aspen Publishers, Inc.
New York   Gaithersburg

About Aspen Law & Business
Legal Education Division

Aspen Law & Business is proud to welcome Emanuel Publishing Corporation's highly successful study aids to its list of law school publications. As part of the Aspen family, Steve and Lazar Emanuel will continue their work on these popular titles, widely purchased by students for more than a quarter century. With the addition of the Emanuel titles, Aspen now offers the most comprehensive selection of outstanding publications for the discerning law student.

ASPEN LAW & BUSINESS
A Division of Aspen Publishers, Inc.
A Wolters Kluwer Company
www.aspenpublishers.com

SUMMARY OF CONTENTS

TABLE OF CONTENTS

Preface

Thank you for buying this book.

The *CrunchTime* Series is intended for people who want Emanuel quality, but don't have the time or money to buy and use the full-length *Emanuel Law Outline* on a subject. We've designed the Series to be used in the last few weeks (or even less) before your final exams.

This book includes the following features, most of which have been extracted from the corresponding *Emanuel Law Outline*:

- *Flow Charts* — We've reduced many of the principles of *Property* to a series of 6 Flow Charts, created specially for this book and never published elsewhere. We think these will be especially useful on open-book exams. The Flow Charts begin on p. 1.

- *Capsule Summary* — This is a 70-page or so summary of the subject. We've carefully crafted it to cover the things you're most likely to be asked on an exam. The Capsule Summary starts on p. 25.

- *Exam Tips* — We've compiled these by reviewing dozens of actual past essay and multiple-choice questions asked in past law-school and bar exams, and extracting the issues and "tricks" that surface most often on exams. The Exam Tips start on p. 103.

- *Short-Answer* questions — These questions are generally in a Yes/No format, with a "mini-essay" explaining each one. The questions start on p. 155.

- *Multiple-Choice* questions — These are in a Multistate-Bar-Exam style, and were adapted from a book we publish called *The Finz Multistate Method*. They start on p. 199.

- *Essay* questions — These questions are actual ones asked on law school or bar exams. They start on p. 223.

We hope you find this book helpful and instructive.

Good luck.

Steve Emanuel,
Larchmont NY
November, 2001

FLOW CHARTS

TABLE OF CONTENTS
to
FLOW CHARTS

Fig.

Figure 1
Adverse Possession

Use this chart to determine whether "A", the potential adverse possessor, has acquired title to Blackacre by adverse possession from "O," the record owner.

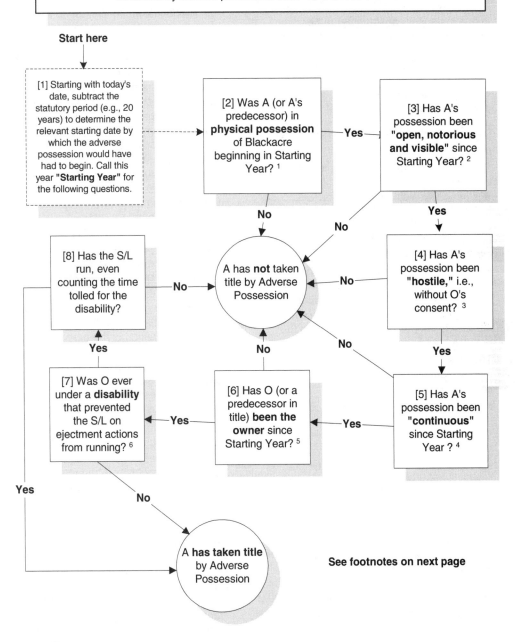

See footnotes on next page

Notes to
Figure 1 (Adverse Possession)

[1] Courts often say that the possession must be "actual." Most important: At least a reasonable percentage of the land claimed by the adverse possessor must be actually used.

In one instance "constructive" rather than "actual" possession will suffice: If A is record owner of an adjacent parcel and is confused about the boundaries (so that A believes he owns a strip that's actually owned of record by O), A's actual ownership of the adjacent piece plus "constructive" ownership of O's strip will suffice -- here, A just needs to show that he regarded the strip as his own (e.g., he fenced it in.)

[2] The idea is that A must behave in such a way towards the property that O would realize that A is asserting a claim. If O has actual notice of A's claim, that's enough. If O does not have actual notice, then the question is whether A's use is similar to that which a typical owner of similar property would make.

Example: In rural areas, A's building of a fence around the property would probably suffice, since that's all that many actual owners do. But in a suburb or city, probably more (e.g., actually spending time on the property, or improving it) would be required.

[3] The idea is that A's possession must be inconsistent with O's rights, and without O's consent.

Most important: If A is O's tenant, A's possession is not hostile, unless A repudiates the lease and says he's claiming ownership.

If A claims under a grant of title from someone other than O -- even if the grant is invalid -- that's enough to meet the hostility requirement. For instance, in the case of a boundary dispute, if A honestly but mistakenly believes that he has received title to a "strip" that really belongs to adjacent owner O, A meets the "hostile possession" requirement.

[4] For "seasonal" property, the continuity-of-possession requirement is met as long as A makes the same seasonal use each year that a real owner would be likely to make.

Example: A claims title by adverse possession to a summer house in the mountains. If A shows that he used the house every summer during the statutory period, this will suffice for the continuity requirement.

Keep in mind that on the adverse side, "tacking" is allowed for purposes of the continuity requirement -- as long as A and A's "predecessors in title," so to speak, have occupied for the whole period, that's enough.

Example: A1 owns Whiteacre, adjacent to Blackacre, owned by O. Due to a mistake in A1's deed, A1 thinks that he owns a 20-foot-wide strip between the two parcels that really belongs to O. A1 holds for 10 years. A1 then sells to A2, with a deed that (falsely) recites that the strip is part of Whiteacre. A2 holds for 10 more years. Assuming a 20-year statutory period, A2 now owns the strip (assuming the other requirements like "open, notorious" are met) -- his 10 years get "tacked" to A1's 10 years.

[5] There is in effect "tacking" on the owner's side as well -- so an owner's time to sue can be used up by possession that was adverse to the prior owner.

Example: O1 owns Blackacre beginning in 1980, the same time that A comes into hostile possession of the property. O1 sells to O2 in 1990. Assuming a 20-year period, A owns the property in 2000, because O2 is charged with the time A possessed hostilely to O2's predecessor in title (O1) just as with the time A possessed hostilely to O2.

[6] Infancy is the most common disability you should look out for.

Example: O receives a bequest of Blackacre in 1970, when O is 10. Assume that the statute treats people under 21 as having a disability for purposes of ejectment actions. A enters hostilely in 1970. Assume a 20-year statute, with a typical disability provision. In 1990, A doesn't own the property yet, because the time O was under 21 does not count towards the 20 years. (But O probably faces a time limit [e.g., 10 years after turning 21], and loses his right to regain the property -- and A takes by adverse possession -- once that time limit passes.)

Figure 2
Freehold Estates

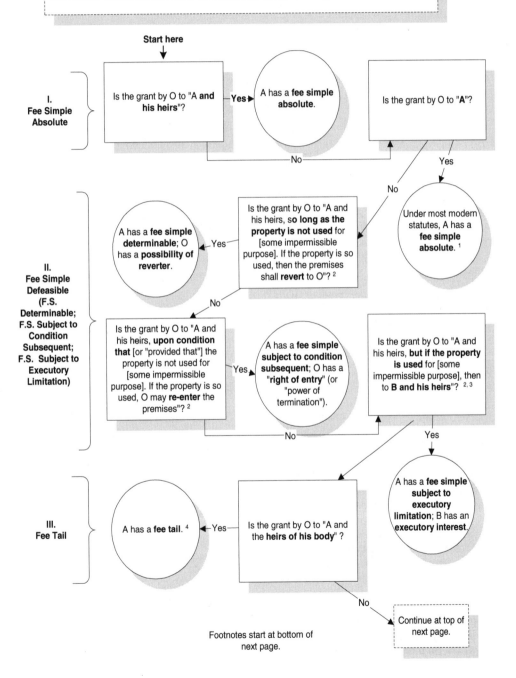

Use this chart to determine what freehold estate is created by particular words of grant. O is the conveyor; A is the recipient of the grant. Where a future interest is also created, B is the recipient of that interest. Unless otherwise noted, the common-law treatment of the grant is all that is discussed.

Start here

I. Fee Simple Absolute

Is the grant by O to "A **and his heirs**"? —Yes▶ A has a **fee simple absolute**.

—No—

Is the grant by O to "**A**"?

Yes / No

Under most modern statutes, A has a **fee simple absolute**. [1]

II. Fee Simple Defeasible (F.S. Determinable; F.S. Subject to Condition Subsequent; F.S. Subject to Executory Limitation)

A has a **fee simple determinable**; O has a **possibility of reverter**. —Yes— Is the grant by O to "A and his heirs, **so long as the property is not used** for [some impermissible purpose]. If the property is so used, then the premises shall **revert** to O"? [2]

—No—

Is the grant by O to "A and his heirs, **upon condition that** [or "provided that"] the property is not used for [some impermissible purpose]. If the property is so used, O may **re-enter** the premises"? [2] —Yes▶ A has a **fee simple subject to condition subsequent**; O has a "**right of entry**" (or "power of termination").

—No—

Is the grant by O to "A and his heirs, **but if the property is used** for [some impermissible purpose], then to **B and his heirs**"? [2, 3]

Yes

A has a **fee simple subject to executory limitation**; B has an **executory interest**.

III. Fee Tail

A has a **fee tail**. [4] —Yes— Is the grant by O to "A and the **heirs of his body**"?

—No—

Footnotes start at bottom of next page.

Continue at top of next page.

Figure 2 (cont.)
Freehold Estates (p. 2)

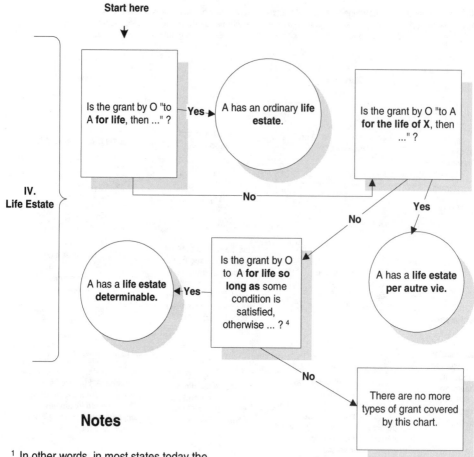

Notes

[1] In other words, in most states today the language "to A and his heirs" is not necessary for creating a fee simple absolute -- a plain old "to A" suffices.

[2] When you deal with any kind of fee simple defeasible (i.e., a fee simple that is not absolute and can therefore end), your main job is to distinguish between the fee simple determinable (f.s.d.) and the fee simple subject to condition subsequent (f.s.s.c.s.). The distinction is that the f.s.d. ends automatically on the happening of the stated event, and the f.s.s.c.s. only ends upon both the happening of the event and some affirmative action by the holder of the reversionary interest (i.e., a suit or an attempt to re-take the premises). If in doubt, resolve ambiguity in favor of f.s.s.c.s., since courts try to avoid forfeitures.

Example 1 (fee simple determinable): Grant by O "to A, so long as the premises continue to be used as a house of Islamic worship. If the property ceases to be so used, it shall revert to O." (Note the use of "revert" [not "re-enter"], indicating that the change happens automatically.)

Example 2 (fee simple subject to condition subsequent): Grant by O "to A, upon condition that the property continues to be used as a house for Islamic worship. If the property ceases to be so used, O or his heirs may re-enter the premises." (Note that

Notes (cont.) to
Figure 2 (Freehold Estates)

the change happens only if O or his heirs affirmatively takes action to re-enter.)

3 Apart from "use" restrictions, a common fee simple subject to executory limitation involves A's "<u>death without issue</u>." Assuming (as is likely) that the court interprets this type of bequest to refer to A's death without <u>survivors</u> (not the running out of his line at some future time after his death with survivors), the bequest is a f.s. subject to executory limitation if the gift over is to some third person (not to O or O's heirs).

<u>Example</u>: O grants "to A and his heirs, but if A shall die without issue, then to B and his heirs." Because the court will probably interpret this to refer to a "definite failure of issue" (i.e., A's failure to die with survivors), the state of title is: A has a fee simple subject to executory limitation; B has an executory interest.

4 Keep in mind that states vary tremendously in how they treat a grant that would, at common law, create a fee tail. For instance, a slight majority of states convert the fee tail into a fee simple absolute.

5 Use the same rules of interpretation as for fees simple that may be determinable. Thus if the life estate is to be cut off automatically upon the happening of the stated event, it's a life estate determinable; if O's heirs have a right of reentry, it's a life estate subject to condition subsequent; and if title moves to a third person on the stated event, it's a life estate subject to executory limitation.

<u>Example</u>: O grants "to A, my wife, for life, but if A should re-marry, then to my son S." Title is: life estate in A subject to executory limitation; executory interest in S.

Figure 3
Future Interests

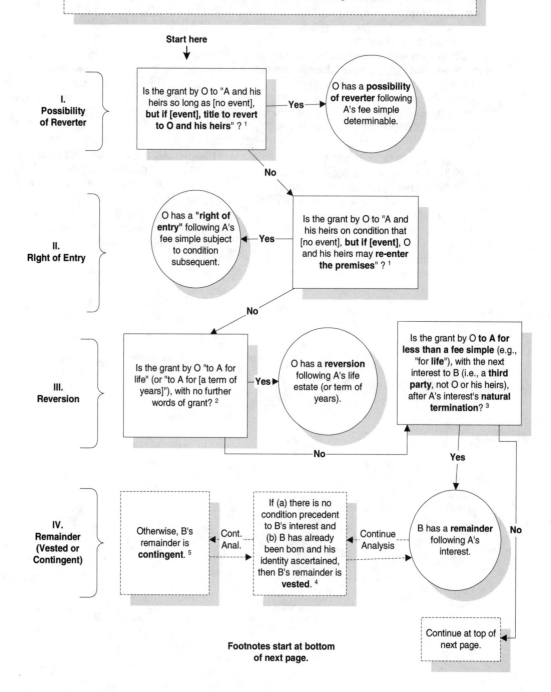

Use this chart to determine what future estate is created by particular words of grant. O is the conveyor; A is the recipient of freehold interest; B is the third-party recipient of the future interest, if any. Unless otherwise noted, the common-law treatment of the grant is all that is discussed.

Start here

I. Possibility of Reverter

Is the grant by O to "A and his heirs so long as [no event], **but if [event], title to revert to O and his heirs**" ? [1]

→ **Yes** → O has a **possibility of reverter** following A's fee simple determinable.

No

II. Right of Entry

Is the grant by O to "A and his heirs on condition that [no event], **but if [event], O and his heirs may re-enter the premises**" ? [1]

← **Yes** ← O has a **"right of entry"** following A's fee simple subject to condition subsequent.

No

III. Reversion

Is the grant by O "to A for life" (or "to A for [a term of years]"), with no further words of grant? [2]

→ **Yes** → O has a **reversion** following A's life estate (or term of years).

No

Is the grant by O **to A for less than a fee simple** (e.g., "for **life**"), with the next interest to B (i.e., a **third party**, not O or his heirs), after A's interest's **natural termination**? [3]

Yes ↓

No →

IV. Remainder (Vested or Contingent)

Otherwise, B's remainder is **contingent**. [5]

← **Cont. Anal.** ←

If (a) there is no condition precedent to B's interest and (b) B has already been born and his identity ascertained, then B's remainder is **vested**. [4]

← **Continue Analysis** ←

B has a **remainder** following A's interest.

Continue at top of next page.

Footnotes start at bottom of next page.

Figure 3 (cont.)
Future Interests (p. 2)

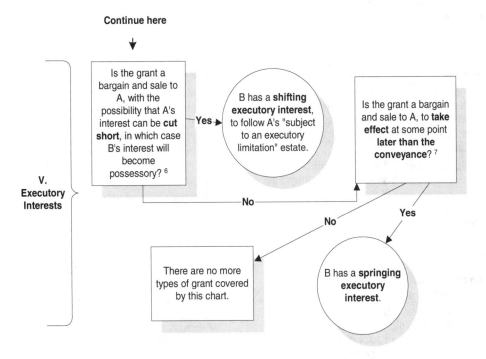

Notes

[1] Your main job is to <u>distinguish</u> between a <u>possibility of reverter</u> and a <u>right of entry</u>, since the two are quite similar. Both are reversionary interests -- that is, they vest in the original grantor and his heirs (O in our chart), not in some third person. The <u>possibility of reverter</u> follows a <u>fee simple determinable</u>. The <u>right of entry</u> follows a <u>fee simple subject to condition subsequent</u>. For examples of each, see note 1 to Figure 2 above.

[2] A <u>reversion</u> is the estate that's created when the holder of a vested estate (most often, a fee simple) <u>transfers to another a smaller estate</u>. The reversion is the interest which remains in the grantor.

Note that the grantor can create a reversion even if the grantor starts with a vested estate that's <u>less than a fee simple</u>. <u>Example</u>: O holds a fee tail. O conveys "to A for A's life." O has a reversion in fee tail.

[3] For a <u>remainder</u> to exist, <u>three requirements</u> must be satisfied: (1) a grantor (O) must <u>convey a present possessory estate</u> to one transferee (A); (2) the grantor (O) must <u>create a non-possessory estate in another transferee</u> (B) by the <u>same instrument</u>; and (C) the second, non-possessory estate must be capable of becoming possessory only on the <u>"natural" expiration</u> (as opposed to the cutting short) of the prior estate.

Notes (cont.) to
Figure 3 (Future Interests)

Example: O conveys "to A for life, then to B and his heirs." B has a remainder, because: (1) O conveyed a present possessory interest to A (the life estate); (2) by the same instrument O created a non-possessory estate in a third person (B); and (3) B's estate will automatically become possessory when A's estate naturally expires.

4 For there not to be a condition precedent, the remainder must become possessory "whenever and however the prior estate terminates."

Example: O conveys "to A for A's life, remainder to B and his heirs." Assuming that B is a named individual who is alive on the date of the conveyance, this is a vested remainder, because: (1) there's no condition precedent attached to B's interest (it will become possessory no matter how or when A's life interest ends); and (2) the person holding it, B, has already been born and is clearly identified in the instrument.

Note that there are 3 types of vested remainders: (1) remainders indefeasibly vested; (2) remainders subject to open; and (3) remainders subject to complete defeasance (including subject to divestment).

Example 1 (indefeasibly vested): Consider the above example, "to A for A's life, remainder to B and his heirs". This is "indefeasibly vested" because no matter what happens, B or his heirs are certain to have their interest become possessory eventually.

Example 2 (vested subject to open): This occurs when there is a gift to a class (usually the "children" of some named person) and one class member already exists and is identified, but others may be added later. Thus, O conveys "to A for life, remainder to B's children and their heirs." At the time of conveyance, B has only one child, C. At the moment of conveyance, the remainder is "vested subject to open" because we know C has part or all of the remainder, but if B has additional kids, the remainder will "open" to allow those additional kids to take. Once either A or B dies, the remainder will no longer be subject to open.

Example 3 (vested subject to divestment): O conveys "to A for life, then to B and his heirs, but if B dies without issue, then to C and his heirs." If B dies without issue while A is still alive, B's remainder is "divested" (cut short), in favor of C's executory interest.

5 All remainders that are not vested are contingent. So you are looking for a remainder where either: (1) there's a condition precedent to the interest's becoming possessory; or (2) the holder has either not yet come into existence or not yet been identified.

Example 1 (remainder that's contingent because of a condition precedent): O conveys "to A for life, then, if B is living at A's death, to B in fee simple." B must meet the condition of surviving A for his remainder to become possessory; therefore, the remainder is contingent.

Example 2 (remainder that's contingent because the holder is not yet in existence or identified): O conveys "to A for life, then to the children of B." At the time of conveyance, B has no children. (Once B has a child, the remainder becomes vested subject to open).

Note that a remainder that's contingent when it comes into existence can (and often does) later become vested. For instance, in Example 2 above, while B has no children the remainder is contingent, but once the first child is born, the remainder becomes vested (though subject to "open" in favor of later-born children).

Notice that a big job you'll have is to distinguish between a remainder that's vested subject to divestment and a remainder that's contingent because it's subject to a condition precedent. The distinction is solely linguistic, not substantive. Look for a separate clause that begins with "but if..." -- this signals a clause that divests, rather than a condition precedent, and thus indicates a vested remainder subject to divestment rather than a contingent remainder.

Notes (cont.) to
Figure 3 (Future Interests)

Example 1 (vested subject to divestment): O conveys "to A for life, remainder to B and his heirs, but if B dies before A, then to C and his heirs." The remainder to B is vested (because in the clause that creates it there's no condition precedent to its becoming possessory), and then the separate "but if" clause serves to divest -- cut short -- that remainder in favor of C.

Example 2 (contingent because of a condition precedent): O conveys "to A for life, then if B survives A, remainder to B and his heirs, otherwise to C and his heirs." This has exactly the same effect as Example 1, but the remainder to B is contingent because the thing that could prevent B's remainder from ever becoming possessory is contained in the same clause as the grant of the interest itself (i.e., there's no separate "but if" clause that cuts B's interest short).

[6] Example: O bargains and sells land "to A and his heirs, but if liquor is ever sold on the premises, then to B and his heirs." The "but if" clause cuts A's interest short. Since the estate then goes to a third person (i.e., not to O and his heirs), that third-party interest is called an executory interest, of the "shifting" variety.

[7] Example: O wants to reassure his prospective son-in-law A that if A marries O's daughter D A will get Blackacre. Therefore, O bargains and sells Blackacre "to A and his heirs from and after the date of A's marriage to D." This is an executory interest of the "springing" variety, since: (1) it benefits a third party (not the grantor), and (2) it will take effect at some point after the grant (i.e., seisin will "spring" out of O).

Figure 4
Rule Against Perpetuities

Use this chart to determine whether: (1) a particular interest is subject to the Rule Against Perpetuities (RAP); and (2) if it is, whether the interest is void for violation of the Rule. Unless otherwise noted, the chart assumes that the common-law version of the RAP is in force.

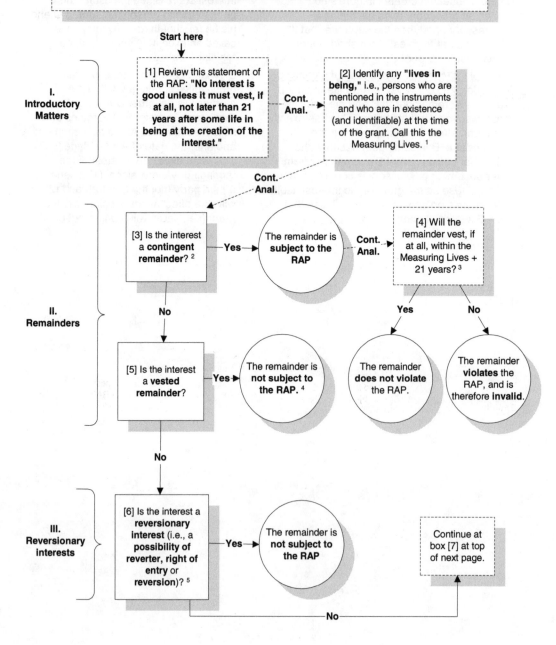

Footnotes start after p. 2 of chart.

Figure 4 (cont.)
Rule Against Perpetuities (p. 2)

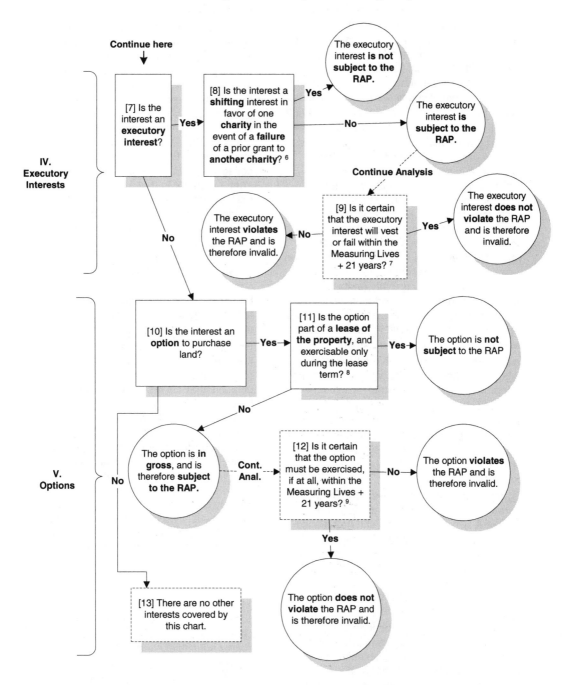

Continue here

**IV.
Executory
Interests**

[7] Is the interest an **executory interest**?

[8] Is the interest a **shifting** interest in favor of one **charity** in the event of a **failure** of a prior grant to **another charity**? [6]

Yes → The executory interest **is not subject to the RAP.**

No → The executory interest **is subject to the RAP.**

Continue Analysis

[9] Is it certain that the executory interest will vest or fail within the Measuring Lives + 21 years? [7]

No → The executory interest **violates** the RAP and is therefore invalid.

Yes → The executory interest **does not violate** the RAP and is therefore invalid.

No

**V.
Options**

[10] Is the interest an **option** to purchase land?

[11] Is the option part of a **lease of the property**, and exercisable only during the lease term? [8]

Yes → The option is **not subject** to the RAP

No → The option is **in gross**, and is therefore **subject to the RAP.**

No

[12] Is it certain that the option must be exercised, if at all, within the Measuring Lives + 21 years? [9]

Cont. Anal.

No → The option **violates** the RAP and is therefore invalid.

Yes → The option **does not violate** the RAP and is therefore invalid.

[13] There are no other interests covered by this chart.

Footnotes start on next page.

Notes to
Figure 4 (Rule Against Perpetuities)

[1] For the interest to be valid, it's enough that there's even one Measuring Life that is certain to end no more than 21 years before the gift vests or fails. But you need to look at <u>each identified life</u> in the gift to see whether it may qualify as that Measuring Life (though you can stop looking if you find one that qualifies).

<u>Example</u>: O conveys "to A and his heirs, but if B shall be living 30 years from today, to B's oldest then-surviving child." The question is whether the gift to B's child is valid. First, evaluate A to see whether he can be a Measuring Life that will cause the gift to succeed: the answer is "no," because A might die to tomorrow (and his heirs would take), and the gift to B's surviving child wouldn't necessarily take or fail within the next 21 years. Next, evaluate B to see whether he can be a successful Measuring Life. Here, the answer is "yes": B is currently (at the moment of the conveyance) alive and identified, and at the moment of truth, 30 years from now, B will have to be alive for the gift to succeed, so B can be a successful Measuring Life.

In the case of an interest that follows a <u>life estate</u>, the Measuring Life will have to be the person who has the life estate.

[2] It's absolutely vital that you figure out whether a remainder is vested or contingent, because the RAP applies to contingent remainders but not to vested ones (since they've already vested at the moment the interest was created).

[3] <u>Example</u>: In 1990, O conveys "to A or his heirs for the life of X, remainder to the oldest child of A living at X's death who has a child who has graduated from a 4-year college." In 1990, A has only one child, B, who has a child C, who was born in 1976. A never has any other children. In 1998, C graduates from Harvard. In 2000, X dies. You have to decide whether the gift to B is valid under the RAP.

B's interest was, at the time of the conveyance, a contingent remainder (since we didn't know, in 1990, which child of A, if any, would be the oldest child to have a child who graduates from college). X will clearly have to be our Measuring Life, since the remainder can only vest following X's death.

Now, viewed from the moment of the conveyance in 1990 (and under the common law we always have to evaluate the possibility of an RAP violation <u>as of the moment of the gift</u>, not based on how things actually turn out), it is possible that: (1) C will never graduate from college; (2) B will have no other children; and (3) A will have a child born after 1990, call her D, who will in turn have a child (call her E) who will graduate from college, but not until more than 21 years after X's death. In that (admittedly unlikely) scenario, the gift to D would be vesting more than 21 years after the death of X, our measuring life. (D can't be a measuring life because she hasn't been born by 1990, the time of the conveyance). Therefore, under the common-law the gift to B is void, even though in the actual event it turned out that C graduated (and B thus qualified for the gift) well before X's death.

[4] <u>Example</u>: In 1990, O conveys "to A for life, remainder to A's children for life, remainder to B and his heirs." It is possible that A's last surviving child will be one who has not been born as of 1990, and who will live more than 21 years longer than any of A's other children born before the date of the conveyance. It is also possible that, following the last child's death, possession will go not to B (who may already be dead) but to an heir or devisee of B not yet living at the time of the 1990 conveyance. Nonetheless, the gift to B and his heirs (which may not become possessory for many decades) does not violate the Rule Against Perpetuities, because that gift is a vested remainder, which vested in interest (though not in possession) in 1990 on the date of the conveyance, and vested remainders are simply not subject to the RAP.

[5] <u>Example</u>: O bequeaths Blackacre in 1900 "to A and his heirs for as long as liquor is not sold on the premises; if such sales occur, the property is to revert to O and

Notes (Cont.) to
Figure 4 (Rule Against Perpetuities)

his heirs." A is 65 at the time. In 1995, at a time when O's sole lineal descendant is his great-granddaughter X, A's great-grandchild B opens a liquor store on the premises.

This act will cause the property to revert automatically to X. Even though the possibility of reverter is becoming possessory much more than 21 years after the end of any measuring life that existed in 1900, the possibility will not violate the RAP. That's because possibilities of reverter, like other reversionary interests, are simply not subject to the common-law RAP.

[6] Example: O bequeaths Blackacre in 1990 "to the American Red Cross, but if the Red Cross should ever cease to be a charity certified as tax-exempt under the Internal Revenue Code, then to the Salvation Army." It's possible that 200 years from now, the Red Cross could lose its tax certification, and the property could go to the Salvation Army. But this would not violate the RAP, because of the exception for executory interests in a charity (here, the Salvation Army) that follow an estate subject to executory limitation in another charity (here, the Red Cross).

[7] Example: O bequeaths Blackacre, a vacant parcel, in 1950 "to the City of Akron, but if the property should ever cease to be used as a public park, title shall pass to A and his heirs." In 1960, the city stops using the park. A is still alive. Does he get the property?

Answer: no. A's interest is an executory interest (following the city's fee simple subject to executory limitation). Since the passing of title *could* have occurred more than lives in being in 1950 + 21 years, A's interest violates the RAP. That's true even though it turned out that the interest vested well within the life of a measuring life (A's life) -- what counts at common law is whether there *could have been* an illegally-late vesting, not whether

there actually was one.

[8] Example: In 1900, O leases Blackacre to XYZ Corp. for 99 years. The lease also provides that at any time during the lease term, XYZ or its successor can exercise the option for $1 million + 10% "interest" for each year after 1901. In 1995, long after O is dead, XYZ purports to exercise its option.

Because the option was part of a lease arrangement (and exercisable only during the lease term), the option is not subject to the RAP, and there is therefore no barrier to XYZ's exercise of it.

[9] Example: In 1950, O owns an estate, Blackacre, next to A's estate, Whiteacre. To preserve open space, O grants to "A and his heirs" an option to purchase Blackacre for its then fair market value "at any time during the next 50 years, provided that for 10 years following the exercise of such option the optionee shall not be entitled to build on the property." A grants to "O and his heirs" a matching option. In 1980, O proposes to sell Blackacre to B, a stranger. A asserts that he holds a valid option, and that O must therefore sell to him instead of to B. Will a court agree with A?

Answer: no. A's option is "in gross," i.e., not associated with a lease. Therefore, the option is subject to the RAP. As of 1950, it was possible that at sometime in the next 50 years, O would be dead, and his "heir" (the person who would have come into ownership of the option) would be someone who was not born until after 1950 (e.g., a grandchild of O born in 1975). In that event, the option would not have "vested" (i.e., be exercised) until more than 21 years after the death of all lives in being in 1950, which would have been an RAP violation. Therefore, A's option violates the RAP, even though he is in fact someone who was very much alive in 1950 and is himself trying to exercise.

Figure 5
Creation of Easements

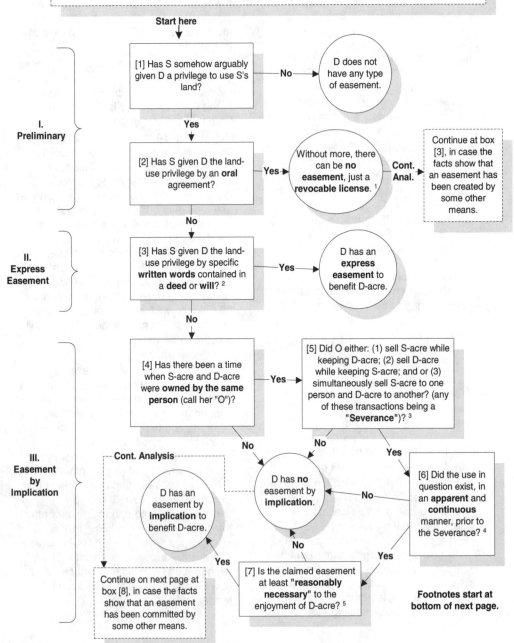

Use this chart to figure out whether an easement has been created, and if so, what type. For simplicity, the chart assumes that the easement, if any, is an easement appurtenant (i.e., there is a dominant estate which is benefitted by the easement). "S" is the owner of the would-be Servient estate (called "S-acre") and "D" is the owner of the would-be Dominant estate (called "D-acre"). Remember that S-acre (the Servient estate) is the estate that is burdened by the easement, and D-acre (the Dominant estate) is the estate that is benefitted by the easement.

Start here

I. Preliminary

[1] Has S somehow arguably given D a privilege to use S's land?

— **No** → D does not have any type of easement.

Yes

[2] Has S given D the land-use privilege by an **oral** agreement?

— **Yes** → Without more, there can be **no easement**, just a **revocable license**. [1]

Cont. Anal. → Continue at box [3], in case the facts show that an easement has been created by some other means.

No

II. Express Easement

[3] Has S given D the land-use privilege by specific **written words** contained in a **deed** or **will**? [2]

— **Yes** → D has an **express easement** to benefit D-acre.

No

III. Easement by Implication

[4] Has there been a time when S-acre and D-acre were **owned by the same person** (call her "O")?

— **Yes** → [5] Did O either: (1) sell S-acre while keeping D-acre; (2) sell D-acre while keeping S-acre; and or (3) simultaneously sell S-acre to one person and D-acre to another? (any of these transactions being a **"Severance"**)? [3]

No

- **Cont. Analysis** -

D has an easement by **implication** to benefit D-acre.

D has **no** easement by **implication**.

[5] **No** / **Yes**

[6] Did the use in question exist, in an **apparent** and **continuous** manner, prior to the Severance? [4]

— **No** → D has **no** easement by implication.

Continue on next page at box [8], in case the facts show that an easement has been committed by some other means.

Yes

[7] Is the claimed easement at least **"reasonably necessary"** to the enjoyment of D-acre? [5]

No (up to "D has no easement")

Yes

Footnotes start at bottom of next page.

Figure 5 (cont.)
Creation of Easements (p. 2)

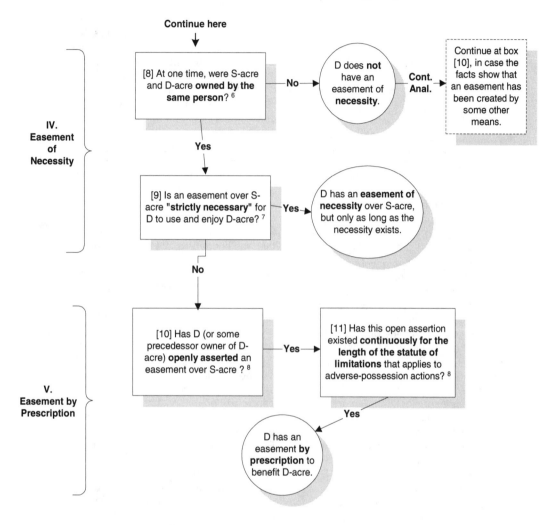

Notes

Notes continued on next page

[1] In other words, there is a Statute of Frauds for express easements. Something that would otherwise be an express easement is turned into a license (i.e., a revocable right to use another's property) by the absence of a writing.

Example: S says to D, "You can cut across my property anytime you want to get to the fishing pond behind my house. I'll never revoke this right, and you can transfer it to anyone who buys your house." Because there is no writing, this grant is a license, not an easement (even though it purports to be irrevocable). Therefore, S (or his successors in interest) can revoke whenever they want.

[2] This can happen by either "grant" or "reservation".

Example 1 (grant): S, owner of S-acre and D, owner of D-acre, are adjacent landowners. S signs a deed (it's a deed even though the only interest it's transferring is an easement) granting D and his assigns

Notes (Cont.) to
Figure 5 (Creation of Easements)

the perpetual right to cross S-acre to get to a fishing pond behind S-acre. The deed has created a valid express easement by grant; the benefit of the easement passes with ownership of D-acre, and the burden passes with ownership of S-acre.

Example 2 (reservation): O owns both S-acre and D-acre, adjacent parcels. There is a pond behind S-acre that O enjoys using. O sells S-acre to S via deed. The deed reserves to O and his assigns (i.e., anyone who comes into ownership of D-acre) the perpetual right to cross S-acre to get to the pond. This deed has created an express easement by reservation.

3   Example 1 (O sells S-acre while keeping D-acre): O two adjacent one-acre parcels, each with a building on it. The road crosses in front of the front parcel, S-acre. The back parcel, D-acre, is behind S-acre, so that the only way to get from D-acre to the road is to cross along a strip of S-acre. O sells S-acre, the front parcel, to S, while keeping D-acre. The deed says nothing about any easement. This arrangement meets the Severance requirement, and if the other requirements (in boxes [6] and [7]) are satisfied, O and any successor owners of D-acre will have reserved for themselves an easement by implication to cross S-acre to get to the road.

Example 2 (O sells D-acre while keeping S-acre): Same basic facts as Example 1. Now, however, O sells D-acre, the back parcel, to D, while keeping S-acre. This arrangement, too, meets the Severance arrangement and if the two other requirements (boxes [6] and [7]) are met will result in D's receiving an easement by implication (enforceable by D's successors in interest as well) to cross S-acre to get to the road.

Example 3 (O sells both parcels): Same basic facts as Examples 1 and 2. Now, however, O simultaneously sells D-acre

to D and S-acre to S. Neither deed says anything about any easement. Again, the Severance requirement is met, so that if the two other requirements (boxes [6] and [7]) are satisfied, D and his assigns will have an easement by implication, enforceable against S and his assigns, to cross S-acre to get to the road.

4   Example: On the facts of Examples 1-3 in Note 3, suppose that O's daughter lived in the house in D-acre, and crossed over S-acre (where O lived) to get to the road virtually every day for several years before O sold either property. Since O knew or could easily have discovered that this was happening, the use will meet the "apparent and continuous" requirement. Note that some courts don't even strictly require an actual use prior to Severance, and merely treat such a use as one factor tending to indicate that an implied easement was created.

Although the use has to be "apparent," this doesn't necessarily mean "visible" -- it's enough that one in O's position could easily have learned of the use. This principle often means that utility pipes going underground from the dominant estate to the servient estate qualify.

Example: Same basic set-up as in the examples in Note 3. Now, however, we're interested in the sewer pipes that run from the basement of the house on S-acre along the floor of the basement of D-acre, and out into the public sewer located in the road. Assuming that the occupant of D-acre (O, let's assume) either knew or could reasonably have discovered that the pipes ran along the D-acre basement, this will met the "apparent" requirement, so that an implied easement in favor of the pipes will be found to exist (assuming that the "reasonably necessary" requirement of box [7] is also met).

5   The required degree of necessity is typically higher when the easement is by grant than when it is reserved -- in the

Notes continued on next page

Notes (Cont.) to
Figure 5 (Creation of Easements)

reservation situation, most courts require "strict" or "absolute" necessity, not just "reasonable" necessity. Thus on the Examples in Note 3 above, in Example 1 O would have to make a stronger showing of necessity than D would have to make in Example 2. (Probably Example 3 would be treated like Example 1, i.e., viewed as a reservation as against S.)

[6] Notice that although prior co-ownership is required for an easement-of-necessity, there is <u>no requirement</u> of an <u>actual past use</u>, as there is in the easement-by-implication case.

[7] Since the necessity must be "strict" rather than merely "reasonable," the classic illustration of easement of necessity is <u>access from a landlocked parcel</u> to a public road.

<u>Example</u>: O owns S-acre and D-acre, adjacent parcels. S-acre fronts on the only public road, and backs onto D-acre. X-acre runs alongside both S-acre and D-acre. Persons on D-acre therefore have to pass either through S-acre or along X-acre to get to the street. In 1980, O sells S-acre to S and D-acre to D, with no mention of any easement on either deed. Beginning in 1980, D uses a dirt road on X-acre to get to the street. In 1998, X, the owner of X-acre, destroys the road and blocks access to his property from D-acre. There is a path along S-acre that would make it convenient for people to get from D-acre to the road, and the use of this path would not be hugely inconvenient for D. On these facts, S

will probably be able to convince a court to find that an easement by necessity over the S-acre path exists to benefit D-acre, even though no use of this path existed when D-acre and S-acre were under common ownership by O. But if the need for the easement ever disappears (e.g., a new public road is built adjacent to S-acre), the easement by necessity will be automatically extinguished.

[8] The "open" and "continuous" requirements are interpreted much the same way as they are in the fee-simple-by-adverse-possession scenario. Note, however, that "hostile" use is not requirement.

<u>Example</u>: D owns D-acre, adjacent to S-acre, owned by S. Beginning in 1980, S allows D and other members of D's household to walk along a dirth path at the edge of S-acre to get from D-acre to a swimming hole on public property adjacent to S-acre. (There is another way for people on D-acre to get to the swimming hole, but it's less convenient). During each swimming season, D and his family use this path quite frequently. Then, in 2001, S sells his property to X, who immediately blocks the path. If the jurisdiction has a 20-year statute of limitations on ejectment actions (the statute of limitations that would apply to an adverse possession suit involving actual title to S-acre), D will be found to have obtained an easement by prescription in 2000, and X will not be permitted to block the path.

Figure 6
Determining Who Wins under a Recording Act

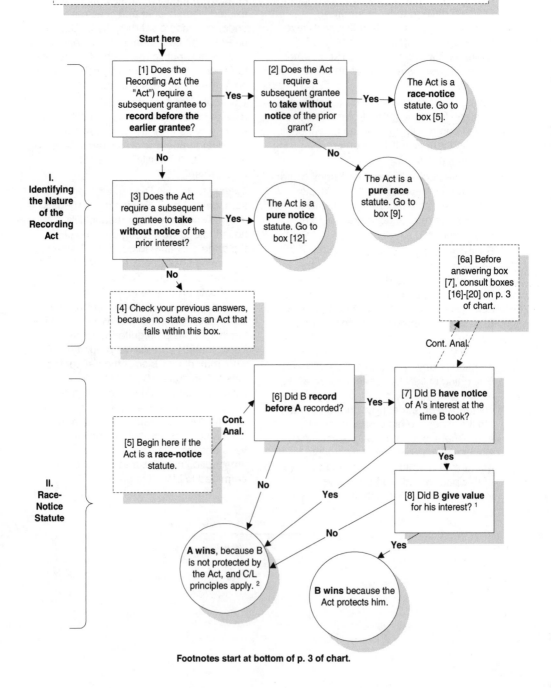

Use this chart to figure out who wins in a contest between two grantees. A is the first (in time) to receive a grant; B is the second to receive the grant. A and B do not necessarily have to have received their grant from the same grantor to be covered by this chart. (For the special problems if they've taken from different grantors, see box [17] and the footnote thereto.)

Start here

I. Identifying the Nature of the Recording Act

[1] Does the Recording Act (the "Act") require a subsequent grantee to **record before the earlier grantee**?

—Yes→

[2] Does the Act require a subsequent grantee to **take without notice** of the prior grant?

—Yes→

The Act is a **race-notice** statute. Go to box [5].

No

No

The Act is a **pure race** statute. Go to box [9].

[3] Does the Act require a subsequent grantee to **take without notice** of the prior interest?

—Yes→

The Act is a **pure notice** statute. Go to box [12].

No

[4] Check your previous answers, because no state has an Act that falls within this box.

[6a] Before answering box [7], consult boxes [16]-[20] on p. 3 of chart.

Cont. Anal.

II. Race-Notice Statute

[6] Did B **record before A** recorded?

—Yes→

[7] Did B **have notice** of A's interest at the time B took?

Cont. Anal.

[5] Begin here if the Act is a **race-notice** statute.

No

Yes

Yes

[8] Did B **give value** for his interest? [1]

A wins, because B is not protected by the Act, and C/L principles apply. [2]

No

Yes

B wins because the Act protects him.

Footnotes start at bottom of p. 3 of chart.

Figure 6 (cont.)
Determining Who Wins under a Recording Act (p. 2)

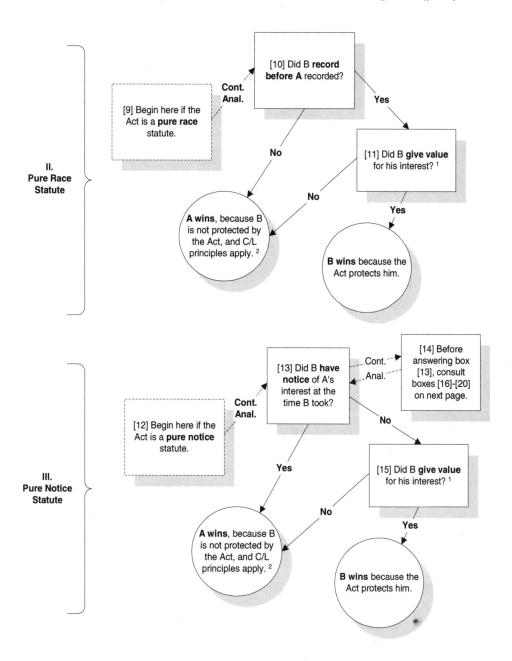

Footnotes start at bottom of next page.

Figure 6 (cont.)

Determining Who Wins under a Recording Act (p. 3)

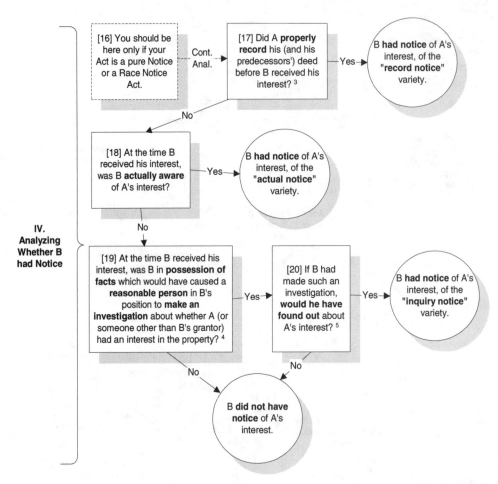

Notes

¹ In the substantial majority of states (though not in all), the recording act protects only "<u>purchasers for value</u>." The most significant thing to watch out for is that a <u>donee</u> -- one who <u>receives the property as a gift</u> -- is <u>not</u> a purchaser for value.

If the grantee has received the property in return for paying real, but less than market-value, consideration, the "purchaser for value" requirement is probably satisfied. Similarly, a mortgage lender who makes a loan to the "grantor" and receives a mortgage in return qualifies as a "purchaser

for value."

² Recording acts by their nature are only designed to protect the later grantee (B), not the earlier one (A). Therefore, if B does not qualify for protection, the Act simply doesn't apply. Then, the case is decided according to common-law principles. At common law, the first-granted interest takes priority over the later-granted interest, so A wins.

³ In deciding whether A "properly" recorded, the most important thing to worry about is whether A recorded his whole "<u>chain of title.</u>" That is, A must have recorded any

Notes continued on next page

Notes (Cont.) to
Figure 6 (Determining Who Wins Under a Recording Act)

previously-unrecorded deeds leading to his deed, in a way that would have enabled a searcher in B's position to find A's deed using standard searching principles.

Be especially careful about whether A properly recorded his whole chain when A and B <u>took from different grantors</u>, because that's when the chain-of-title concept is likely to make the most difference.

<u>Example</u>: A owns Blackacre. A conveys to B, and B records. B conveys to C, and C does not record. B conveys a second time, to D, and D records. C conveys to E, and E records his own deed, but not the deed from B to C. D now wants to sell to F. F checks the records. He will find the deed from B to C, and the deed from A to B. But F will never have occasion to discover that there was an unrecorded deed from B to C. F will also therefore also never look in the grantor index under C, so he'll fail to find the C-to-E deed even though that deed is recorded. Therefore, on these facts E will be found not to have "properly" recorded his deed, since he didn't record his whole chain. Consequently, F will not have "record notice" of E's interest.

4 There are two main ways in which B may know facts that would cause a reasonable person to make an investigation: (1) there are <u>references</u>, in the recorded deeds that are part of A's chain of title, to another interest, which is either completely unrecorded or recorded outside A's chain of title; or (2) the property is in the physical <u>possession</u> of someone who is not the record owner, and whose possession is inconsistent with the record title.

<u>Example 1 (reference in recorded deed)</u>: O conveys mineral rights on O's property to X. The mineral-rights deed is never recorded. O then conveys the fee simple to A. This deed mentions that the conveyance is "subject to the mineral rights previously conveyed by O to X."

The O-to-A deed is properly recorded. A now conveys to B, who promptly records. B then discovers that X is mining the minerals, and sues to stop X. B will be found to have been in possession, at the time he took from A, of facts that would have led a reasonable person in his position to make an investigation about the mineral rights.

<u>Example 2 (possession)</u>: Same basic facts as Example 1. Now, however, assume that the O-to-A deed is silent about mineral rights, but further assume that X has built a large oil well on the property that, at the time B buys from A, is busy pumping away. Here, too, B will be found to have been in possession of facts that would have led a reasonable person in his position to make an investigation about the mineral rights -- courts presume that a reasonable buyer will conduct a physical inspection of the property.

5 Generally, on exam questions, the answer to this question will be "yes."

<u>Example 1</u>: Same facts as Example 1 in note 4. Once B knew of the reference in the O-to-A deed to the O-to-X minerals conveyance, inquiry of either A, O or X (or even physical inspection of the now-mined property) would almost certainly have caused B to learn that the mineral rights had indeed been conveyed to X. In that event, B would be deemed to be on inquiry notice, and he wouldn't be a purchaser without notice. Consequently, in a notice or race-notice state, he'd lose in a contest with X.

<u>Example 2</u>: Same facts as Example 2 in note 4. Once B physically inspected the property, he would see the oil well, would be able to find out who was operating the well, and would learn that X, the operator, had a valid interest. Therefore, B would be deemed to be on inquiry notice, and he wouldn't be a purchaser without notice. As in Example 1, consequently, B would lose in a contest with X, in a notice or race-notice state.

CAPSULE SUMMARY

SUMMARY OF CONTENTS
OF CAPSULE SUMMARY

CAPSULE SUMMARY

Chapter numbers are to the chapters in the full-length
Emanuel Law Outline on Property, 5th Edition.

CHAPTER 2

POSSESSION AND TRANSFER OF PERSONAL PROPERTY

I. RIGHTS OF POSSESSORS

A. Wild animals: Once a person has gained possession of a *wild animal*, he has rights in that animal superior to those of the rest of the world.

B. Finders of lost articles: The finder of *lost property* holds it *in trust for the benefit of the true owner,* as a bailee. But the finder has rights *superior* to those of everyone except the true owner.

> **Example:** P finds logs floating in bay. He takes them and moors them with rope. The logs break loose, and are found by D, who takes them and refuses to return them to P. P may recover the value of the logs from D. P's possession is the equivalent of ownership as against anyone but the true owner.

1. Statutes of limitations: Although the possessor of goods holds them in trust for the true owner, all states have *statutes of limitations*, at the end of which the true owner can no longer recover the good from the possessor. Usually, the statute of limitations does not start to run until the true owner knows or with reasonable diligence should know the possessor's identity.

II. *BONA FIDE* PURCHASERS

A. *Bona fide purchasers:* The problem of the *"bona fide purchaser"* arises when one who is in *wrongful possession of goods* (e.g., a thief, defrauder, finder, etc.) sells them to one who *buys for value* and *without knowledge* that the seller has no title. (This buyer is the "bona fide purchaser" or *b.f.p.*)

1. General rule: The general rule is that *a seller cannot convey better title than that which he holds* (but subject to exceptions summarized below).

a. Stolen goods: This general rule is always applied when the seller (or his predecessor in title) has *stolen* the property.

> **Example:** X steals a car from P and sells it to Y, who ultimately sells it for fair value to D, who does not know it is stolen. P may recover the car from D, because a possessor of stolen goods can never convey good title, even to a b.f.p.

2. Exceptions: But where the goods are acquired from the original owner not by outright theft, but by less blatant forms of dishonesty and/or crime, the b.f.p. may be protected.

    a. "Voidable" title: First, a b.f.p. who takes from one who has a *"voidable"* title (as opposed to the "void" title that a thief has) will be protected. Thus if B obtains goods from A by *fraud* (e.g., B pays with counterfeit money or a bad check), B gets a voidable title, and if he immediately re-sells the goods to C, a b.f.p., A cannot get them back from C.

    b. Estoppel: Also, the owner may lose to the b.f.p. by the principle of *estoppel*. If A expressly or impliedly represents that B is the owner of goods or has the authority to sell them, A cannot recover if C buys the goods in good faith from B. Today, one who entrusts goods to a *merchant* who deals in goods of that type gives the merchant power to transfer full ownership rights to a b.f.p. See UCC §2-402(2).

        Example: Consumer leaves his watch with Jeweler for repairs. Jeweler is in the business of selling used watches as well as repairing them. Jeweler sells the watch to Purchaser, who pays fair market value and does not suspect that Jeweler does not own the watch. Consumer may not recover from Purchaser.

III. BAILMENTS

A. Bailments: A *bailment* is the *rightful possession* of goods by one who is *not their owner*.

B. Duty during custody: During the time that the bailee (the person holding the goods) has the object in his possession, he is *not an insurer* of it. He is liable only for *lack of care*, but the precise standard depends on who is benefitted:

1. Mutual benefit: If the bailment is beneficial to *both parties*, the bailee must use *ordinary diligence* to protect the bailed object from damage or loss.

    Example: A hotel which takes guests' possessions and keeps them in its safe is liable for lack of ordinary care, such as where it fails to use reasonable anti-theft measures.

2. Sole benefit of bailor: If the benefit is solely for the bailor's benefit, the bailee is liable only for *gross negligence*.

3. Sole benefit of bailee: If the bailment is solely for the benefit of the *bailee* (i.e., the bailor lends the object to the bailee for the latter's use), the bailee is required to use *extraordinary care* in protecting the goods from loss or damage (but he is still not an insurer, and is liable only if some degree of fault is shown).

4. Contractual limitation: The modern trend is that the parties may change these rules by *contractual* provisions. But even by contract, the bailee generally may not relieve himself from liability for *gross* negligence.

    a. Acceptance: Also, for such a provision to be binding, the bailor must know of it and *"accept"* it.

Example: P puts his car into a commercial garage run by D. The claim check asserts that D has no liability for negligence. The provision will be binding only if D can prove that P knew of and accepted this provision — D probably cannot make this showing, since P can argue that he regarded the claim check as merely a receipt.

IV. GIFTS

A. Definition: A gift is a *present transfer* of property by one person to another *without any consideration* or compensation.

B. Not revocable: A gift is generally *not revocable* once made; that is, the donor cannot "take back" the gift. (But gifts "*causa mortis*," i.e., made in contemplation of death, are revocable if the donor escapes from the peril of death which prompted the gift.)

C. Three requirements: There are three requirements for the making of a valid gift: (1) there must be a *delivery* from the donor to the donee; (2) the donor must possess an *intent* to make a present gift; and (3) the donee must *accept* the gift.

   1. Delivery: For the *delivery* requirement to be met, *control* of the subject matter of the gift must pass from donor to donee. Thus a mere oral statement that a gift is being made will not suffice.

      Example: O says orally to P, "I'm hereby giving you ownership of my valuable painting," but O does not give P the painting or any written instrument referring to the painting. There is no gift, and O still owns the painting.

      a. Symbolic and constructive delivery: *"Symbolic"* or *"constructive"* delivery will suffice in the case of property which cannot be physically delivered (e.g., *intangibles*, such as the right to collect a debt from another person), or which would be very inconvenient to deliver (e.g., heavy furniture). That is, delivery of something *representing* the gift, or of something that gives the donee a *means of obtaining* the gift, will suffice.

      Example: O is bedridden and cannot get to his locked bank safe-deposit box in another city. O gives P the key to the box, and tells P that the contents of the box now belong to P. Probably the transfer of the key will meet the delivery requirement as a "constructive delivery" of the box.

      b. Written instrument: Most courts today hold that a *written instrument* (even if it is not under seal) is a valid substitute for physical delivery of the subject matter of the gift.

      Example: O writes a letter to P saying, "I am hereby giving you my 500 shares of ABC stock as a present." Most courts today will hold that this letter is a written instrument the delivery of which to P meets the delivery requirement, so that physical transfer of the shares themselves is not necessary to make a gift of the shares. But a minority of courts would disagree.

      c. Gifts *causa mortis*: Courts are generally hostile to gifts *causa mortis* (in contemplation of death). Therefore, they frequently impose *stricter requirements* for delivery in such cases than where the gift is made *inter vivos* with no expectation of death. For instance, courts are less likely to accept symbolic and constructive delivery in lieu of actual physical transfer of the subject matter of the gift.

   i.   Revocation: Also, gifts *causa mortis* may be **revoked** if the donor does not die of the contemplated peril (and most courts hold that revocation is **automatic** if the donor recovers).

2.   Intent: In addition to delivery, there must be an **intent** on the part of the donor to make a gift. The intent must be to make a **present** transfer, not a transfer to take effect in the future. (A promise to make a **future** gift is not enforceable because of lack of consideration.)

   a.   Present gift of future enjoyment: However, a gift will be enforced if the court finds that it is a present gift of the **right** to the subject matter, even though the **enjoyment** of the subject matter is postponed to a later date.

   Example: O writes to P, "I am now giving you title to my valuable painting, but I want to keep possession for the rest of my life." Most courts would hold that the gift is enforceable, because it was a present gift of ownership, even though enjoyment was postponed to the future.

3.   Acceptance: The requirement that the gift be **accepted** by the donee has little practical importance. Even if the donee does not know of the gift (because delivery is made to a third person to hold for the benefit of the donee), the acceptance requirement is usually found to be met. However, if the donee **repudiates** the gift, then there is no gift.

D. Bank accounts: One common kind of gift arises out of the creation of a **joint bank account**. For instance, A may deposit in an account called "A and B jointly, with right of survivorship," or "A in trust for B." (The form "A in trust for B" is called a **"Totten Trust"**).

1.   Survivorship rights: Then, if B survives A, B will generally be entitled to **take the balance** of the account unless there is clear evidence that A did not intend this result. Also, the modern rule is that the fact that A reserved the right to **withdraw** funds during his lifetime does not change the fact that B gets the funds on A's death.

2.   Rights of parties *inter vivos*:   While both parties to the bank account are still **alive**, ownership of the funds depends on the type of account.

   a.   Totten trust: If the account is a **Totten Trust** ("A in trust for B"), or the account is in A's name, but with a clause stating "payable on death to B," the courts generally presume that during A's life he has the right to withdraw all funds (but subject to rebuttal by B's showing that A intended an immediate gift). In the case of a **joint** account, the modern trend seems to be that during the lifetime of both, the funds belong to the parties in proportion to the net contributions of each, in the absence of a contrary intent. See Uniform Probate Code.

C<small>HAPTER</small> 3

ADVERSE POSSESSION

I. ADVERSE POSSESSION GENERALLY

A. Function: All states have ***statutes of limitation*** that eventually bar the owner of property from suing to ***recover possession*** from one who has wrongfully entered the property. (Suits to recover property are called *"ejectment"* suits.) Once the limitations period has passed, the wrongful possessor effectively gets ***title*** to the land. This title is said to have been gained by *"**adverse possession**."*

   1. Clears title: The doctrine of adverse possession also furnishes the additional benefit of ***clearing titles to land***.

      Example: A state has a 20-year statute of limitations on ejectment actions. X claims that he holds title to Blackacre, and wants to sell it to Y. Y will only have to check the land records going back 20 years — plus perhaps some additional period to cover the possibility that the running of the statute of limitations might have been "tolled" for some reason — in order to check X's claim of ownership. The fact that, say, 100 years ago X's alleged "predecessor in title" took the property by wrongfully entering on it, is irrelevant, since the right of the rightful possessor to regain possession has long since been barred by the statute of limitations.

B. Requirements generally: To obtain title by adverse possession, the possessor must satisfy four main requirements: (1) he must actually ***possess*** the property, and this possession must be *"**open, notorious and visible**"*; (2) the possession must be *"**hostile**,"* i.e., without the owner's consent; (3) the possession must be ***continuous***; and (4) the possession must be for at least the length of the ***statutory period*** (perhaps longer if the owner was under a disability).

II. OPEN, NOTORIOUS AND VISIBLE

A. "Open, notorious and visible" requirement: The adverse possessor's use of the land must be *"**open, notorious and visible**."* Usually, this means that the possessor's use of the property must be similar to that which a typical owner of ***similar property*** would make.

      Example: Blackacre is undeveloped wild land suitable only for hunting and fishing. If D builds a small hunting cabin on the land, and enters several times per year to hunt and fish, this will meet the "open, notorious and visible" requirement if a typical owner of similar property would make such limited use. But it would not qualify if a typical owner would use the property more extensively, build a much bigger dwelling, etc.

III. "HOSTILE" POSSESSION

A. "Hostile" possession: The adverse possession must be *"**hostile**."* This merely means that possession must be ***without the owner's consent***.

Example: T occupies Blackacre under a lease from O, the record owner. T's possession of the premises is not "hostile" since it is with O's consent, so even if T resides for more than the statutory period, he does not become the owner by adverse possession.

B. Bad faith possessor: A *minority* of courts impose the additional requirement that the possessor must have a *bona fide belief* that he has *title* to the property. Thus in these minority states, a mere *"squatter"* never gets title.

C. Boundary disputes: Adverse possession is most frequently used to resolve mistakes about the location of *boundary lines*. Most courts hold that one who possesses an adjoining landowner's land, under the mistaken belief that he has only possessed up to the boundary of his own land, meets the requirement of "hostile" possession and can become an owner by adverse possession.

Example: O is the true owner of Blackacre, and A is the true owner of the adjoining parcel, Whiteacre. When A moves onto Whiteacre, he mistakenly believes that his land goes all the way up to a creek, but the creek is in fact 15 yards into Blackacre. Accordingly, A builds a fence up to the creek, and uses the enclosed portion of Blackacre for farming. At the end of the statutory period, most courts would hold that A becomes the owner of the 15-yard portion by adverse possession.

IV. CONTINUITY OF POSSESSION

A. Continuity of possession: The adverse possession must be *"continuous"* throughout the statutory period, as a general rule.

1. Interruption by owner: Thus if the owner *re-enters the property* in order to regain possession, this will be an interruption of the adverse possession. When this happens, the adverse possessor must start his occupancy *from scratch*.

B. Tacking: Possession by two adverse possessors, one after the other, may be *"tacked"* if the two are in *"privity"* with each other. That is, their periods of ownership can be *added together* for purposes of meeting the statutory period.

Example: A, who owns Whiteacre, adversely possesses a small strip of the adjacent Blackacre, due to confusion about boundaries. A adversely possesses that piece of Blackacre for 15 years; he then sells Whiteacre to P, who holds for another seven years (and who adversely possesses the same strip). A's 15 years of possession can be "tacked" to P's seven years, so that P meets a 20-year limitations period. (In most courts, this is true whether A's deed to P recited the false boundary lines that A and B believe to be correct, or recited the true boundary lines that do not include part of Blackacre.)

1. No privity: But if the two successive adverse possessors are not in *"privity,"* i.e., do not have some continuity of interest, then *tacking will not be allowed*.

Example: A adversely possesses Blackacre for 15 years. He then abandons the property. B then enters for another seven years. B cannot "tack" his holding period to A's holding period, since they had no continuity of interest. But if A had purported to give B his interest by oral gift, deed, bequest or inheritance, then B could tack.

V. MISCELLANEOUS

A. Length of time: The length of the holding period for adverse possession varies from state to state. It is usually 15 years or longer.

   1. Disabilities: If the true owner of property is under a *disability*, in nearly all states he is given *extra time* within which to bring an ejectment action.

      Example: Statutes often hold that the running of the limitations period is suspended until the true owner becomes 21. Usually, the person is given an additional time, say 10 years, to sue after he reaches 21.

   2. Tacking on owner's side: There is effectively "tacking" on the *owner's* as well as the possessor's side.

      Example: O is the owner of Blackacre in 1950, when A enters and begins to adversely possess. In 1960, O conveys to X. Under a 21-year statute, A will gain adverse possession in 1971, even though he has not held for 21 years against either O or X separately.

B. Rights of adverse possessor: Once the statutory period expires, the adverse possessor effectively gets *title*. However, the possessor usually cannot *record* title (since he has no deed). But he can apply for a judicial determination of adverse possession, and if he gets it, that determination can be recorded as if it were a deed.

   1. Need to inspect: Since a title gained by adverse possession usually cannot be recorded, a buyer of property cannot be sure that the record owner still owns it (and that the record owner can therefore convey a good deed) unless the buyer *physically inspects* the property.

   2. Scope of property obtained: Normally, the possessor acquires title only to the portion of the property *"actually"* occupied.

      a. Constructive adverse possession: But there is one important exception: by the doctrine of *"constructive"* adverse possession, one who enters property under *"color of title"* (i.e., a written instrument that is defective for some reason) will gain title to the *entire area described in the instrument*, even if he "actually" possesses only a portion.

C. Conflicts: If there is a conflict between two person's whose interests are solely possessory, the general rule is that the *first possessor has priority over the subsequent one*.

CHAPTER 4

FREEHOLD ESTATES

I. INTRODUCTION

A. Estates generally: One does not really "own" Blackacre. Instead, one owns an "estate in Blackacre." Traditionally, there are two types of estates: *freehold* and *nonfreehold*.

1. **Freehold estates:**   The three freehold estates are: (1) the *fee simple* (which may be either absolute or defeasible); (2) the *fee tail*; and (3) the *life estate*.

2. **Non-freehold:**   The non-freehold estates are: (1) the estate for *years*; (2) the *periodic estate*; and (3) the *estate at will*.

II. THE FEE SIMPLE

A. Fee simple absolute: The *fee simple absolute* is the most unrestricted and longest estate.

1. **Inheritable:**   The fee simple absolute is *inheritable* under intestacy statutes. Thus if the owner of a fee simple absolute dies, the property passes to the people deemed to be his "heirs" under the intestacy statute of the state where the land is located.

2. **Words to create:**   Generally, a fee simple absolute is created by using the words *"and his heirs."* Thus at common law, the only way for O to convey a fee simple absolute to A is for O to convey "to A and his heirs."

    a. **Abolished:**   But most states have *abolished* the requirement that the phrase "and his heirs" be used. Thus in most states, if O conveys "to A," this will give A a fee simple absolute.

B. Fee simple defeasible: The holder of a fee simple *defeasible* may hold or convey the property, but he and those who take from him must use the property *subject to a restriction*.

1. **Three types:**   There are three types: (1) the fee simple *determinable*; (2) the fee simple *subject to a condition subsequent*; and (3) the fee simple *subject to an executory limitation*.

2. **Determinable:**   A fee simple *determinable* is a fee simple which *automatically* comes to an end when a stated event occurs (or, perhaps, fails to occur).

    a. **Restriction on uses:**   Most often, the fee simple determinable is used to *prevent the property from being put to a certain use* which the grantor opposes. The limitation controls even after the property changes hands numerous times.

        Example: O owns Blackacre in fee simple. He sells the property "to A and his heirs so long as the premises are not used for the sale of alcoholic beverages." A then purports to convey a fee simple absolute to B, who builds a bar. When the first alcoholic beverage is sold, B's interest *automatically* ends, and the property reverts to O (or his heirs).

    b. **Possibility of reverter:**   The creator of a fee simple determinable is always left with a *"possibility of reverter,"* i.e., the possibility that title will revert to him if the stated event occurs.

        Example: In the above example, O, following the conveyance, is left with a possibility of reverter if alcohol is sold.

    c. **Statute of limitations:**   Many states have enacted *statutes of limitation* which bar a possibility of reverter after a certain period. Some statutes begin to run after the fee simple determinable is created, others don't start to run until the stated event occurs.

    d. **Words creating:** A fee simple determinable is usually created by words that make it clear that the estate is to end *automatically* upon the occurrence of the stated event. Such words include "so long as…," or "until…," or "during…." Also, if the conveyance says that the property is to *"revert"* to the grantor, that's a sign of a fee simple determinable.

3. **Fee simple subject to condition subsequent:** The fee simple *subject to a condition subsequent* is also geared to the happening of a particular event, but unlike the fee simple determinable, the fee simple subject to a condition subsequent *does not automatically end* when the event occurs. Instead, the grantor has a *right of entry,* i.e., a right to *take back* the property — but nothing happens until he *affirmatively exercises that right*.

    a. **Words creating:** The words that create a fee simple subject to condition subsequent usually have a "conditional" flavor, such as *"upon express condition that…,"* or *"provided that…."* Also, most courts require that there also be a statement that the grantor may *enter the property* to terminate the estate if the stated event occurs.

    Example: O conveys Blackacre to A and his heirs "but upon condition that no alcohol is ever served; if alcohol is served, Grantor or his heirs may re-enter the property and terminate the estate." A has a fee simple subject to condition subsequent.

    b. **Distinguishing from fee simple determinable:** A key difference between the fee simple subject to condition subsequent and the fee simple determinable relates to the *statute of limitations*. When an f.s. determinable is involved, the holders of the possibility of reverter often have a long or unlimited time to sue (see above). But in the case of an f.s. subject to condition subsequent, the statute of limitations usually starts to run upon the occurrence of the stated event, and usually is for a very *short* period — so if the holder of the right of entry does not promptly re-enter or sue, he will lose the right.

4. **Fee simple subject to executory limitation:** A fee simple *subject to an executory limitation* provides for the estate to pass to a *third person* (one other than the grantor) upon the happening of the stated event.

    Example: O conveys "to A and his heirs, but if A dies without children surviving him, then to B and his heirs." A has a fee simple subject to an executory limitation.

III. THE FEE TAIL

A. Fee tail generally: The *fee tail* allows the owner of land to ensure that the property *remains within his family* indefinitely. If O conveys a fee tail to his son, A, and the fee tail is enforced, then upon A's death the property will go to A's heir, then to that heir's heir, etc. — A and his decedents can never convey the property outside the family line. (If they try to do so, then the property reverts to O's heirs.)

1. **Words to create:** The most common way of creating a fee tail is by a grant "to A and the *heirs of his body*."

    a. **Death without issue:** Also, a *minority* of states recognize a fee tail where the conveyance is by O "to A and his heirs, but if A dies without issue, then to O's heirs." But *most* states hold that this means that O gets back the property only if A *himself* dies without children or grandchildren, not that O's line gets it whenever A's *line* dies out.

B. **Modern treatment:** Today, in most states a grant or bequest that would be a fee tail at common law is simply *converted* by statute to a *fee simple absolute*. (But a minority of states follow various approaches, including life estate to the grantee, with a remainder in fee simple to his issue.) No states today fully enforce the fee tail as a method of ensuring that property will descend along bloodlines and will not be conveyed outside the family tree.

IV. THE LIFE ESTATE

A. **Life estate generally:** A *life estate* is an interest which lasts for the lifetime of a person. Ordinarily, the lifetime by which the life estate is "measured" is that of the holder of the life estate.

> **Example:** O conveys "to A for his lifetime, then to B in fee simple."

1. **Phrase creating:** A life estate is usually created by the words "to A during his life" or "to A for life."

2. **Defeasible:** A life estate may be *defeasible*, just as a fee simple may be.

> **Example:** O conveys "to A, for so long as she shall remain my widow, then to my son B." A has a life estate determinable.

3. **Life estate per autre vie:** There can be a life estate that is measured by the life of someone other than the grantee. This is called a life estate *"per autre vie"* ("by another life").

> **Example:** O conveys "to A for the life of B, then to C and his heirs." A has a life estate per autre vie.

    a. **Grantee dies before end of measuring life:** Today, if the grantee of a life estate per autre vie dies before the end of the measuring life, the balance of the estate is treated as personal property, which passes by will or by intestacy. Thus in the above example, if A died before B, A's interest would pass as provided in A's will or under the intestacy statute.

B. **Duties and powers of life tenant:**

1. **Duties:** The life tenant has a number of duties vis a vis the future interest. Most importantly, he may not commit *waste*, i.e., he may not unreasonably impair the value which the property will have when the holder of the future interest takes possession. Thus he must make reasonable repairs, not demolish the structure, pay all property taxes, etc.

2. **Powers:** The life tenant *cannot convey a fee simple*, or any other estate greater than the life estate he holds. But he may convey the interest which he does hold, or a lesser one.

> **Example:** If A holds a life estate, he may convey to B either for the life of A, or for a term of years.

CHAPTER 5

FUTURE INTERESTS

I. FUTURE INTERESTS GENERALLY

A. Five future interests: There are five future estates: (1) the possibility of reverter; (2) the right of entry; (3) the reversion; (4) the remainder; and (5) the executory interest.

II. POSSIBILITY OF REVERTER; RIGHT OF ENTRY

A. Possibility of reverter and right of entry: The *possibility of reverter* and the *right of entry* follow the fee simple determinable and the fee simple subject to a condition subsequent, respectively.

1. **Possibility of reverter:** When the owner of a fee simple absolute transfers a fee simple *determinable*, the grantor automatically retains a *possibility of reverter*. All states allow this possibility of reverter to be *inherited*, or to be devised by will; most but not all states also allow it to be conveyed *inter vivos*.

2. **Right of entry:** If the holder of an interest in land (e.g., a fee simple absolute) conveys his interest but attaches a *condition subsequent*, the transferor has a *"right of entry."* Most commonly, one who holds a fee simple absolute and who then conveys a fee simple subject to condition subsequent has a right of entry.

> **Example:** O owns Blackacre in fee simple absolute. He conveys "to A and his heirs, on condition that liquor never be sold on the premises; if liquor is sold thereon, O or his heirs may re-enter the premises." The conveyance to A is a fee simple subject to condition subsequent, and O therefore reserves a right of entry.

   a. **Incident to reversion:** Often, a transferor who holds a right of entry also holds a *reversion*. Thus the typical lease contains various right of entry clauses (e.g., the right to re-enter if the tenant does not pay rent), as well as a reversion at the end of the lease term.

   b. **Alienability:** If the right of entry is incident to a reversion (as in the prior paragraph), it *passes with the reversion*. (Thus if a landlord sells his property, he will be deemed to have also sold his right of entry to the buyer.) If the right of entry is *not* incident to a reversion, in most states the right of entry may be left by will and passes under the intestacy statute, but may not be conveyed *inter vivos*. (But some states allow even the *inter vivos* conveyance).

III. REVERSIONS

A. Reversions generally: A *reversion* is created when the holder of a vested estate transfers to another a *smaller estate*; the reversion is the interest which *remains in the grantor*.

> **Example:** A holds a fee simple absolute in Blackacre. He conveys "to B for life." A is deemed to have retained a "reversion," which will become possessory in A (or his heirs) upon B's death.

1. Distinguishing from possibility of reverter: Distinguish between a reversion and a possibility of reverter. If the grantor has given away a fee simple determinable, he retains only a possibility of reverter. If he has given away something *less* than a fee simple, he retains a reversion.

2. Alienability: Reversions are completely alienable: they may pass by will, by intestacy or by *inter vivos* conveyance.

IV. REMAINDERS

A. Remainders generally: A *remainder* is a future interest which can become possessory only upon the *expiration* of a *prior possessory interest*, created by the *same instrument*.

1. Requirements: So there are three requirements: (1) the grantor must convey a present *possessory* estate to one transferee; (2) he must create a non-possessory estate in *another* transferee by the *same instrument*; and (3) the second, non-possessory, estate (the remainder) must be capable of becoming possessory only on the *"natural"* expiration (as opposed to the cutting short) of the prior estate.

> **Example:** O conveys "to A for life, remainder to B and his heirs." B has a remainder because: (1) a present interest was created in A; (2) a future interest was created in someone other than A, by the same instrument; and (3) the second interest (the remainder) will become possessory only after the natural expiration of the first one (i.e., after A's death).

2. Following a term of years: Today, we refer to an estate *following a term of years* as a remainder.

> **Example:** O conveys "to A for 10 years, then to B and his heirs." Today, B is said to have a remainder, even though this would not have been called a remainder at common law.

3. Distinguished from reversion: Distinguish between the remainder and the reversion. Most importantly, the remainder is created in someone *other than the transferor*, whereas the reversion is an interest left in the transferor after he has conveyed an interest to someone else.

4. No remainder after fee simple determinable: There cannot be a remainder after any kind of fee simple, including after a *fee simple determinable*. If an interest is created in a third person to follow a fee simple determinable, that interest is called an "executory interest," not a remainder.

B. Vested remainders: A remainder is *"vested"* (as opposed to "contingent") if: (1) no *condition precedent* is attached to it; and (2) the person holding it has already been *born*, and his identity is *ascertained*.

> **Example:** O conveys Blackacre "to A for life, remainder to B and his heirs." B has a vested remainder, since his identity is ascertained, and there is no condition precedent which must be satisfied in order for his interest to become possessory.

1. **Meaning of "condition precedent":**   No condition precedent is deemed to exist so long as the remainder will become possessory *"whenever and however the prior estate terminates."* Thus in the above example, no matter how and when A's life estate ends, B's estate will immediately become possessory; therefore, B's remainder is vested.

C. Contingent remainders: All remainders that are not vested are *contingent*.   A remainder will be contingent rather than vested if: (1) it is subject to a *condition precedent*; *or* (2) it is created in favor of a person who is either *unborn* or *unascertained* at the time of creation.

1. **Condition precedent:**   The "condition precedent" branch of "contingent" means that if some condition must be met before the remainder could *possibly become possessory*, the remainder is contingent.

> **Example:** O conveys "to A for life, then, if B is living at A's death, to B in fee simple." B must meet the condition precedent of surviving A, before his remainder can possibly become possessory. Therefore, B's remainder is contingent.

   a. **Distinguish from condition subsequent:**   Distinguish between condition precedent (making the remainder contingent) and condition subsequent (making the remainder vested). If the condition is incorporated into the clause which gives the gift to the remainderman, then the remainder is contingent. But if one clause creates the remainder and a separate *subsequent* clause takes the remainder away, the remainder is vested (subject to divestment by the condition subsequent).

> **Example:** O conveys "to A for life, remainder to B and his heirs, but if B dies before A, to C and his heirs." B's remainder is vested, not contingent, because the condition is not part of the clause giving B his interest, but is instead part of a second added clause. But if the conveyance was "to A for life, then if B survives A, to B and his heirs; otherwise to C and his heirs", B's remainder would be contingent because the condition is incorporated into the very gift to B, making it a condition precedent.

> **Note:** The key phrase *"but if"* indicates a condition subsequent rather than a condition precedent, so it's a clue to a vested rather than a contingent remainder.

2. **Unborn or unascertained:**   A remainder is also contingent rather than vested if it is held by a person who, at the time the remainder is created, is either (1) *unborn* or (2) *not yet ascertained*.

Example of unborn: O conveys "to A for life, then to the children of B." At the time of the conveyance, B has no children. Therefore, the remainder in the unborn children is contingent. (But a remainder in favor of unborn children, like any other contingent remainder, may *become vested* due to later events. Thus if prior to A's death, B has a child, X, X will now have a vested remainder "subject to open" (in favor of any other children of B born before A's death).)

Example of unascertained: O conveys "to A for life, then to A's heirs." Assuming that the Rule in Shelley's Case (discussed below) is not in force, the heirs have a remainder, and it is contingent. That's because until A dies, it is impossible to say who his heirs are. (At A's death, the remainder will both vest and become possessory.)

3. **Destructibility of contingent remainders:** At common law, a contingent remainder is deemed *"destroyed"* unless it *vests at or before the termination of the preceding freehold estates*. This is the doctrine of *"destructibility of contingent remainders"*.

    Example: O conveys "to A for life, remainder to the first son of A who reaches 21." At A's death, he has one son, B, age 16. Since B did not meet the contingency (becoming 21) by the time the prior estate (A's life estate) expired, B's contingent remainder is destroyed. Therefore, O's reversion becomes possessory.

    a. **Normal expiration:** One way the contingent remainder can be destroyed is if the preceding freehold estates *naturally terminate* before the condition precedent is satisfied. This is the case in the above example.

    b. **Destruction by merger:** A contingent remainder can also be destroyed because the estate preceding it (usually a life estate) is *merged into* another, larger, estate. The doctrine of merger says that whenever *successive vested estates* are owned by the *same person*, the smaller of the two estates is *absorbed* by the larger.

        Example: O conveys "to A for life, remainder to A's first son for life if he reaches 21, remainder to B and his heirs." When A has a 19-year-old son, A conveys his life estate to B. Since B now has two successive vested estates (the life estate and B's own vested remainder in fee simple), the smaller estate — the life estate — is merged into the fee simple and disappears. Since the son's remainder has not yet vested when A's life estate disappears, the son's contingent remainder is destroyed.

    c. **Destructibility rule today:** About half the states have passed statutes *abolishing the destructibility of contingent remainders*. Some additional states reach this result by case law.

D. **Why it makes a difference:** Here are the main consequences of the vested/contingent distinction:

1. **Rule Against Perpetuities:** The consequence that most significantly lives on today relates to the *Rule Against Perpetuities*. Contingent remainders are subject to the Rule Against Perpetuities, but vested remainders are not.

2. **Transferability:** At common law, the two types of remainders differed sharply with respect to *transferability*. Vested remainders have always been transferable *inter vivos*. Contingent remainders, on the other hand, were basically not transferable *inter vivos*. But today, in most states, contingent remainders, too, are transferable *inter vivos*.

3. **Destruction:** At common law a contingent remainder was *destroyed* if it did not vest upon termination of the proceeding life estate (the doctrine of "destruction of contingent remainders discussed above.") There was no comparable doctrine destroying vested remainders. But this distinction is not as significant today, because as noted above most states have abolished the doctrine of destruction of contingent remainders.

V. RULE IN SHELLEY'S CASE

A. Rule generally: The *Rule in Shelley's Case* provides: *if a will or conveyance creates a freehold in A, and purports to create a remainder in A's heirs* (or in the heirs of A's body), and the estates are *both legal or both equitable, the remainder becomes a remainder in A*. Usually, the result is that A ends up getting a fee simple.

> **Example:** O conveys "to A for life, remainder to A's heirs." If there were no Rule in Shelley's Case, the state of the title would be: life estate in A, contingent remainder in A's heirs, reversion in O. But by operation of the Rule in Shelley's Case, the state of the title becomes: life estate in A, remainder in A (not A's heirs). Then, by the doctrine of merger, A's life estate will merge into his remainder in fee simple, and A simply holds a present fee simple.

1. **Freehold in ancestor:** For the Rule to apply, there must be a *freehold estate* given to the ancestor. Basically, this means that the ancestor must have a *life estate*.

2. **Remainder in heirs or heirs of the body:** There must be a *remainder*, and it must be in the *heirs of the ancestor*, or in the *heirs of the ancestor's body*.

   a. **Can't be executory interest:** This means that the heirs (or heirs of the body) cannot have an *executory interest* (as opposed to a remainder).

3. **Life estate and remainder separated by other estate:** The Rule applies even if there is *another estate* between the life estate and the remainder. Thus the Rule may apply even though there is no *subsequent merger* of the life estate and the remainder.

   > **Example:** O conveys "to A for life, remainder to B for life, remainder to A's heirs." Since there is both a life estate in A and a remainder in his heirs, the Rule in Shelley's Case applies, to transform the remainder into one in A. But there is no merger, because of the vested life estate in B separating the two. Thus the title is: life estate in A, vested remainder for life in B, vested remainder in fee simple in A.

B. Modern treatment: About two-thirds of the states have enacted statutes *abolishing the Rule*. But the remaining states still apply the common-law version. Also, some of the statutory abolitions apply only to wills, not to *inter-vivos* deeds.

VI. DOCTRINE OF WORTHIER TITLE

A. Doctrine generally: The Doctrine of Worthier Title provides that *one cannot, either by conveyance or will, give a remainder to one's own heirs*. (We are interested only in the "conveyance," or *"inter vivos,"* aspect of the Doctrine, since that is the only aspect that remains important today.)

1. Consequence: The consequence of the Doctrine of Worthier Title is that if the owner of a fee simple attempts to create a life estate or fee tail estate, with a remainder to his own heirs, the remainder is *void*. Thus the grantor *keeps a reversion*. (This is why the Doctrine is sometimes called the *"rule forbidding remainders to grantors' heirs."*)

> **Example:** O conveys "to A for life, remainder to O's heirs." The Doctrine of Worthier Title makes the remainder void. Consequently, O is left with a reversion. He is thus free to convey the reversion to a third party; if he does so, his heirs will get nothing when he dies, even if he dies intestate.

B. Rule of construction: In most states, the Doctrine has been transformed into a *rule of construction*. That is, the Doctrine only applies where the grantor's language, and the surrounding circumstances, indicate that he *intended to keep a reversion*. So in most states, the Doctrine today just establishes a presumption that a reversion rather than a remainder in the grantor's heirs is really intended.

VII. EXECUTORY INTERESTS AND THE STATUTE OF USES

A. Statute of Uses: The Statute of Uses provides that any *equitable estate* is *converted into the corresponding legal estate*.

1. Equitable estates: An equitable estate is similar to a trust: if O conveys "to T and his heirs, to the use of A and his heirs," then T's estate is "legal" and A's estate is "equitable." (So look for the phrase "to the use of," which means that the person named following the phrase gets an equitable interest.)

2. Operation of Statute: The Statute of Uses converts any equitable estate into the corresponding legal estate.

> **Example:** O conveys Blackacre "to T and his heirs, to the use of A and his heirs." The Statute of Uses transforms A's equitable fee simple into a legal fee simple. T's legal estate is nullified. So the state of title is simply: legal fee simple in A.

B. Modern executory interests: The Statute of Uses makes possible modern *"shift*ing" *executory interests*.

1.Shifting executory interests: A *"shifting* executory interest" is a legal estate in someone other than the grantor, that *cuts short* a prior legal interest.

Example: O, who owns Blackacre, "bargains and sells" it — i.e., he creates an equitable estate in it — "to A and his heirs, but if the premises are ever used for other than residential purposes, then to B and his heirs." The bargain and sale raises a use in A in fee simple subject to condition subsequent, and a use in B. The Statute of Uses executes both of these uses, so title becomes: fee simple in A subject to an executory limitation, and a shifting executory interest in fee simple in B. If A or his heirs fail to use the property for residential purposes, the gift over to B will take effect.

2. **Distinguish equitable interest from remainder:** Distinguish between an equitable interest and a remainder. The difference is that a remainder *never cuts off* a prior interest, but merely awaits the prior interest's *natural termination*. An executory interest, by contrast, *divests* or *cuts off* a prior interest before the latter's natural termination.

   Example 1: O bargains and sells "to A for life, then to B and his heirs if B survives A, otherwise to C and his heirs." B and C each have contingent remainders.

   Example 2: O bargains and sells "to A for life, then to B and his heirs, but if B should die before A, to C and his heirs." Here B's interest is vested subject to divestment because the "but if…" divesting language comes in a separate clause, and C's interest is therefore an executory interest.

3. **Statute of Uses today:** The Statute of Uses is still in force. Thus a "bargain and sale" deed will generally create a legal estate. Even where the Statute is not in force, the modern deed can be used to produce the same result (e.g., shifting executory interests, which will cut off prior interests).

VIII. THE RULE AGAINST PERPETUITIES

A. Rule Against Perpetuities generally:

1. **Statement of Rule:** The Rule Against Perpetuities can be summarized as follows: *"No interest is good unless it must vest, if at all, not later than 21 years after some life in being at the creation of the interest."* Try to memorize this phrase.

2. **Paraphrase:** Paraphrasing, an interest is invalid unless it can be said, with absolute certainty, that it will either *vest or fail to vest*, before the end of a period equal to: (1) a life in existence (and specified in the document creating the interest) at the time the interest is created plus (2) an additional 21 years.

   Example: O conveys Blackacre "to A for life, remainder to the first son of A whenever born who becomes a clergyman." At the date of the conveyance, A has no son who is presently a clergyman. Viewing the matter from the date of the conveyance, it is possible to imagine a situation in which the remainder to the son could vest later than lives in being plus 21 years. Thus A's son could be born to A after the date of the conveyance, and this son could become a clergyman more than 21 years after the death of A, and more than 21 years after the death of all of A's sons living at the time of the conveyance. (A and

A's sons living at the time of the conveyance are the "measuring lives," since they're living people specifically mentioned in the conveyance.) Since this remote vesting is possible — even though unlikely — the contingent remainder is *invalid*. This is so even though it *actually turns out* that A has a son alive before the date of the conveyance who ultimately becomes a clergyman.

3. **Judged in advance:** As the above example shows, the common-law version of the Rule requires that the validity of the interest be judged *at the time it is created*, not at the time the interest actually vests. So if it is *theoretically possible* (even though very unlikely) that the interest will vest later than 21 years after the expiration of lives in being, the interest is invalid. This is true even if it actually turns out that the interest vests before the end of lives in being plus 21 years. (But see the discussion of "wait and see" statutes below.)

B. Applicability of Rule to various estates:

1. **Contingent remainders:** The Rule applies to *contingent remainders*.

    Example: O conveys "to A for life, remainder to the first son of A to reach the age of 25 and his heirs." At the time of the conveyance, A does not have a son who has reached the age of 25. The remainder in the unborn son is contingent, rather than vested, since it is not yet known which son if any will reach the age of 25. Since there is a possibility of remote vesting, the gift to the oldest son violates the Rule and is invalid.

2. **Vested remainder:** A *vested* remainder, by contrast, can *never* violate the Rule, because a vested remainder *vests at the moment it is created*.

    Example: O conveys "to A for life, remainder to A's children for life, remainder to B and his heirs." The gift to B and his heirs does not violate the Rule, because that gift is a vested remainder, which vested in interest (though not in possession) on the date of the conveyance. Therefore, even though the remainder to B and his heirs might not become possessory until later than lives in being plus 21 years (as where A's last surviving child is one who was not born on the date of conveyance, and who dies after age 21), the gift to B is valid.

3. **Reversion:** The Rule does *not* apply to *reversionary interests* (reversions, possibilities of reverter, and rights of entry). These are deemed to vest as soon as they are created.

4. **Executory interests:** The Rule applies to *executory interests*, because such interests are *not vested* at their creation.

    Example: O conveys "to the City of Klamath Falls, so long as the city maintains a library on the property, then to A and his heirs." The executory interest in A violates the Rule, because it might vest beyond lives in being plus 21 years — the city might maintain a library on the property longer than any life in being at the time of the gift plus 21 years. Therefore, instead of the executory interest in A being valid, O and his heirs have a possibility of reverter which will become possessory if the city ever stops using the library.

5. **Options to purchase land:** An *option* to *purchase land* will often be subject to the Rule.

a. **Option as part of lease:** If an option to purchase property is part of a *lease* of that property and is exercisable only during the lease term, then the option is *not* subject to the Rule.

b. **Option "in gross":** But if the option is *not* part of a lease or other property interest, most states hold that the Rule *does* apply. Such an unattached option is called an option *"in gross."*

Example: O sells Blackacre to A, with the condition that if at any time the property is used for the sale of alcohol, O or his heirs may repurchase the property for the amount originally paid by A. Since there is no time limit to this option, and since the option is not attached to any lease or continuing interest by O, the option is void as a violation of the Rule.

C. **"Lives in being":** Normally, "lives in being" means one or more persons who are *actually mentioned* in the conveyance or bequest. These are sometimes called *"measuring lives."*

Example: O conveys "to my daughter D for life, then to her first child to reach the age of 21." D is childless at the date of the conveyance. D is the "life in being" or "measuring life." The contingent remainder to D's oldest child is valid, because we know that any child D may eventually have will reach 21 within 21 years after D's death.

D. **Special situations:** At common law, there are some remote possibilities that nonetheless count for the purposes of the Rule:

1. **Fertile octogenarian:** There is a conclusive presumption that any person, regardless of age or physical condition, is capable of *having children*. This is the *"fertile octogenarian"* rule, which will sometimes make a reasonable gift invalid.

    Example: T conveys "to A for life, then to A's surviving children for life, then to the surviving children of B." At the time of T's death, B has three children, and B herself is 80 years old. But it is conceivable that B could now have another child, and that that child would take after lives in being plus 21 years — for instance, all of A's children might be born after T's death, and might die more than 21 years after T's death. Therefore, B's three now-living children will not take anything since their interest violates the Rule. It doesn't matter that B could not possibly have any further children as a medical matter.

2. **Unborn widow:** Similarly, if an interest is created which will flow through the *"widow"* of X (by naming and relying on her in determining when the interest will vest), the common-law view is that the interest *must fail*. This is the *"unborn widow"* rule.

    Example: In 1995, T bequeaths Blackacre "to A for life, then to A's widow, then to the issue of A and A's widow who survive them." At T's death, A is married to B. It is possible that B will either predecease or divorce A, and A will then marry someone born after 1995 (we'll call her C.) C would be not be a life-in-being in 1995, the time of the bequest. Since the contingent remainder to the issue can't vest without referring to the life of C, it is not certain to vest within 21 years of the relevant lives that were in being *at the time the remainder was created* (C might live longer than 21 years after the death of A). Therefore, the contingent remainder to the issue of A and "A's widow" must fail.) (But a modern court might accept evidence that T intended "A's widow" to refer to B in particular, in which case the gift will be valid.)

3. **Class gifts:** If a gift is made to all members of a *class*, the entire gift fails unless it can be said that *each member of the class* must have his interest vest or fail within lives in being plus 21 years. This rule will be triggered if the class could *obtain new members* following a testator's death.

> **Example:** T bequeaths property "to A, then to A's surviving children who attain the age of 25." At the time of the bequest, A has two children, B and C. It is possible that another child (called hypothetically "D"), will be born after T's death. Since A, B and C might all die prior to D's fourth birthday, D's interest would then vest too remotely (more than 21 years after the deaths of A, B and C, the measuring lives). Therefore, not only is the gift invalid as to children born after T's death, but it is also invalid as to B and C, according to the strict common-law approach.

E. **"Wait and see" statutes:** Many states reject the common-law principle that if a scenario could be imagined whereby the interest might vest too remotely, it is invalid regardless of how things actually turn out. These states have adopted *"wait and see"* statutes, by which if the interest actually vests within lives in being at the time of creation plus 21 years, the fact that things might have worked out differently is irrelevant.

> **Example:** O conveys Blackacre "to A and his heirs, but if A or his heirs ever uses Blackacre for other than residential purposes, to B and his heirs." At common law, the executory interest in B is void, since the premises might stop being used for residential purposes more than lives in being plus 21 years. But under the wait-and-see test, if the property ceases to be used for residential purposes within 21 years after the death of the survivor of O, A and B, the gift over to B and his heirs is valid.

1. **Effect on fertile octogenarian and unborn widow cases:** The wait-and-see approach virtually knocks out the fertile octogenarian and unborn widow cases. So long as the octogenarian does not in fact have a child, or the widow referred to in the instrument in fact turns out to be someone born prior to the instrument, the Rule Against Perpetuities is not violated.

IX. RESTRAINTS ON ALIENATION

A. **Restraints generally void:** A *restraint on the alienation* of a *fee simple* is generally *void*.

> **Example:** O conveys Blackacre "to A and his heirs, but no conveyance by A to any third party shall be valid." Since this restricts the alienation of a fee simple, the restriction will be void, and A may convey to whomever he wishes.

1. **Life estates:** But a *life estate* may be subjected to restraints on alienation.

Example: O conveys "to A for life, but A shall have no right to convey his interest; then to B and his heirs." The restraint upon A's life estate will generally be upheld.

2. **Use restrictions:** *Use restrictions* will generally be *upheld*.

    Example: O conveys "to A and his heirs, provided that the property not be used for non-residential purposes." This use restriction will be upheld, and will not be struck down as a restraint upon alienation.

3. **Defeasible estates:** The defeasible estates (e.g., fee simple determinable) are also enforced, even though they are in a sense restraints on alienation.

    Example: O conveys "to A and his heirs, but if the property is ever used for the purposes of sale of alcohol, Grantor or his heirs may re-enter." This will be enforced even though it to some extent restrains alienability.

CHAPTER 6

MARITAL ESTATES

I. THE COMMON-LAW SYSTEM — RIGHTS DURING MARRIAGE

A. The common-law system generally: All but eight states govern marital property in a way that is derived from traditional common-law principles.

B. The feudal system: The feudal system gave the husband extreme dominion over his wife's property, by means of the doctrines of coverture and *jure uxoris*.

1. **Personal property (coverture):** Under the doctrine of *"coverture"*, all personal property owned by the wife at the time of the marriage became the property of the husband.

2. **Real property *(jure uxoris):*** Under the doctrine of *"jure uxoris"*, the husband had the right to *possess* all his wife's lands during the marriage, and to spend the rents and profits of the land as he wished.

C. Married Women's Property Acts: All states have enacted Married Women's Property Acts, which undo couverture and *jure uxoris*, give the woman equality, and protect her assets from her husband's creditors.

II. THE COMMON-LAW SYSTEM — EFFECT OF DIVORCE

A. Traditional "title" view: Under traditional common-law principles, if the parties were *divorced*, the division of their property depended heavily on who held formal legal *"title"* to the property.

1. **Title in husband's name:** Most significantly, if the legal title to property was held by one spouse alone, that spouse *retained title upon divorce*. This was usually to the husband's advantage.

B. Modern "equitable distribution": Today, every common-law property state has *abolished* the "title" approach to property division at divorce. Instead, all have substituted by statute a doctrine called *"equitable distribution,"* by which property is divided by the court according to the demands of fairness, not based on who has title.

    1. What property is covered: Most states allow the court to divide only *"marital property"* under equitable distribution principles. Usually, marital property is defined to include only property *acquired during the marriage from the earnings of the parties.* (So property acquired *before marriage*, or acquired by one spouse through a *gift or bequest* to that spouse, is not included in the assets to be distributed.)

III. THE COMMON-LAW SYSTEM — DEATH OF A SPOUSE

A. Dower and curtesy: At common law, the surviving spouse was provided for by the doctrines of "dower" and "curtesy".

    1. Dower: A widow (W) received *"dower."* This was defined as a *life estate* in *one-third* of the *lands* of which H was seised at any time during the marriage, provided that H's interest was *inheritable by the issue* of the marriage (if any). So any land owned in *fee simple* by H alone, or by H and a third person as tenants in common, qualified for dower. (But there was no dower in a life estate held by H, even a life estate per autre vie.)

        a. Dower inchoate: While H was alive, W got a right of *dower inchoate* as soon as H became seized. This meant that any conveyance of the freehold by H to a third party did not affect the right of dower inchoate, so after H died W could still demand her dower rights from the person who bought from H.

    2. Curtesy: A widower (H) was entitled to *"curtesy."* This was a life estate in *each piece* of real estate in which W held a freehold interest during their marriage, provided the freehold was inheritable by issue born alive of the marriage. (So if H and W were childless, and W predeceased H, H had no right of curtesy).

    3. Abolished in most jurisdictions: In all but six American jurisdictions, dower and curtesy have been *abolished*.

    4. Practical importance: Where dower and curtesy still exist, the main consequence is that *both husband and wife* must *sign any deed* if the recipient is to take free and clear of the right, even if only one spouse holds title.

        a. Elective share available: In the six remaining dower and/or curtesy states, the survivor may take an "elective share" (see below) instead, which is almost always more generous.

B. Modern "elective share" statutes: The modern substitute for dower and curtesy is the *"elective share."* The surviving spouse has the right to *renounce the will*, and instead receive a designated portion of the estate.

    1. Effect: The effect of an elective share statute (which all common-law property states but Georgia have) is that *one spouse cannot "disinherit" the other.*

2. **Size of share:** Most commonly, the elective share is *one-half* or *one-third*. Both personal and real property are covered.

3. **Length of marriage irrelevant:** Most elective share statutes treat the *length of marriage* as *irrelevant* — a woman widowed after one day of marriage gets the same share of her husband's estate as one married for 50 years.

IV. COMMUNITY PROPERTY

A. **Community property generally:** In eight states, the rights of husband and wife in property is governed by the *civil-law* concept of *"community property"*. These states are Arizona, California, Idaho, Louisiana, New Mexico, Nevada, Texas and Washington.

1. **General approach:** The key tenet of community property is that property acquired during the marriage (with exceptions) belongs *jointly* to husband and wife from the moment it is acquired. Thus upon *divorce* or *death*, the property is treated as belonging *half to each spouse*.

B. **What is "community property":** All property acquired during the marriage is *presumed* to be community property (though this presumption may be rebutted by showing it falls within one of the classes of "separate property" described below).

1. **Before marriage:** Property acquired by either spouse *before marriage* is separate, not community, property.

2. **Gift or inheritance:** Property acquired by *gift, inheritance or bequest*, even *after marriage*, is separate property.

3. **Earnings:** Income produced by either spouse's *labor* is community property.

> **Example:** H is an employee. His salary is community property. Also, if he gets stock in his employer, pension rights, or insurance as part of his job, these probably also are fruits of his labor and therefore community property.

C. **Divorce:** Generally, if *divorce* occurs, the community property is *evenly divided*.

D. **Death:** Upon the *death* of one of the parties, the community property is treated as having belonged half to the deceased spouse and half to the surviving spouse. A deceased spouse's half is thus subject to his right to devise it by will to whomever he wishes.

> **Example:** H and W hold Blackacre as community property. H dies, and his will gives whatever interest he has to S, his son by a prior marriage. S and W will hold the property as tenants in common, each with an undivided one-half interest.

V. HOMESTEAD EXEMPTION

A. **Homestead exemptions:** Most states have enacted *"homestead exemptions."* Exempted property may not be seized and sold by *creditors*. Usually, the family's *residence* is exempt from seizure, but only up to a certain dollar limit. Also, homestead exemptions do not bar a *mortgagee* from foreclosing — the exemption only protects against seizure by "general" or "unsecured" creditors.

CHAPTER 7

CONCURRENT OWNERSHIP

I. CONCURRENT OWNERSHIP GENERALLY

A. Three types: There are three ways in which two or more people may own present possessory interests in the same property: (1) joint tenancy (which includes the right of survivorship); (2) tenancy in common (which does not have the right of survivorship); and (3) tenancy by the entirety (which exists only between husband and wife, and which includes not only survivorship but "indestructibility.")

II. JOINT TENANCY

A. Joint tenancy generally: In a *joint tenancy*, two or more people own a *single, unified* interest in real or personal property.

  1. General attributes: Here are the most important attributes of a joint tenancy:

    a. Survivorship: Each joint tenant has a *right of survivorship*. That is, if there are two joint tenants, and one dies, the other becomes *sole owner* of the interest that the two of them had previously held jointly.

    b. Possession: Each joint tenant is entitled to *occupy* the *entire* premises, subject only to the same right of occupancy by the other tenant(s).

    c. Equal shares: Since the joint tenants have identical interests, they must have "equal shares." Thus one joint tenant cannot have a one-fourth interest, say, with the other having a three-fourths interest.

B. Creation: A joint tenancy must be created by a *single instrument* (deed or will), and must be created in both or all joint tenants at the *same time*.

  1. Language used: Usually, a joint tenancy is created by specific language: "To A and B as joint tenants with right of survivorship."

  2. Conveyance by A to A and B: At common law, A (owner of a fee simple) *cannot* create a joint tenancy between himself and another by conveying "to A and B as joint tenants." But many states, by statute or case law, now permit this result.

C. Severance: There are a number of ways in which a joint tenancy may be *severed*, i.e., *destroyed*. Severance normally results in the creation of a *tenancy in common*.

  1. Conveyance by one joint tenant: A joint tenant may *convey* his interest to a *third party*. Such a conveyance has the effect of destroying the joint tenancy. (*Example*: A and B hold Blackacre as joint tenants. A conveys his interest to C. This conveyance destroys the joint tenancy, so that B and C now become tenants in common, not joint tenants.)

    a. Three or more joint tenants: If there are *three* or more original joint tenants, a conveyance by one of them to a stranger will produce a tenancy in common as between the stranger and the remaining original joint tenants, but the joint tenancy will continue as between the original members.

Example: A, B and C hold Blackacre as joint tenants. A conveys his interest to X. Now, X will hold an undivided one-third interest in the property as a tenant in common with B and C. B and C hold a two-thirds interest, but they hold this interest as joint tenants with each other, not as tenants in common. Thus if X dies, his interest goes to his heirs or devisees. But if B dies, his interest goes to C.

2. **Granting of mortgage:** Courts are split as to whether the *granting of a mortgage* by one joint tenant severs the joint tenancy. In so-called "title theory" states, the mortgage is treated as a conveyance, and thus severs the joint tenancy (so that the mortgagee can foreclose on the undivided one-half interest of the mortgagor, but the interest of the other party is not affected). In "lien theory" states, the mortgage does not sever the joint tenancy; in some but not all lien theory states, if the mortgagee dies first, the other joint tenant takes the whole property free and clear of the mortgage.

3. **Lease:** Most courts seem to hold that a *lease* issued by one joint tenant does not act as a severance.

III. TENANCY IN COMMON

A. **Tenancy in common:** Whereas in a joint tenancy each party has an equal interest in the whole, in a "tenancy in common" each tenant has a *separate "undivided"* interest.

1. **No right of survivorship:** The most important difference between the tenancy in common and the joint tenancy is that there is *no right of survivorship* between tenants in common. Thus each tenant in common can make a *testamentary transfer* of his interest; if he dies intestate, his interest will pass under the statute of descent.

    Example: A and B take title to Blackacre as tenants in common. They have equal shares. A dies, without a will, leaving only one relative, a son, S. Title to Blackacre is now: a one-half undivided interest in S, and a one-half undivided interest in B.

2. **Unequal shares:** Tenants in common may have *unequal shares* (unlike joint tenants).

    Example: A and B may hold as tenants in common, with A holding an "undivided one-quarter interest" and B an "undivided three-quarters interest."

    a. **Rebuttable presumption of equality:** If the conveyance does not specify the size of the interests, there is a *rebuttable presumption* that *equal* shares were intended.

3. **Presumption favoring:** Most states have a *presumption* in *favor* of tenancies in common, rather than joint tenancies, so long as the co-tenants are not husband and wife. But this can be rebutted by clear evidence showing that the parties intended to create a joint tenancy.

4. **Heirs:** Apart from a conveyance directly creating a tenancy in common, a tenancy in common can result from operation of law, including the *intestacy* statute:

if the intestacy statute specifies that two persons are to take an equal interest as co-heirs, they take as tenants in common.

> **Example:** A, fee simple owner of Blackacre, dies without a will. His sole surviving relatives are a son, S, and a daughter, D. The intestacy statute says that heirs who are children take "equally." S and D will take title to Blackacre as tenants in common, each holding an undivided one-half interest.

IV. TENANCY BY THE ENTIRETY

A. Tenancy by the entirety generally: At common law, any conveyance to two persons who were *husband and wife* resulted automatically in a *"tenancy by the entirety."*

   1. Usually abolished: Only 22 states retain the tenancy by the entirety. Even in these states, it is no longer the case (as it was at common law) that a conveyance to husband and wife necessarily creates a tenancy by the entirety — instead, there is usually just a rebuttable *presumption* that a conveyance to a husband and wife is intended to create a tenancy by the entirety.

   2. No severance: The key feature of the tenancy by the entirety is that it is *not subject to severance*. So long as both parties are alive, and remain husband and wife, neither one can break the tenancy. Most significantly, each spouse knows that if he or she survives the other, he/she will get a *complete interest*.

   > **Example:** H and W hold Blackacre as tenants by the entirety. H conveys his interest to X. In all states, if W survives H, W will get the property outright and X will get nothing. (But in some states, the conveyance will be effective to the limited extent that if H survives W, X, not H, will get the property.)

   3. Divorce: If the parties are *divorced*, the tenancy by the entirety *ends*. The parties are then treated as owning equal shares (usually as tenants in common).

V. RELATIONS BETWEEN CO-TENANTS

A. Possession: Regardless of the form of co-tenancy, each co-tenant has the *right to occupy the entire premises*, subject only to a similar right in the other co-tenants. (But the parties may make an *agreement* to the contrary.)

   1. No duty to account: If the property is solely occupied by one of the co-tenants, he normally has *no duty to account* for the value of his exclusive possession (e.g., he has no duty to pay the non-occupying co-tenant one-half of what a normal rent would be). But there are two main exceptions:

   a. Ouster: If the occupying tenant *refuses to permit* the other tenant equal occupancy, then he is said to have *"ousted"* the other tenant, and must *account* to the ousted co-tenant for the latter's share of the *fair rental value* of the premises.

   b. Depletion: Also, the occupying tenant will have a duty to account if he *depletes the land*.

   > **Example:** A and B are co-tenants of Blackacre. A mines coal from the property. A must split the profits with B.

B. Payments made by one tenant: If one tenant makes *payments* on behalf of the property (e.g., property tax, mortgage payments, repairs, etc.), that tenant does *not* have an automatic right to *collect* the share from the other tenants. However, the tenant making the payment may *deduct* the payment from rents he collects from third parties; also, he will be reimbursed for these payments "off the top" before any proceeds from a *sale* are distributed.

C. Partition: Any tenant in common or joint tenant (but not a tenant by the entirety) may bring an equitable action for *partition*. By this means, the court will either *divide* the property, or order it *sold* and the proceeds distributed.

CHAPTER 8

LANDLORD AND TENANT

I. INTRODUCTION

A. Various types: There are four estates that involve a landlord-tenant relationship: (1) the tenancy for *years*; (2) the *periodic* tenancy; (3) the tenancy *at will*; and (4) the tenancy at *sufference*.

B. Statute of Frauds: Under the original English Statute of Frauds, any lease for *more than three years* must be *in writing*. (Otherwise, it merely creates an "estate at will.") In the U.S., most statutes now require a writing for all leases for *more than one year*.

    1. Option to renew: In calculating whether a lease is for more than one year (so that it probably has to be in writing), most courts add together the fixed term and any period for which the tenant has the *option* to *renew*.

C. The estate for years: Most leases are *estates for years*. An estate for years is any estate which is for a *fixed period of time*. (So even a six-month lease is an "estate for years.")

    1. Certain term: For a lease to be an estate for years, the beginning date and end date must be *fixed*.

    2. Automatic termination: Because an estate for years contains its own termination date, *no additional notice of termination* need be given by either party — on the last day, the tenancy simply ends, and the tenant must leave the premises.

D. Periodic tenancy: The *periodic tenancy* is one which *continues* from one period to the next *automatically*, unless either party terminates it at the end of a period by notice. Thus a year-to-year tenancy, or a month-to-month one, would be periodic.

    1. Creation by implication: Normally a periodic tenancy is created by *implication*. Thus a lease with no stated duration (e.g., T agrees to pay L "$200 per month," but with no end period) creates a periodic tenancy. Also, if a tenant *holds over*, and the landlord accepts rent, probably a periodic tenancy is created.

    2. Termination: A periodic tenancy will automatically be *renewed* for a further period unless one party gives a valid *notice of termination*.

a. Common law: At common law, six months' notice was needed to terminate a year-to-year tenancy, and a full period's notice was necessary when the period was less than a year (e.g., 30 days notice for a month-to-month tenancy). Also, at common law, the notice had to set the *end of a period* as the termination date.

b. Modern: Most states today require only 30 days notice for any tenancy, even year-to-year. Notice today must still generally be effective as of the end of a period, but if the notice is not sufficiently in advance of one period, it is automatically applicable to the following period.

Example: L and T have a month-to-tenancy; if one gives the other notice of termination on January 4, this will be effective as of February 28.

E. At-will tenancy: A *tenancy at will* is a tenancy which has *no stated duration* and which may be *terminated at any time* by either party.

    1. Implication: Usually a tenancy at will, like a periodic tenancy, is created by *implication*. For instance, if T takes possession with L's permission, with no term stated and no period for paying rent defined (so that the lease is not even a periodic one), it will probably be at will. Also, a few courts hold that if one party has the option to terminate at will, the other party has a similar option so that the tenancy is at will.

F. Tenancy at sufferance: There is only one situation in which the "tenancy at sufferance" exists: where a tenant *holds over* at the end of a valid lease. Here, the landlord has a *right of election*, between: (1) *evicting* the tenant; and (2) holding him to *another term* as tenant. (If L elects to hold T to another term, most courts hold that a periodic tenancy is then created, and the length of the period is determined by the way rent was computed under the lease which terminated.)

II.   TENANT'S RIGHT OF POSSESSION AND ENJOYMENT

A. Tenant's right of possession: Courts are split about whether L impliedly warrants to T that he will deliver *actual possession* at the start of the lease term. The question usually arises when a prior tenant *holds over*.

    1. "American" view: The so-called *"American"* view is that the landlord has a duty to deliver *only* legal possession, *not actual possession*. Despite the name, at most a slight majority of American courts follow this rule.

    2. "English" rule: Other courts follow the so-called *"English"* rule, by which L *does* have a duty to deliver actual possession. In courts following this rule, T has the right to *terminate the lease* and recover damages for the breach if the prior tenant holds over and L does not oust him. Alternatively, T may continue the lease and get damages for the period until the prior tenant is removed.

B. Quiet enjoyment: T has the right of *"quiet enjoyment"* of the leased premises. This right can be violated in two main ways: (1) by claims of *"paramount title"*; and (2) by acts of L, or persons claiming under him, which interfere with T's *possession or use* of the premises.

1. **Claims of paramount title:** L, by making the lease, impliedly warrants that he has *legal power* to give possession to T for the term of the lease. If someone else successfully asserts a claim to the property which is superior to T's claim under the lease (a claim of *"paramount title"*), L has breached this warranty. Thus suppose that X shows that L does not have title to the premises at all (because X has title), or that X shows that L has previously leased the premises to X, or that X shows that X holds a mortgage on the premises, and is entitled to foreclose because L has not made mortgage payments — in all of these instances, X's claim of paramount title constitutes a breach by L of his implied warranty.

    a. **Before T takes possession:** If T discovers the paramount title *before* he takes possession, he may *terminate the lease*.

    b. **After T takes possession:** Once T takes possession, he may *not* terminate the lease (or refuse to pay rent) merely on the grounds that a third person *holds* a paramount title. (It is sometimes said that T is *"estopped to deny L's title"* to the leased property.) On the other hand, if the third person then *asserts* his paramount title in such a way that T is *evicted*, T may terminate the lease and recover damages.

2. **Interference by landlord or third person:** If L himself, or someone claiming under L, *interferes* with T's *use* of the premises, this will be a breach of the covenant of quiet enjoyment.

    a. **Conduct by other tenants:** If the conduct of *other tenants* makes the premises uninhabitable for T, the traditional view is that L is *not* responsible (unless the other tenants use their portion for immoral or lewd purposes, or conduct their acts in the *common areas*). But the *modern trend* is to impute the acts of other tenants to L where these acts are *in violation of the other leases*, and L could have prevented the conduct by eviction or otherwise.

       Example: Suppose that other tenants make a great deal of noise in violation of their leases, so that L could evict them, but does not. The modern trend, but not the traditional rule, is that T may terminate the lease.

    b. **Constructive eviction:** If T's claim is merely that his *use* or *enjoyment* of the property has been substantially impaired (e.g., excessive noise, terrible odors) the eviction is *"constructive"*. When T is constructively evicted, even if this is L's fault, T is not entitled to terminate or stop paying rent unless he *abandons the premises*.

       Example: Other tenants make so much noise that T's use is severely impaired. If T remains in the premises, he may not reduce the rent payments to L; he must leave and terminate the lease, or else pay the full lease amount.

C. **Condemnation:** If the government uses its right of eminent domain to *condemn* all or part of the leased premises, T may have a remedy.

    1. **Total taking:** If the *entire* premises are taken, the *lease terminates*, and T does not have to pay the rent.

    2. **Partial:** But if only a *portion* of the premises is taken (even a major part), at common law the lease is *not terminated*. Also, T must *continue paying the full*

rent (though he gets an appropriate portion of any condemnation award which L collects from the government). However, the modern trend is to let T terminate if the condemnation *"significantly interferes"* with his use, and to give him a reduction in rent even for a small interference.

D. Illegality: If T intends to use the property for *illegal purposes*, and L knows this fact, the court will probably treat the lease as *unenforceable*, especially if the illegality would be a serious one (e.g., crack distribution).

    1. Variance or permit: If the use intended by T requires a *variance* or *permit*, and T is unable to get the variance or permit after the lease is signed, most courts hold that the lease *remains valid*.

III. CONDITION OF THE PREMISES

A. Common-law view: At common law, T takes the premises *as is*. L is *not* deemed to have made any implied warranty that the premises are *fit* or *habitable*. Nor does L have any *duty to repair* defects arising during the course of the lease (unless the parties explicitly provide that he does).

    1. Independence of covenants: Also, the common law applies the doctrine of *"independence of covenants"* in leases. Thus even if L does expressly promise to repair (or warrants that the premises are habitable), if he breaches this promise T must still pay rent. T may sue for damages, but he is stuck in the uninhabitable living conditions.

    2. Constructive eviction: However, even at common law, T can raise the defense of *"constructive eviction"* — he can terminate the lease if he can show that the premises are virtually uninhabitable. But he can only assert constructive eviction if he first *leaves the premises*, something which a poor tenant in uninhabitable residential space can rarely afford to do.

B. Modern implied warranty of habitability: But today, the vast majority of states (either by statute or case law) impose some kind of *implied warranty of habitability*. That is, if L leases residential premises to T, he impliedly warrants that the premises are in at least *good enough condition to be lived in*. If L breaches this warranty, T may (among other remedies) withhold rent, and use the withheld rent to make the repairs himself.

    1. Waiver of known pre-existing defects: Some (but by no means all) courts hold that if T *knows* of the defect *before he moves in*, he will be held to have *waived* the defect, so that the implied warranty of habitability does not apply to that defect. (If the defect is one which T neither discovered nor reasonably could have discovered before moving in, then all courts agree that an otherwise-applicable implied warranty of habitability protects T against the defect.)

    2. Standards for determining "habitability": All courts agree that the existence of a *building code violation* is at least *evidence* of uninhabitability. However, most courts require that to prove uninhabitability, T must show that the conditions not only violate the building code, but are also a *substantial threat to T's health or safety*. (Conversely, most courts hold that if conditions *are* a substantial threat to T's health or safety, the warranty is breached even if there is no building code violation.)

    a. Relevance of nature of building: Some (but not all) courts hold that the *age of the building* and the *amount of rent charged* may be considered in determining whether there has been a breach. Thus a given condition might be a breach of the warranty as to a new luxury highrise, but not as to an old low-rent structure.

3. Kinds of leases:

    a. Residential: Most *statutes* imposing an implied warranty of habitability apply to *all residential* leases (though some apply merely to units in multiple dwellings, so that a single-family house would not be covered).

    b. Commercial leases: Most statutes and cases do *not* impose an implied warranty of habitability as to *commercial* leases.

4. Waiver in lease: Generally, a clause in the lease expressly stating that there is no implied warranty is usually *not effective*. (But some statutes, such as the URLTA, will enforce a deal in which T promises, in a *separate writing*, and for adequate consideration such as a lower rent, to *make repairs himself*.)

5. Remedies: If T shows a breach of the implied warranty of habitability, he may have a number of *remedies*:

    a. Terminate lease: T may usually *vacate the premises* and *terminate* the lease (after he puts L on notice and L still refuses to make the repairs).

    b. Withhold rent: T may also *withhold rent* until the defects have been cured. (But most statutes, and some cases, require T to *deposit* the rent in some sort of escrow account.)

    c. Use rent for repairs: Many cases and statutes allow T to *make the repairs* and then to *deduct the reasonable costs* of those repairs from the rent. T must usually give L advance notice of his intent to make the repairs and to deduct (so that L can make the repairs himself to avoid the loss of rent).

6. Retaliatory eviction barred: By the doctrine of *"retaliatory eviction,"* L usually may not terminate a periodic lease, or deny T's request for a new lease at the conclusion of a tenancy for years, on account of T's assertion of the right to habitable premises. The doctrine is most likely to be applied where L tries to terminate the tenancy in retaliation for T's complaints made to a housing authority about *code violations*. Also, some courts apply the doctrine where the non-renewal or termination is in retaliation for T's withholding of rent or his joining in a tenants' organization.

C. Destruction of premises: If the premises are suddenly *destroyed* or *damaged* (by fire, flood, lightning or other natural elements), at common law T must *keep paying rent*, and may not terminate the lease.

1. Modern view: But most states have now passed *statutes* changing this common-law rule — if the premises are destroyed or damaged so that they are no longer habitable, T may now usually *terminate the lease* and stop paying rent. Also, some courts have reached this result by case law. (But T usually cannot recover damages, so termination of the lease is his only remedy.)

IV. TORT LIABILITY OF LANDLORD AND TENANT

A. Tenant's tort liability: T, during the time he is in possession of the premises, is treated *like an owner*, for purposes of his *tort liability* to others who come onto the property. (*Example*: Since L would have a duty to warn a social guest, or licensee, of known dangers, T has a similar duty to warn of dangers that he is aware of.)

B. Landlord's liability:

1. **Common law:**   At common law, L is generally *not liable* for physical injury to T, or to persons who are on the leased property with T's consent. That is, L has no general duty to use reasonable care to make or keep the premises safe. However, there are a number of *exceptions* (including some developed by courts recently), including the following:

    a. **Concealment:**   L is liable if he *conceals*, or *fails to disclose*, a dangerous defect existing at the start of the lease of which he is *aware*.

        i.   **L should know but does not:**   Most courts also hold that if L does not have actual knowledge but *should know* about the danger, based on facts that he does know, he will be liable for failing to warn.

        ii. **No duty of inspection:**   But L has *no duty of inspection*, i.e., no obligation to inspect the property to find out whether there are hidden defects.

    b. **Liability to persons other than T:**   Nearly all courts hold that if L would be liable to T, he is also liable to *persons on the premises with T's consent*. (But if L has told T about the defect, L will not be liable to T's guests even if T did not pass on the warning.)

    c. **Areas under L's control:**   L has a duty to use *reasonable care* to keep the *common areas* safe (e.g., lobbies, elevator, corridor, etc.).

        i.   **Security against criminals:**   Most courts now require L to use reasonable care to prevent *unauthorized access* to the building.

            Example: L, the owner of an apartment building, fails to repair the building's outer lock after being told that it is broken. X enters, and mugs T. Most courts would hold L liable for not using reasonable care to secure the building.

    d. **Repairs negligently performed:**   If L *attempts* to make a repair, he will be liable if the repair is done negligently, and L has made the condition more dangerous or lulled T into a false feeling of security. (But if L's negligent repair does not make the condition worse or lull T, the courts are split as to whether L is liable if T is injured.)

    e. **L contracts to repair:**   If a *clause in the lease* requires L to make *repairs* or otherwise keep the premises safe, L will be liable in tort if he fails to use reasonable care and T is injured. Also, L is probably liable to *third persons* on the premises with T's consent in this situation.

    f.   **L's legal duties:** If *building codes* or other laws impose a duty on L to keep the premises safe, L will generally be liable in tort if he fails in this duty. Probably L will also be liable if he breaches an implied warranty of habitability, and the uninhabitable condition causes injury to T or T's guest.

    g.   **Admission of public:** If L has reason to believe that T will *hold the premises open to the public*, and L has reason to know that a dangerous condition exists, L will be liable for resulting physical harm to the public. (L usually has an affirmative *duty to inspect* in this situation.)

2.   **General "reasonable care" theory:** Some recent cases have simply *rejected* the common law view that L has no general duty to use reasonable care. Under these cases, P does not have to fit within one of the above exceptions, and merely has to show that: (1) L failed to use reasonable care and (2) the lack of reasonable care proximately caused P's injury.

3.   **Exculpatory clauses:** At least in the case of a *residential* lease, most courts today *refuse* to enforce an *"exculpatory clause"* in a lease, that is, a clause purporting to relieve L of tort liability for his negligence. About half the states accomplish this by statute, and some others by case law.

V.   TENANT'S DUTIES

A. Duty to pay rent: T of course has a duty to *pay rent*.

    1.   **Breach of L's duties:** Most courts today hold that if L *materially breaches* his implied or express obligations (e.g., the implied warranty of habitability), T is temporarily *relieved* from continuing to pay rent.

B. Duty to repair: At common law, T had an implied duty to make *minor repairs*.

    1.   **Modern rule:** However, most courts today do not impose this duty on T (and indeed, most impose it on L under the doctrine of implied warranty of habitability, at least for residential leases).

C. Fixtures: A *fixture* is an item of personal property which is *attached* to the land (e.g., lighting, built-in bookcases, etc.).

    1.   **Right to affix:** T is usually allowed to *attach* fixtures if this would not unfairly damage the value of L's reversion.

    2.   **Right to remove:** Similarly, most courts today say that T may *remove* a fixture installed by him if this removal will not damage L's interests (so that T must normally *restore* the premises to the way they were before the fixture was attached).

D. Duty to behave reasonably: T has the implied duty to *behave reasonably* in his use of the premises.

    Examples: T must not unreasonably disturb other tenants, and must obey reasonable regulations posted by the landlord.

VI. LANDLORD'S REMEDIES

A. Security deposits:

1. **Interest:** In many states, L is required by statute to pay *interest* on the security deposit.

2. **Right to keep:** Once the lease terminates, L must *return* the deposit to T, after subtracting any damages. If T abandons the lease before the end of the lease term and L re-lets, L must *immediately* return the deposit (after subtracting damages).

3. **Commingle:** L may normally *commingle* the security deposit with his own funds.

4. **Purchaser's obligation:** Courts are split as to whether one who *purchases* L's interest in the property must account to T for the end of the deposit at the end of the lease term.

B. Acceleration clause: Most leases contain an *acceleration of rent* clause, by which if T fails to pay rent promptly or otherwise breaches the lease, L may require that all of the rent for the rest of the lease term is payable at once.

1. **Generally valid:** Most courts *enforce* such acceleration clauses. (But if L decides to sue for enforcement of the acceleration clause, he may not also demand possession of the premises.)

C. Eviction:

1. **Express forfeiture clause:** Most leases explicitly give L the right to *terminate the lease* if T fails to pay rent or violates any other lease provision. Such clauses will be enforced, but only if T's breach is *material*. (*Example*: If T is merely a couple days late with the rent on one or two occasions, the court will probably not allow L to terminate the lease.)

2. **Summary proceedings:** In most states, if L is entitled to terminate the lease and regain possession (or if T holds over at the end of the lease term and L wants to get him out), L may do so by *"summary proceedings,"* which provide for a *speedy trial* of L's right to immediate possession. Summary proceedings usually work by *limiting the defenses* which T may assert.

   Example: Some summary proceeding statutes prevent T from asserting the breach of the implied warranty of habitability as a defense in L's action to regain possession for non-payment of rent.

D. Damages for holdover: If T *holds over* after the lease terminates, L is entitled to *damages* as well as eviction.

E. Abandonment: If T *abandons* the premises (and defaults on the rent) before the scheduled end of the lease term, L has three basic choices: (1) to *accept a surrender* of the premises, thus terminating the lease; (2) to *re-let* on T's behalf; and (3) to leave the premises *vacant* and sue for rent as it comes due.

1. **Accept surrender:** L may treat T's abandonment as a *surrender*, and accept it. This has the effect of *terminating* the lease, so that *no further rent becomes due from T*. (If T takes possession and/or leases to someone else, and does not notify T

that he is acting on T's behalf, then this will probably be held to be an acceptance of surrender, causing T's rent obligation to end.)

2. **Re-letting on T's account:** L may *re-let on T's behalf*, if he notifies T that he is doing so. This has two advantages to L: (1) T remains liable for all rents coming due, if no new tenant is found; and (2) if a new tenant is found who pays a lesser rent, T is still liable for the difference between this and the original rent due under the L-T lease. (Courts are split on whether L must give the surplus to T if L relets for a *higher* amount.)

3. **Leave vacant:** Courts are split on whether L has the right to *leave the premises vacant*, and hold L to the lease. Usually, the question is phrased, "Does L have the duty to mitigate?"

   a. **Traditional view:** The traditional view is that L has *no duty to mitigate*, i.e., no duty to try to find a new tenant.

   b. **Duty to mitigate:** But an increasing minority of courts now hold that L *does have a duty to mitigate*, by attempting to find a suitable replacement tenant. In these courts, if L does not make such an effort, T is off the hook.

VII. TRANSFER AND SALE BY LESSOR; ASSIGNMENT AND SUBLETTING BY LESSEE

A. **Generally allowed:** Unless the parties to a lease agree otherwise, either may *transfer* his interest. Thus L may sell his reversion in the property, and T may either *assign* or *sublease* his right to occupy.

   1. **Distinguish assignment from sublease:** Be sure to distinguish *sublease* from *assignment*. An assignment is the transfer by T of his *entire interest* in the leased premises. Thus he must transfer the *entire remaining length* of the term of his lease. A *sublease* is the transfer by T of *less* than his entire interest.

      Example: T's lease has one year to go. T transfers the first 11.5 months of this interest to T1. In most states, this is a sublease, not an assignment.

      a. **Significance:** The main significance of this distinction is that if T assigns to T1, T1 is *personally liable* to *pay rent* to L, even if he makes no express promise to L or T that he will do so. If T merely subleases to T1, T1 is not personally liable to L for the rent (absent an explicit promise).

B. **Running of benefit and burden:** Determine whether a particular promise *runs with the land*, either as to benefit or burden. If the *benefit runs*, then an assignee of the promisee can sue to enforce; if the *burden runs*, an assignee of the promisor will be liable. If neither the burden nor benefit runs, then the promisor's assignee is not liable, and promisee's assignee cannot sue.

   Example 1 (benefit runs): In the L-T lease, T promises to make repairs. This promise "touches and concerns the land" both as to benefit and burden, so benefit and burden run. Thus if T assigns to T1, T1 is personally liable for making the repairs. Conversely, if L assigns to L1, L1 can sue T (and T1 if T has assigned to T1) to enforce this promise.

Example 2 (burdens runs, but benefit does not): In the L-T lease, T promises not to compete with L's use of certain other property. If T assigns to T1, T1 is liable not to compete. But if L assigns to L1, in most states L1 cannot enforce the promise against either T or T1.

1. **"Touch and concern" test:** The burden runs if the promise *"touches and concerns"* the promisor's assignee's interest in the land. Similarly, the benefit runs if the promise "touches and concerns" the promisee's assignee's interest in the property.

2. **Normally both or neither:** Normally, either the benefit and burden will both run, or neither will run. (The non-competition situation described in Example 2 above is one of the few examples where this is not true.)

C. **Rights after T assigns:** Here are the rights of the parties after T assigns to T1 his rights under the L-T lease:

1. **T's liability to L:** After the assignment, T *remains liable* to L (whether T's promise to L does or does not "touch and concern" the land).

   Example: T remains liable for the rent after assignment to T1. This is true even if L consents to the assignment, and even if L accepts some rent payments from T1.

2. **T's rights against T1:** After the assignment, T1 becomes *primarily liable*, and T is only secondarily liable. Therefore, if L sues T when T1 does not make the rent payments, T can then sue T1 for the amount that T has had to pay (even if T1 never expressly assumed the lease duties at the time of the assignment).

3. **L's rights against T1:** Assuming that T1 does not make any specific promises of performance when he takes the assignment, T1 is liable only for those promises made by T whose burden *runs with the land*.

   Example 1: T1 is liable to L for *rent*, since the burden of T's original rent promise ran with the land. Thus T1 must make the rent payments even if he did not expressly promise either T or L that he would make these payments.

   Example 2: In the original L-T lease, T promises to keep the premises insured. Assume that the burden of this promise does not run with the land (the majority rule). If T assigns to T1 and T1 does not make any promise of insurance, T1 is not liable for failing to insure the property (though L can terminate the lease for breach if T1 does not do so).

   a. **Assignment by assignee:** But T1 remains liable (even on promises whose burdens run with the land) only for the period when he is in *actual possession*. If he *re-assigns*, he is *not liable* for breaches by the subsequent assignee.

   Example: T assigns to T1. T1 remains in possession for six months, then assigns to T2. T1 is liable for the rent that accrued during the six months he was in possession, but not for any rents accruing after he left possession and T2 took possession.

  b. **Assumption:** However, if T1 *assumes* the lease (i.e., expressly promises T that T1 will obey all terms of the L-T lease), then T1 is liable both to T and L for all T's obligations, including those accruing after T1 re-assigns to T2.

D. Assignment by L: Now, assume that L assigns his rights to L1. Here, the same rule applies: L1 has the burden of covenants whose burden runs with the land, and has the benefit of covenants whose benefit runs with the land.

  1. **Repair obligation:** Thus if L promised T that he would keep the premises in repair, L1 is liable for making the repairs after the sale. (Also, the implied warranty of habitability, if it applies at all, probably binds L1 just as it bound L.)

E. Agreement by the parties about transfer: All of the above assumes that the lease itself contains no provisions restricting transfer. Most leases, however, contain a promise by T that he will *not assign or sublease his interest without L's consent.*

  1. **Generally enforced:** Most states *enforce* such a clause, even if L is completely *unreasonable* in refusing to consent to the transfer.

     a. **Strict construction and waiver:** However, courts construe such anti-transfer clauses strictly, and are quick to hold that L *waived* the benefit of the clause.

        Example: If L knowingly accepts rents from T1 he will probably be held to have waived his right to refuse to consent to the transfer.

     b. **Consent to second transfer:** Also, if L consents (or waives his objection to) a particular transfer, he is usually held to have also waived his right to a *subsequent* transfer, under the rule of *Dumpor's Case.* (*Example*: L consents to T's assignment to T1. In most states, L is also held to consent to T1's further assignment to T2.)

  2. **Modern trend:** An increasing minority of states hold (often by statute) that even if the lease says that L has an *unconditional* right to refuse to consent to a transfer by T, the *consent may not be unreasonably withheld*. (In such a state, L should get a lease provision giving him the right to *make his own deal* directly with T1 — this way, if T1 is willing to pay more than the original lease amount, L, not T, gets the benefit.)

CHAPTER 9

EASEMENTS AND PROMISES CONCERNING LAND

I. EASEMENTS GENERALLY

A. Definition: An *easement* is a privilege to *use the land of another*.

  1. **Affirmative easement:** An *affirmative* easement is one entitling its holder to *do a physical act* on another's land.

Example: A, who owns Blackacre, gives B a *right of way* over Blackacre, so that B can pass from his own property to a street which adjoins Blackacre. B holds an affirmative easement.

2. **Negative easement:** A *negative* easement is one which enables its holder to *prevent* the owner of land from making certain uses of that land. These are rare.

> **Example:** A owns Whiteacre, which is next to the ocean; B owns Blackacre, which is separated from the ocean by Whiteacre. A gives B an easement of "light and air," which assures B that A will not build anything on Whiteacre which would block B's view of the ocean. B holds a negative easement.

B. **Appurtenant vs. in gross:** Distinguish between easements that are *appurtenant* to a particular piece of land, and those that are *"in gross."*

1. **Appurtenant:** An easement *appurtenant* is one which benefits its holder in the use of a *certain piece of land*. The land for whose benefit the appurtenant easement is created is called the *"dominant tenement."* The land that is burdened or used is called the *"servient tenement."*

> **Example:** Blackacre, owned by S, stands between Whiteacre, owned by D, and the public road. S gives D the right to pass over a defined part of Blackacre to get from Whiteacre to the road. This right of way is an easement that is appurtenant to Whiteacre — Blackacre is the servient tenement, and Whiteacre is the dominant tenement.

    a. **Test for:** For an easement to be appurtenant, its benefit must be intimately *tied to a particular piece of land* (the dominant tenement).

2. **Easement in gross:** An easement *in gross* is one whose benefit is *not tied* to any particular parcel.

> **Example:** O, who owns Blackacre, gives E, who lives across town, the right to come onto Blackacre anytime he wants, and use O's swimming pool. Since the grant is not given because of E's ownership of nearby land, the easement is in gross.

3. **Profit:** Related to easements is something called the *"profit a prendre."* A profit is the right to go onto the land of another and *remove the soil or a product of it*. Thus the right to mine *minerals*, drill *oil*, or capture wild game or fish, are all profits. (In the U.S., profits are functionally identical to easements.)

II. CREATION OF EASEMENTS

A. **Four ways to create:** There are four ways to create an easement: (1) by an *express* grant; (2) by *implication*; (3) by strict *necessity*; and (4) by *prescription*.

B. **Express creation:** If a easement is created by a *deed* or a *will*, it is *"express."*

1. **Statute of Frauds:** An express easement *must be in writing*. This is required by the Statute of Frauds.

2. **Reservation in grantor:** Often, an express easement is created when the owner of land conveys the land to someone else, and *reserves for himself* an easement in it. This is called an "easement by reservation."

> **Example:** A deeds Blackacre to B, with a statement in the deed that "A hereby retains a right of way over the eastern eight feet of the property."

3. **Creation in stranger to deed:** At common law, it was *not* possible for an owner to convey land to one person, and to establish by the same deed an easement in a *third person*. (Thus an easement could not be created in a *"stranger to the deed."*) But most modern courts have *abandoned* this rule.

> **Example:** O owns two parcels, 1 and 2. O sells parcel 1 to P, without recording any easement over parcel 2 in favor of parcel 1. O then deeds parcel 2 to D, with a statement in the deed, "Easement reserved in favor of P or his successors to parcel 1." Today, this easement will be enforced even though P was not a party to the O-D deed.

C. **Creation by implication:** An easement by *implication* may sometimes be created. If so, it does *not have to satisfy the statute of frauds.*

1. **Requirements:** There are three requirements for an easement by implication: (1) land must be *divided up* (or "severed"), so that the owner of a parcel is either selling part and retaining part, or subdividing the property and selling pieces to different grantees; (2) the use for which the implied easement is claimed must have *existed prior to the severance*; and (3) the easement must be at least *reasonably necessary* to the enjoyment of the dominant tenement.

2. **Severance:** An easement will only be implied where the owner of a parcel *sells part and retains part*, or *sells pieces simultaneously* to more than one grantee. This is the requirement of *"severance."*

> **Example:** A and B are neighboring landowners. A new street is built adjoining B's property, and A can only get to this street by crossing B's property. A crosses B's property at a particular spot for several years, then sells to C. C has no easement by implication across B's property, because there was never any conveyance between A and B, required for the creation of an easement by implication.

3. **Prior use:** The use for which the easement is claimed must have existed *prior* to the severance of ownership.

4. **Necessity:** According to most courts, the easement must be *reasonably necessary* to the enjoyment of what is claimed to be the dominant tenement. Courts are stricter in imposing this requirement where the easement is created by *grant* (i.e., in favor of the grantee), than where the easement is *reserved* (i.e., in favor of the grantor).

> **Example of easement by implication:** O owns two houses side by side on one parcel. To give the garage behind house no. 1 access to the street, he builds a driveway which runs between the two houses. O then conveys house no. 2, including part of the land and the driveway, to A. An implied easement

in favor of house no. 1, and against the land on which house no. 2 is located, will be reserved with respect to the driveway. Also, if O conveys house no. 1, an implied easement in favor of that house will be created against the land of house no. 2. This is because: (1) O was the owner of both tenements just before the easement came into being; (2) the use existed prior to the severance of the two tenements; and (3) the easement is reasonably necessary to the enjoyment of house no. 1's garage.

5. **Easement of light and air:** An easement of *"light and air"* (the right to have one's view remain unobstructed) *cannot* be created by implication, in most states.

D. **Easement by necessity:** The courts will find an "easement by *necessity"* if two parcels are so situated that an easement over one is *"strictly necessary"* to the enjoyment of the other.

1. **Common grantor:** The courts require that *at one time*, both the alleged dominant tenement and the alleged servient tenement were owned by the same person.

2. **No prior use:** But unlike the easement by implication, there does not have to have been a *"prior use,"* that is, the easement does not have to have been used prior to the time the two parcels were split up.

> **Example:** O owns parcel 1 and parcel 2, which adjoin each other. In 1950, he sells parcel 1 to P and parcel 2 to D. In 1960, an old road serving parcel 1 is closed, and a new one is built so that the only way to get from parcel 1 to the road is by crossing parcel 2. Because both parcels were owned originally by the same owner, O, the courts will grant parcel 1 an easement over parcel 2 to get to the road, even though no such easement was in use at the time O split up the ownership of the parcels.

3. **Landlocked parcels:** The most common example of an easement by necessity is where a parcel is *landlocked*, so that access to a public road can only be gained via a right of way over adjoining property (as in the above example).

E. **Easement by prescription:** An easement by *"prescription"* is one that is gained under principles of *adverse possession*. If a person uses another's land for more than the statute of limitations period governing ejectment actions, he gains an easement by prescription.

> **Example:** In state X, the statute of limitations on actions to recover possession of real estate (ejectment actions) is 21 years. A, the owner of lot 1, uses a path over lot 2, owned by B, for 21 years. Assuming that the use meets the requirements discussed below (e.g., use must be "adverse," not "permissive"), after the 21 years A gains an easement by prescription, and may use the path as a right of way forever afterwards.

1. **When statute starts to run:** The statutory period does not begin to run until the owner of the servient tenement *gains a cause of action* against the owner of the dominant tenement. Therefore, an easement of *"light and air"* cannot be acquired by prescription (since the owner of the servient tenement never can sue the owner of the dominant tenement, because the latter merely looks out over the former's property, rather than trespassing upon it).

2. **Adverse use:** The use must be *adverse* to the rights of the holder of the servient tenement, and without the latter's *permission*.

> **Example:** P and D are next-door neighbors. Solely out of friendship, D agrees that P may use D's driveway to get to P's garage. P thanks D for this, and does not say that he is asserting an actual legal right to use the driveway. P's use is therefore not adverse, so even if the usage continues longer than the statute of limitations, no easement by prescription will be gained. Instead, the use is merely a *license*, which is revocable at will by D.

3. **Continuous and uninterrupted:** The use must be *continuous and uninterrupted* throughout the statutory period. Thus if the use is so *infrequent* that a reasonable landowner would not be likely to protest, the continuity requirement is not satisfied.

4. **Tacking:** There can be *tacking* on the dominant side of the prescriptive easement.

> **Example:** In a state with a 21-year statute of limitations on ejectment, A, the owner of Blackacre, uses a path across Whiteacre for 12 years. He then sells Blackacre to B, who uses the same path for an additional 9 years. At the end of this 9 years, B will have an easement by prescription, because he is in privity of estate with A and therefore can tack his use onto A's use.

III. SCOPE OF EASEMENTS

A. **Prescriptive easement:** If the easement is created by *prescription*, the *scope* of the allowable use is determined by looking at the use that took place during the statutory period. Therefore, a use that is substantially *broader* (or more burdensome to the servient tenement) than existed during the time when the statute of limitations was running, will *not* be allowed.

B. **Development of dominant estate:** Regardless of how the easement was created (e.g., whether by implication, prescription, etc.), the court will allow a use that increases dues to the *normal, foreseeable development* of the dominant estate, so long as this does not impose an *unreasonable burden* on the servient estate.

> **Example:** A right-of-way easement is created by prescription in favor of the sole house then located on a dominant tenement. After the easement is created, two more houses are built on the dominant property. The residents of all three houses may use the right of way, since the basic use — as a pedestrian right of way — remains unchanged, the increased use is a function of normal development, and the increase in the burden is slight.

C. **Use for benefit of additional property:** The holder of the dominant estate is normally *not* allowed to *extend his use* of the easement so that *additional property* owned by him (or by others) is benefitted.

> **Example:** W, the owner of Whiteacre, gives B, the owner of Blackacre, an express easement by which B may cross W's property to get from the road to a house on Blackacre. B then buys an adjoining parcel, Greenacre, tears down the house on

Whiteacre, builds a new house on Greenacre, and extends the path represented by the easement through Blackacre (which he still owns) to get to the new house on Greenacre. W will be able to enjoin this extended use, since the easement is now being used to benefit additional property beyond Blackacre, the originally-contemplated dominant estate.

IV. TRANSFER AND SUBDIVISION OF EASEMENTS

A. Transfer of burden: When the title to the *servient estate* is *transferred*, the burden of the easement *remains* with the property.

> **Example:** O, the owner of Blackacre, gives A, a neighboring landowner, an express right of way over Blackacre. O then sells Blackacre to B. After the sale, A's easement remains valid against Blackacre.

B. Transfer of benefit: Whether the *benefit* of an easement "runs with the land" (i.e., is *enforceable by an assignee*) depends on whether the easement is appurtenant or in gross.

1. **Transfer of easements appurtenant:** An easement *appurtenant* (one where the benefit applies to particular land only) normally *passes with the transfer of the dominant estate*. (Thus in the above example, if A sells his land to X, X may enforce the easement against either O or one who bought from O.)

    a. **Subdivision:** Also, if the dominant estate is *sub-divided* into smaller lots sold to different people, and the geography is such that each of the smaller lots can benefit from the easement, then each will generally be permitted to do so. (But this will not happen if this would result in an extreme *increase* in the burden to the servient estate.)

2. **Easements in gross:** But easements *in gross* are different.

    a. **Common law:** At common law, easements in gross are *not transferable*.

    > **Example:** O owns Blackacre, which adjoins a public beach. O gives A, a friend of his who lives in a different city, the right to park in O's driveway and walk across A's land to the beach. Since this easement is "in gross" — it is not intimately tied to particular land held by A — at common law it is not transferable by A to anyone else.

    b. **Modern view:** Today, courts continue to apply this rule of non-transferability to easements that are *"personal"* (as in the above example). But courts will often find that a *commercial* easement was intended to be transferable and will therefore hold it to be so.

    > **Example:** O gives the telephone company the right to string wires over his land. Today, because of the commercial nature of this easement in gross, most courts would hold that the phone company can assign this right to some other outfit that takes over the phone operations.

V. TERMINATION OF EASEMENTS

A. Abandonment: Unlike estates in land, an easement may be *terminated* by *abandonment* in some circumstances.

1. **Words alone insufficient:** The easement holder's *words alone* will *never* be sufficient to constitute an abandonment.

2. **Intent plus conduct:** But if the easement holder *intends* to abandon an easement, and takes *actions* manifesting that intent, he will be held to have abandoned the easement, and it will be extinguished.

    a. **Non-use:** For instance, *non-use* may on particular facts be action which manifests the easement holder's intent to abandon, in which case the abandonment will be effective.

       Example: A owns a summer cottage, which holds an appurtenant easement to use a driveway on B's next-door property. If A uses the cottage each year for three years, and fails to ever use the driveway, he may be held to have intended to abandon the easement. But if A's non-use for three years is because he doesn't even use the cottage, then no intent to abandon will be found, and therefore there will be no abandonment.

VI. LICENSES

A. Definition: A *license* is a right to use the licensor's land that is *revocable* at the will of the licensor. This revocability is the main thing that distinguishes licenses from easements. (But there are a couple of exceptions to the revocability of licenses, described below.)

1. **No Statute of Frauds:** A license is *not* required to satisfy the *Statute of Frauds*, so it may be created *orally*.

2. **Illustrations:** Some licenses are much like easements, except for revocability (e.g., O orally gives A the right to use O's driveway to get from A's land to the public highway; this would be an easement if it were in writing, but is a license because it is oral). Other licenses are much more transitory. For instance, a *ticket* to a sports event or concert is a license; similarly, the right to use a *parking lot* is generally only a license.

B. Exceptions to revocability: There are a couple of exceptions to the general rule that licenses are revocable at the grantor's will.

1. **Oral license acted upon:** Most important, a license is *irrevocable* if its use would have been an easement except for failure to meet the Statute of Frauds, and the licensee makes *substantial expenditures* on the land in *reliance* on the licensor's promise that the license will be permanent or of long duration.

    Example: P orally gives D permission to build a roadway across P's land so that D can get from his land to the public highway. D expends substantial money digging and paving the road. P attempts to revoke, and sues D for trespass. A court would probably hold that the license, though oral, was irrevocable because of D's substantial reliance expenditures.

VII. COVENANTS RUNNING WITH THE LAND

A. Definition: Like easements, *"covenants"* may under some circumstances run with the land. A covenant running with the land is simply a contract between two parties which, because it meets certain technical requirements, has the additional quality that it is *binding against one who later buys the promisor's land*, and/or *enforceable by one who later buys the promisee's land*.

1. Legal relief: When we use the term "covenant," we are talking about a promise that is subject to *legal* rather than equitable relief. That is, when a covenant is breached the relief granted is *money damages*, not an injunction or decree of specific performance. (An injunction or specific performance may be granted for breach of what is called an "equitable servitude," discussed below.)

B. Statute of Frauds: For a covenant to run with the land, it must be *in writing*.

C. Running with the land: The only interesting question about covenants is, When do they *run with the land*?

1. Running of burden and benefit: More specifically, we want to know: (1) When does the *burden* run (so that the promisor's assignee is bound)? and (2) When does the *benefit* run (so that the promisee's assignee can sue for damages if the covenant is breached)? We have to worry about: (1) the "touch and concern" requirement; and (2) the privity requirements.

    a. "Touch and concern": For the burden to run, the burden must *"touch and concern"* the promisor's land. Similarly, for the benefit to run, the benefit must "touch and concern" the promisee's land.

    b. Privity: Also, for the burden to run, there must be *"privity of estate,"* which usually means both a land transfer between the promisor and promisee ("horizontal" privity) plus a succession of estate from promisor to promisor's assignee ("vertical" privity). For the benefit to run, horizontal privity is sometimes required, but vertical privity is generally not. (See further discussion immediately below).

2. Privity between promisor and promisee ("horizontal" privity): Where a court requires *"horizontal" privity*, it means that there must be some land transfer between the original promisor and the original promisee.

    a. Running of burden: In America, *horizontal privity is required in order for the burden to run*. This mainly means that if the original parties are "strangers to title," the burden will not run. Thus two *neighboring landowners* cannot get together and agree that neither will use his property for a certain purpose, and have this restriction be binding on a subsequent purchaser from either of them.

    Example: A and B, neighboring landowners, agree in writing that neither will tear down his house to erect a new structure. B sells his property to X, who tears down that house. A cannot sue X for damages, because the burden of the covenant does not run with the land. This is so because there was never any land transfer between A and B, and thus no horizontal privity between them.

i. **Requirement satisfied:** But the horizontal requirement is satisfied if the original promisor and promisee have some land-transfer relationship.

> **Example:** A owns two parcels, each with a house on it. He sells one of the parcels to B. In the transfer agreement, A and B each promises the other that he will not tear down the house to build a new structure. B then re-conveys his parcel to X, who tears down the house. Now, A can sue X for damages, because there was horizontal privity between A and B, in the sense of a land transfer between them.

b. **Running of benefit:** Most courts hold that there must also be horizontal privity for the *benefit* to run. (Nearly all courts hold that the same privity rule that applies to running of burden applies to running of benefit; since most courts require horizontal privity for running of burden, they also require it for running of benefit.)

Example: A and B own adjacent parcels. They each agree not to tear down their house and rebuild. A conveys to X; B tears down and rebuilds. Assuming that the state, like most, requires horizontal privity for the burden to run, it will apply the same rule for running of benefit. In that case, X will not be able to sue B for damages, because the benefit does not run due to lack of horizontal privity between A and B.

3. **Privity between litigants ("vertical" privity):** When a court requires *"vertical"* privity, this refers to the relationship between the promisor and his successor in interest, or the relation between the promisee and his successor.

a. **Running of burden:** For the burden to run, the party against whom it is to be enforced must succeed to the *entire estate* of the original promisor, in the durational sense.

Example: A and B, owners in fee simple of neighboring parcels, each agree to maintain half of a hedge between the properties. B gives a long term lease to X. X fails to maintain his part of the hedge. A cannot sue X for damages, because there is no vertical privity between B and X — when X took a long term lease, he took only part, not all, of B's fee simple.

b. **Running of burden:** But the vertical privity requirement has much less bite on the *benefit* side. The benefit may be enforced by anyone who has taken *possession* of the promisee's property with the promisee's permission.

Example: On the facts of the above example, if A gave a long-term lease to Y, Y could sue B if B failed to maintain his part of the hedge.

i. **Homeowners association:** If P is a homeowners' association set up by a developer to collect annual fees from homeowners in a subdivision (used to maintain any common areas), the association may sue non-payers even though the association owns no property in the development. Thus the requirement of vertical privity is almost completely relieved in this instance.

4. **"Touch and concern" requirement:**

    a. **Running of benefit:** For the *benefit* to run, that benefit must *touch and concern* the promisee's land. But this requirement does not have too much practical bite — most kinds of covenants that have anything to do with real estate (e.g., promises to make repairs, promises not to demolish, promises to pay money to a homeowners association, etc.) are found to "touch and concern" the promisee's land (as well as the promisor's land).

        i. **Burden in gross:** If the benefit touches and concerns the promisee's land, the benefit will run *even though the burden does not*. That is, *the benefit can run even if the burden is "in gross,"* i.e., personal to the promisor.

            Example: D sells land containing a restaurant to P; as part of the transaction, D promises not to operate a competing restaurant within a two mile radius. (Assume that the state holds that a non-compete promise "touches and concerns" the promisee's land.) P then conveys the property to X. X can sue D for breach of the promise — since the benefit touches and concerns the P/X land, the benefit can run even though the burden is "in gross," i.e., personal to D.)

    b. **Running of burden:** For the *burden* to run, that burden must "touch and concern" the promisor's land. But about half of the courts impose an additional significant requirement: these courts hold that the burden will not run if the *benefit* does not touch and concern the promisee's land. (That is, half the courts say that *the burden may not run when the benefit is in gross.*)

        Example: A, the owner of Blackacre, sells it to B. B promises not to operate a liquor store on the property so as not to compete with a similar store owned by A on different property. Assume that the state is one which holds that a non-compete promise does not touch and concern the promisee's land. B then sells Blackacre to C. About half of the courts would hold that A cannot sue C for breach, because the burden will not run where the benefit is in gross, i.e., personal to A.

VIII. EQUITABLE SERVITUDES

A. Generally: The above rules apply where a promise concerning land is sought to be enforced at law, i.e., by the award of damages. But a promise may also be enforced *at equity*, by the award of an *injunction* (ordering the defendant not to do something) or a decree of *specific performance* (ordering the defendant to do something). When a court not only gives equitable relief, but applies it against an *assignee* of the original promisor, the promise is referred to as an *"equitable servitude"* against the burdened land.

    1. **Less rigid requirements:** In general, the technical requirements for establishing an equitable servitude that burdens the land are *less difficult* to meet than the

requirements for covenants at law. Therefore, the law of equitable servitudes is generally more important today than the law of covenants at law.

2. **Affirmative vs. negative:** Most agreements for which equitable enforcement is sought are *negative* in nature — they are usually agreements not to violate certain *building restrictions*. But occasionally, an equitable servitude may involve an *affirmative* promise (e.g., the promise to pay dues to a homeowners' association, or the promise to make certain repairs), at least in American courts.

B. **Privity not required:** The requirements of *privity* are virtually *non-existent* in connection with equitable servitudes. For instance, two *neighboring landowners* that never had any land-transfer relationship between them can, by agreement, impose land-use restrictions that will be binding on assignees.

   Example: A and B, who own adjacent parcels, agree that neither will tear down his house without the other's consent. A and B sell their properties to X and Y, respectively. Assuming requirements of notice are met, X can get an injunction against Y to stop a threatened demolition in violation of the restriction, even though Y may not have expressly agreed to honor the restrictions. By contrast, X could not sue Y for damages under a covenant-at-law theory, because of the lack of horizontal privity between A and B.

C. **"Touch and concern" still required:** Neither the benefit nor the burden of a restrictive covenant will run unless it can be said to *"touch and concern"* the promisor's land (in the case of a running burden) or the promisee's land (in the case of a running benefit). But this requirement has little bite — courts are extremely loose in determining what kind of benefit or burden "touches and concerns" land.

   1. **Running of burden or benefit is in gross:** Courts are in dispute about whether equity will enforce a burden where the benefit is in gross, just as they are in dispute about whether a suit at law for money damages may be awarded in this situation.

D. **Notice to subsequent purchaser:** The most important thing to remember about equitable servitudes is that equity will not enforce an agreement against a subsequent purchaser unless he had *notice* of the restriction. Notice may be either *"actual"* or *"constructive."*

   1. **Actual notice:** Thus if the subsequent purchaser of the burdened land happens to know about the restriction, it is irrelevant that the restriction is not recorded anywhere.

      Example: A and B each agree in writing not to use their properties for anything but residential premises. Neither records this promise in the land records. B assigns to X, and orally tells X, "You should know that I have promised A that I'll never use the property for non-residential purposes." A will be able to enjoin X from making non-residential use of the property, because X was on actual notice of the restriction at the time he bought.

   2. **Recording:** Also, the subsequent purchaser will be deemed to be on notice if he has *"constructive"* knowledge of the restriction. Most importantly, if the restric-

tion is properly **recorded** in the land records, the purchaser is bound even if he does not discover the restriction by the time he buys.

E. Developer's building plan: A general **building plan** formulated by a developer will often bind all parcels in the development. The developer records the plan in the form of a subdivision "plat" or map. To see how the burden and benefit can run to all parcels, assume that Developer (who has recorded a subdivision plat) conveys one parcel to B1 and, subsequently, another parcel to B2. Assume that the deed from Developer to each imposes the requirement that the buyer use the property in accordance with the recorded building plan (e.g., that he not use the property for non-residential uses if the building plan prohibits this).

1. Enforcement by subsequent purchaser: First, consider a suit by B2 against B1. Here, B2 can enjoin B1 against violating the use restrictions. This would probably be true even if the deed from Developer to B1 did *not* expressly mention the plan or the restrictions — the fact that the plan had been publicly filed would probably be enough to put B1 on notice.

2. Enforcement by prior purchaser against subsequent one: Now consider a suit by B1 against B2. This is trickier, because by hypothesis B1 received his property before the restriction against B2 even existed. Nonetheless, B1 can probably get an injunction against any violation by B2. Courts often do this by the doctrine of **"implied reciprocal servitude"** — when B1 acquired his land in expectation that he would get the benefit of subsequently-created servitudes, there was immediately created in him an implied reciprocal servitude against Developer's remaining land (even if Developer did *not* put the restriction in later deeds, including the deed to B2!)

F. Selection of neighbors: Equitable restrictions (as well as covenants at law) may be used to facilitate the **selection of neighbors**. Such agreements will generally be enforced as long as they are **reasonable** in scope (so that they do not constitute an unreasonable "restraint on alienation") and are not in violation of any anti-discrimination law.

> **Example:** Each deed executed by a developer provides that the purchaser must become a member of the homeowners' association, and that the purchaser may not sell his land to anyone who is not a member of the association. It also provides that the association has the right of first refusal to buy any property offered by a member. Such a restriction will generally be enforced, and will give the association's other members (providing that the association has enough money) the practical ability to keep property out of the hands of anyone deemed undesirable. Such a provision is often used by *condominiums* and *co-ops*.

CHAPTER 10

ZONING AND OTHER PUBLIC LAND-USE CONTROLS

I. THE "TAKING" CLAUSE, AND LAND-USE CONTROLS AS IMPLICIT TAKINGS

A. The "Taking" Clause generally: State and federal governments may take private property for public use — this is the power of "eminent domain." However, the Fifth Amendment to the U.S. Constitution provides that "private property [shall not] be taken for public use, without just compensation." This is the so-called "Taking" Clause, made binding on the states by means of the Fourteenth Amendment.

1. **Land-use control as taking:** Normally, land-use controls will *not* constitute a taking for which the government must pay compensation. But very occasionally, a regulation may so drastically interfere with the private owner's use of his property, or with the value of that property, that the court will conclude that there has been an *implicit* "taking."

2. **Damages vs. injunction:** If the court does find an implicit "taking," it will award one or both of the following remedies: (1) it will strike down the regulation, i.e., *enjoin* the government from enforcing it any more; or (2) it will award *damages* to the owner for his lost use or value.

B. Taking/regulation distinction: If the state merely *regulates* property use in a manner consistent with the state's *"police power,"* then no compensation needs to be paid, even though the owner's use of his property or even its value has been substantially diminished. Thus zoning regulations, environmental protection rules, landmark preservation schemes, etc., will usually not constitute a compensable "taking." But if the regulation goes too far, it will become a "taking" even though the state calls it a regulation. Here are some of the principles the courts look to to decide whether a regulation has become a compensable "taking":

1. **Substantial advancement of legitimate state interests:** The land regulation will be a taking unless it *"substantially advances legitimate state interests."*

   a. **Broad range of legitimate interests:** A *broad range* of governmental purposes constitute "legitimate state interests." These include maintaining residential uses (often done by zoning), preserving landmarks, protecting the environment, etc.

   b. **Tight means-end fit:** In order for the regulation to substantially advance legitimate state interests, there must be a fairly *tight fit* between the state interest being promoted and the regulation chosen (more than a mere "rational relation" between means and end).

   Example: The Ps, owners of beachfront property, want to replace their bungalow with a larger home. D, a government body that regulates beachfront construction, prevents the Ps from doing the rebuilding unless the Ps first give the public an easement across the property along the ocean, which would permit people to walk along the beach from the north of the Ps' property to the south and vice versa. D claims that the easement is needed to prevent public views of the beach from being worsened.

Held, for the Ps. The government may have had an interest in encouraging public views of the beaches, but the easement requirement was not substantially related to achievement of that objective, because the easement would only help those already on the beach (who already had good views). [*Nollan v. California Coastal Comm.*]

c. **"Rough proportionality" for give-backs:**   When a city conditions the owner's right to develop his property on some *"give-back"* by the owner, there must be a *"rough proportionality"* between the burdens on the public that the development would bring about, and the benefits to the public from the give-back.

   Example: Owner wants to expand her store. City says, "You may do that, but only if you deed to the public a 15-foot strip of land to be used as a bike pathway." *Held,* this trade-off was an unconstitutional taking of Owner's property, because City didn't show that the public burdens from the extra traffic to Owner's bigger store were "roughly proportional" to the public benefits from the bike path. [*Dolan v. City of Tigard*]

2. **Deprivation of all use:**   If a regulation is found to deny the landowner of *all economically viable use* of his land, this will make the regulation a "taking."

   Example: Regulations prevent a particular owner of vacant land from building any structure on the property. This will probably deprive him of all economically viable use, and will thus be a compensable taking unless necessary to serve some overriding governmental interest, such as prevention of flooding or erosion.

3. **Physical use:**   If the government makes or authorizes a permanent *physical occupation* of the property, this will automatically be found to constitute a taking.

   Example: The state orders O to give the public a permanent *easement* across his property so that the public can get to a beach — this would be a permanent physical occupation, automatically amounting to a compensable taking.

4. **Diminution in value:**   The more drastic the *reduction in value* of the owner's property, the more likely a taking is to be found. This *"diminution in value"* standard is probably the single most important factor.

   Example: Particular land is valuable mostly for the coal to be found under it. The state bars the owner of the mineral rights from doing any coal mining under the land. *Held,* the value of the mining rights was so completely impaired as to amount to a taking.

5. **Prevention of harm:**   A taking will probably *not* be found where the property use being prevented is one that is *harmful* or *"noxious"* to others.

Example: A zoning ordinance may properly prevent the operation of a steel mill in the middle of a residential neighborhood.

C. Damages for temporary taking: If a land-use regulation is so broad that it constitutes a taking, the owner may bring an *"inverse condemnation"* suit. Under such a suit, he may receive *damages* for the *temporary* taking (temporary because the regulation is eventually struck down by the court). See *First English Evangelical Lutheran Church v. L.A. County.*

II. ZONING

A. Generally: The main type of public land-use regulation is *zoning*. Zoning is generally done on the local, municipal, level. The municipality's power to zone comes from the state "police power," or power to act for the general welfare, which is delegated by state statute to the municipality.

1. **Use zoning:** Most zoning is *"use zoning,"* by which the municipality is divided into districts, in each of which only certain uses of land are permitted (e.g., a residential-only district, a commercial district, etc.)

2. **Density controls:** Other zoning laws govern the *density* of population or construction. Thus a town might establish a *minimum lot size* for single-family homes, minimum *set-back* requirements (requiring a certain amount of unbuilt land on some or all sides of the structure), *minimum square footage* for residences, and *height* limits.

B. Legal limits on zoning:

1. **Constitutional limits:** Several different federal constitutional provisions may limit a city's ability to zone in a particular manner:

    a. **Taking Clause:** First, the Fifth Amendment's "Taking" Clause means that if a zoning regulation is so overreaching that it deprives the owner of all economically viable use of his land, or is not substantially related to some legitimate public purpose, the zoning will be treated as a taking for which compensation must be paid. (See the discussion of the Taking Clause above.)

    b. **Procedural due process:** The Fourteenth Amendment's Due Process Clause imposes certain *procedural requirements* on the zoning process. For a zoning action that is *administrative* rather than legislative (e.g., the granting of a variance or special-use permit for a particular property), an owner is entitled to a *hearing*, an impartial tribunal, and an explanation of the government's decision.

    c. **Substantive due process:** If the zoning law fails to bear a *rational relation* to a *permissible state objective*, it may violate the *substantive* aspect of the Due Process Clause.

       Example: A zoning law that limits a district to single-family occupancy, and defines "family" so as to exclude most extended families, violates substantive due process. See *Moore v. City of East Cleveland.*

    d. Equal protection: A zoning law that is adopted for the purpose of excluding racial minorities will trigger strict judicial scrutiny, and will probably be found to be a violation of the ***Equal Protection*** Clause of the Fourteenth Amendment.

  2. Aesthetic zoning: Most courts hold today that ***aesthetic*** considerations may constitute ***one factor*** in a municipality's zoning decision. But aesthetics may not be the ***sole*** factor.

    Example: A city provides that only Georgian Colonial-style houses may be built, because these structures are the most beautiful. A court would probably strike down this regulation on the grounds that although aesthetics may be one factor, they may not be the sole factor.

C. Administration of zoning:

  1. Bodies involved in: Several governmental bodies generally get involved in zoning:

    a. Town council: The ***zoning code*** is enacted by the ***municipal legislature***. Usually this is the ***town council***.

    b. Board of zoning appeals: A "board of adjustment" or "board of zoning appeals" usually exists to award or deny ***variances***, and to hear appeals from the building department's enforcement of the zoning laws.

    c. Planning or zoning commission: The town council generally appoints a ***planning commission*** or zoning commission. The commission generally ***advises*** the town council on (but does not independently determine) the contents of the zoning code.

  2. Variances: Virtually all zoning ordinances have a provision for the granting of ***variances***, i.e., relief in a particular case from the enforcement of an ordinance.

    a. Requirements for: Most states impose these requirements for a variance: (1) denial would result in ***"unnecessary hardship"*** to the owner; (2) the need for the variance is caused by a problem ***unique to the owner's lot*** (not one shared by many lots in the area); and (3) the variance would not be ***inconsistent*** with the overall purpose of the ordinance, or inconsistent with the general welfare of the area.

  3. Special uses: Zoning ordinances also usually provide for ***"special use"*** permits. Typically, a special use permit must be obtained for such things as private schools, hospitals and churches. Generally, an applicant is not entitled to a special use permit "as of right," but only in the discretion of the zoning board; however, usually no showing of "special hardship" has to be made (as is the case for a variance).

  4. Conditional zoning: Many ordinances provide for ***"conditional" zoning***. Under this device, the rezoning of a particular parcel is made subject to the developer's promise to comply with certain conditions, which will protect neighbors.

    Example: O owns a parcel in an area zoned residential-only. If the ordinance allows for conditional zoning, the town might rezone O's parcel for light industry, but only if O agrees to large set-backs, a low floor-space-to-land-area ratio, or other condition.

5. **Non-conforming uses:** When a zoning ordinance is enacted or made more stringent, the pre-existing uses that are now banned by the ordinance are called *"non-conforming uses."* Virtually all ordinances either: (1) grant a non-conforming user a *substantial period* within which he may continue his use; or (2) let him continue that use *indefinitely*.

   a. **Constitutional issue:** Probably it would be a violation of an owner's due process or other constitutional rights for him not to be given at least a substantial period within which to phase out the non-conforming use.

   b. **Amortization:** If the ordinance does give an owner a substantial period to phase out his use (called an *"amortization"* provision), most courts hold that no violation of the owner's constitutional rights results from the fact that he must eventually cease the non-conforming use.

D. **Exclusionary zoning:** *"Exclusionary* zoning" is the use of zoning laws to exclude certain types of persons and uses, particularly *racial and ethnic minorities* and *low-income* persons.

   1. **Examples of exclusion:** A town might exclude certain types of people by putting tight restrictions on the kinds of allowable *residential uses*. Thus a high minimum-acreage requirement, a ban on multiple dwellings, a ban on mobile homes, or a ban on publicly-subsidized housing are all ways a town could try to keep out poor people (and, to the extent that blacks, say, are on average poorer than whites, a way to keep out black people).

   2. **Equal Protection law:** Exclusionary zoning may be attacked as a violation of the *Equal Protection* Clause of the U.S. Constitution. An equal protection argument has the best chance of success when it argues that a town is discriminating on the basis *race* or *national origin*, since these are "suspect classes"; an attack based on the claim that the town is discriminating against the *poor* will probably not succeed (because poverty is not a suspect class).

      a. **Effect vs. purpose:** Also, the plaintiff in an equal protection case will probably only win if the court applies *"strict scrutiny"* to the ordinance. This, in turn, will happen only if the court believes that the town acted with the *purpose* of discriminating on racial or ethnic grounds, not if the ordinance merely has the *effect* of making it harder for minorities to live there.

      b. **Standing:** The *standing* requirements for an equal protection attack in federal court are very difficult. In most instances, P will have to prove that: (1) the zoning rules have prevented a particular project from being built on particular land; and (2) P would probably become a resident of the housing if the zoning limit were overturned and the project built.

   3. **Federal statutory suits:** Zoning may also be attacked in federal court suits based on federal statutory law, especially the Fair Housing Act. Zoning enacted for the purpose of limiting access by racial or ethnic minorities violates the Act.

a. **Effect vs. purpose:**   In a Fair Housing Act suit, P does not have to show a discriminatory purpose behind the zoning enactment. Instead, he merely has to show a discriminatory effect; then, the burden shifts to the defendant town to show that its enactment serves legitimate governmental interests rather than discriminatory ones.

4. **State case law:**   A number of *states*, by case law, have held that zoning may not be used to *exclude the poor*.

   a. *Mt. Laurel cases:*   The most important such cases are the two *Mt. Laurel* cases, in which the New Jersey Supreme Court held that a town must allow its *"fair share"* of the region's demand for low and middle-income housing. According to the *Mt. Laurel* principle, not only may zoning not be used to keep out the poor, but affirmative measures must be taken by a town to cause such housing to be built (e.g., density bonuses given to developers who build some low income housing; cooperation with developers seeking federally-subsidized housing; allowing of mobile homes, etc.) Also, builders must be allowed to seek *site-specific relief* (in which the court orders the builder's parcel to be rezoned to allow the particular project, if the court finds for the developer). [*So. Burlington County NAACP v. Mt. Laurel*]

III. REGULATION OF SUBDIVISION AND GROWTH

A. **Subdivision regulation:**   Towns often extensively regulate the process of *subdivision*. This is the process of dividing a parcel into two or more smaller ones, for resale to different purchasers.

   1. **Sewers and water mains:**   For instance, towns usually have detailed requirements that the developer put in water mains, sewers, gutters, and other drainage facilities.

   2. **Street design:**   Similarly, towns regulate *street design*, and require the developer not only to furnish the land for streets, but to build the streets himself.

B. **Growth control:**   Towns and regions also sometimes attempt to regulate their rate of *growth* (or the *sequence* in which the various parcels of land are developed).

   1. **Generally upheld:**   Generally, growth-control regulations are *upheld* so long as they are reasonable. For instance, a town would probably be entitled to prevent premature subdivision and "urban sprawl" by **prohibit**ing residential construction unless various public facilities (e.g., schools, parks, roads, firehouses, sewers, etc.) were in place first.

      a. **Moratoria and limits:**   In fact, a town ordinance will probably be upheld if it tries to place an absolute *limit* on the number of new units that will be constructed during a particular time period. Even a complete *moratorium* on new residential or commercial construction might be upheld if this was a reasonable way of achieving an important local government goal (e.g., avoiding strain on roads or other public facilities).

IV. HISTORICAL AND ENVIRONMENTAL PRESERVATION

A. Historical preservation: Municipalities often try to protect buildings or districts of great *historical* or *architectural* interest.

1. **Districts and landmarks:** Sometimes, an entire *historical district* is protected. (For instance, the French Quarter in New Orleans is protected because of its great age, uniformity and architectural significance.) Alternatively, sometimes a particular *structure* will be protected because of its historical or architectural significance. In either event, historical preservation schemes generally prohibit the owner from *altering* or *demolishing* the building without a special *permit*.

2. **Generally upheld:** A historic preservation ordinance will generally be *upheld* so long as: (1) it gives reasonably precise *standards* to the board charged with enforcement, so that the board does not behave in an *arbitrary* or *discriminatory* manner; and (2) it does not constitute a "taking" without compensation, in violation of the Fifth Amendment.

   a. **Taking:** The owner's best chance of attacking a scheme is by arguing that it deprives him of all economically viable use of his land, without compensation, in violation of the Fifth Amendment's Taking Clause. But even such arguments are hard to win. For instance, in the *Penn Central* case, the Supreme Court held that a New York City ordinance preventing major changes to Grand Central Terminal, but allowing the owners to continue their present use of the property (as a terminal with office space above it) did not amount to a taking. [*Penn Central Trans. Co. v. City of New York*] (But a prohibition on *all* development of a building beyond the current use might be found to deny the owner all economically viable use of the property, in which case the preservation scheme would be a taking for which compensation must be paid.)

   b. **Transferable Development Rights (TDRs):** Some ordinances avoid "taking" problems by giving the owner "Transferable Development Rights" or "TDRs," by which he may transfer his development rights from the preserved building to other nearby parcels. If in the particular real estate market the TDRs have substantial economic value, this may turn what would otherwise be a "taking" (because the owner is deprived of all economically viable use of his land) into a non-taking.

B. Environmental preservation: Towns and regions also frequently attempt to protect the *environment*. Of special interest are regulations that attempt to maintain *open areas* by limiting or prohibiting certain kinds of development.

1. **Urban park land:** Occasionally, a city may prohibit the development of privately-owned urban *park land*. But prohibiting all development of otherwise-valuable vacant land in the middle of a downtown area is likely to constitute a compensable "taking," because the owner is being deprived of all economically viable use of his land. (But the problems might be eased by allowing TDRs, as discussed above.)

2. Wetlands and coastlands: More frequently, towns and regions try to limit or prohibit development on *wetlands* and *coastland*. By and large, such preservation schemes have been *upheld*, on the grounds that preservation of these areas is a goal of great social importance, outweighing the landowner's interest in land development. (But a permanent ban on development might be a compensable "taking," unless the government shows that construction would be dangerous, as in the case of a coastal area subject to heavy flooding and erosion.)

V. EMINENT DOMAIN

A. Generally: State and federal governments have the power of *eminent domain*, i.e., the power to take private property for public use. Usually this is done through *condemnation proceedings*, in which the government brings a judicial proceeding to obtain title to land that it needs for some public use. Alternatively, the government occasionally simply makes *use* of a landowner's property without bringing formal condemnation proceedings; here, the landowner may bring an *"inverse condemnation"* action, in which he seeks a court declaration that his property has been taken by the government and must be paid for.

The two requirements for the government to use its eminent domain power are:

[1] the property must be put to a *"public use"*; and

[2] *"just compensation"* must be paid.

B. "Public use": The requirement of *"public use"* (imposed by the Taking Clause of the Fifth Amendment) is very *loosely* interpreted. So long as the state's use of its eminent domain power is "rationally related" to a "conceivable public purpose," the public-use requirement is satisfied.

> **Example:** Hawaii condemns lots owned by large landowners, and transfers them to the tenants living on them. *Held*, because there was tremendous inequality in land ownership in Hawaii, this scheme was a rational attempt to remedy a social and economic evil, and therefore satisfied the "public use" requirement. *Hawaii Housing Authority v. Midkiff*.

1. Urban renewal: Thus as part of an *urban renewal* project, a city may condemn private land, then turn it back to a *private developer* for private use. (The renewal program meets the "public use" requirement even if the particular parcel condemned is not a slum.)

C. "Just compensation": In general, the requirement of *"just compensation"* means that the government must pay the *fair market value* of the property at the time of the taking.

1. Highest and best use: This fair market value is usually based on the *"highest and best use"* that may be made of the property (at least under current zoning regulations). Thus if a vacant parcel is zoned for subdivision, the value that must be paid is the value the land would have to a subdivider, not the value based on the current rental value of vacant land.

CHAPTER 11

LAND SALE CONTRACTS, MORTGAGES AND DEEDS

I. LAND SALE CONTRACTS

A. Statute of Frauds: The *Statute of Frauds* is applicable in all states to any contract for the sale of land, or for the sale of any interest in land. Therefore, either the contract itself, or a memorandum of it, must be *in writing*.

    1. Memorandum satisfying: A *memorandum* of the parties' agreement, summarizing some terms but not the entire oral agreement, will satisfy the Statute if it specifies the following: (1) the *names* of the parties; (2) the *land* to be conveyed; (3) normally, the *purchase price*; and (4) the *signature* of the party to be charged (i.e., the party against whom enforcement is sought).

        Example: Seller writes a letter to Buyer, confirming the provisions of their oral contract for the sale of Blackacre. This letter will constitute a sufficient memorandum if Buyer seeks to enforce the contract against Seller, but not if Seller seeks to enforce it against Buyer.

    2. Part performance exception: There is one major exception to the Statute of Frauds for land sale contracts: under the doctrine of *part performance*, a party (either buyer or seller) who has taken action in *reliance* on the contract may be able to gain at least limited enforcement of it.

        a. Acts by vendor: If the vendor *makes a conveyance* under the contract, he will then be able to sue for the agreed-upon price, even if the agreement to pay that price was only oral.

        b. Acts by purchaser: Courts are split as to what acts by the *purchaser* constitute part performance entitling him to specific performance.

            i. Possession plus payment: Many states hold that if the buyer takes *possession*, and also *makes payments*, this will be sufficient part performance that the seller will be required to convey the property.

            ii. Improvements: Also, in many states, a buyer who takes possession and then either makes permanent *improvements*, or changes his position in *reliance*, can require the seller to convey.

            iii. "Unequivocally referable" requirement: Most courts say that the buyer's part performance must be *"unequivocally referable"* to the alleged contract. Thus the buyer must show that the part performance was clearly *in response* to the oral contract, and not explainable by some other aspect of the parties' relationship.

                Example: D orally promises to convey Blackacre to P if P will move in with D and care for D in his old age. P does so. P is distantly related to D. D dies without ever having made the conveyance. If P sues D's estate to enforce the alleged oral agreement, P will probably lose because P's part performance (moving in and caring for P) is not "unequivocally referable" to the oral contract, since P may have been doing it out of affection for a relative.

B. Time for performance: In a suit for damages, the *time* stated in the contract will be deemed to be *of the essence*, unless the parties are shown to have intended otherwise. (*Example*: Seller refuses to close on the date specified in the contract. Buyer may bring a suit for damages for the delay, even if it is only a few days.)

    1. Equity: But in a suit in *equity* (i.e., a suit for *specific performance*), the general rule is that time is *not* of the essence. Therefore, even if the contract specifies a particular closing date, either party may obtain specific performance though he is unable to close on the appointed day (so long as he is ready to perform within a reasonable time after the scheduled day).

        Example: The sale contract specifies a November 1 closing date. Buyer has trouble lining up his financing, so he can't close on November 1. The contract is silent about whether time is of the essence. By November 15, Buyer has his financing lined up, and asks Seller to close. Seller now refuses. In the absence of strong evidence that the parties intended time to be of the essence, Buyer will probably get a court to order Seller to convey even though Buyer missed the November 1 closing date.

C. Marketable title: Nearly all land sale contracts require the vendor to convey a *marketable* title. (Even if the contract is silent on this issue, an obligation to convey a marketable title will be *implied* by the court.)

    1. Definition of "marketable title": A marketable title is one that is *free from reasonable doubt* about whether the seller can convey the rights he purports to convey. Thus it is *not* sufficient that a court would probably hold the title good in a *litigation*. Instead, the title must be *free from reasonable doubt* so that the buyer will be able to resell in the future. The purchaser is not required to *"buy a lawsuit"*.

    2. Defects making title unmarketable: Here are some of the defects that might make title unmarketable:

        a. Record chain: First, anything in the prior chain of title indicating that the vendor does not have the *full interest* which he purports to convey, may be a defect.

        Examples: A substantial variation between the *name* of the grantee of record in one link and the name of the grantor in the following link is a defect. Similarly, a substantial variation in the *description of the land* between one deed and the next may be a defect.

        b. Encumbrances: Second, even if the vendor has valid title to the property, an *encumbrance* on the property will normally constitute a defect.

            i. Mortgage or lien: Thus an outstanding *mortgage* would be an encumbrance making the title unmarketable. (However, the vendor has the right to *pay off the mortgage at the closing*, out of the sale proceeds.) Similarly, *liens* (e.g., a lien for unpaid taxes, or a lien gotten by a judgment creditor) are defects.

ii. **Easement:** An *easement* will be a defect if it reduces the *"full enjoyment"* of the premises.

iii. **Use restrictions:** Similarly, privately-negotiated *use* restrictions (e.g., a covenant whose burden runs with the land, to the effect that only residential structures will be built) can be a defect.

iv.**Land-use and zoning violations:** Most courts hold that violations of *building codes* are *not* encumbrances on title. But a violation of a *zoning ordinance* usually *is* treated as an encumbrance.

3. **Agreement and notice:** But the parties may *agree* that certain kinds of defects will *not* constitute unmarketable title. This agreement will normally take place in the contract of sale.

Example: Buyer and Seller agree that a particular easement held by X across the property will not render title unmarketable. The court will enforce this agreement.

Also, the buyer may be held to be on *notice* of certain defects, and therefore held to have implicitly agreed to take subject to them (e.g., where a right of way across the property is very visible to anyone who looks even casually at the property).

4. **Time for measuring marketability:** Unless the contract specifies otherwise, the vendor's title is not required to be marketable *until the date set for the closing*. Thus the vendor may sign a contract to sell property which he does not yet own (or on which there are several defects in title), and the purchaser cannot cancel the contract prior to the closing date because of this fact.

D. **Remedies for failure to perform:** Where one party fails to perform a land sale contract, the other party may have two remedies: (1) a suit for *damages*; and (2) a suit for *specific performance*.

1. **Damages:** If one party breaches a land sale contract, the other may almost always sue for *money damages*. Generally, P recovers the *difference between the market price and the contract price* (the "benefit of the bargain" rule).

2. **Specific performance:** Usually, an action for *specific performance* may be brought against the defaulting party, whether the defaulter is buyer or seller. Most commonly, the seller changes his mind, and buyer is able to get a decree of specific performance ordering seller to convey the property. (Each parcel of land is deemed unique, so the court presumes that money damages would not be adequate to compensate the buyer.)

3. **Deposit:** If buyer is unable to close on the appointed date, most courts do *not* allow him to recover his *deposit* (on the theory that a suit to recover a deposit is in effect an action at law, and time will be deemed to be of the essence in a suit at law).

E. **Equitable conversion:** For many purposes, the courts treat the *signing of the contract* as vesting in the purchaser *equitable ownership* of the land. (Conversely, the vendor is treated as becoming the equitable owner of the purchase price.)

1. **Risk of loss:** Most courts hold that since the vendee acquires equitable owner-ship of the land as soon as the contract is signed, the ***risk of loss*** immediately ***shifts to him***. This is true even if the vendee never takes ***possession*** prior to the casualty.

   Example: S contracts to sell land to B. Prior to the closing, while S is still in possession, a hurricane destroys the house located on the land. Most courts hold that the loss falls upon B — B must still pay the agreed-upon purchase price, and does not receive any abatement of price, nor does he get his deposit back.

   a. **Exceptions:** But courts following this majority rule have a couple of key ***exceptions*** to it: (1) the vendor bears any loss resulting from his own ***negligence***; and (2) the vendor bears the loss if at the time it occurred, he could not have conveyed title (e.g., because his title was ***unmarketable***).

   b. **Insurance:** But very importantly, courts who place the risk of loss on the purchaser give him the ***benefit of the vendor's insurance***.

II.   MORTGAGES AND INSTALLMENT CONTRACTS

A. **Nature of mortgage:**   A ***mortgage*** is a financing arrangement, in which the person buying property (or one who already owns property) receives a loan, and the property is pledged as security to guarantee repayment of the loan.

   1. **Two documents:**   There are two documents associated with every mortgage: (1) the ***"note"*** (or "bond"); and (2) the ***mortgage*** itself.

      a. **The note:**   The ***note*** is the buyer's personal ***promise to make the repayments***. If there is a foreclosure against the property and the foreclosure sale does not yield enough to cover the outstanding mortgage debt, the note serves as the basis for a ***deficiency judgment*** against the borrower for the balance still due.

      b. **Mortgage:**   The ***mortgage itself*** is a document which gives the lender the right to ***have the property sold*** to repay the loan if the borrower defaults. Since the mortgage in effect gives the mortgagee an interest in the land, the mortgage is ***recorded***.

   2. **Sale of mortgaged property:**   Usually, when mortgaged property is sold the mortgage is paid off at the closing. But property can be sold without paying off the mortgage, either by: (1) having the purchaser take "subject to" the mortgage; or (2) having the purchaser "assume" the mortgage.

      a. **Sale "subject to" mortgage:**   If the purchaser merely takes ***"subject to"*** the mortgage, he is ***not personally liable*** for payment of the mortgage debt. True, the mortgagee can foreclose if the buyer does not make the payments. But the mortgagee may not sue the buyer for any balance still remaining on the loan after foreclosure; that is, the mortgagee may not get a deficiency judgment against the purchaser. (But the mortgagee may in this instance sue the original mortgagor for this balance.)

    b. **Assumption:** If the new buyer *assumes* payment of the mortgage, he is liable, both to the original mortgagor and to the mortgagee, for re-payment of the mortgage loan. Thus the mortgagee can get a deficiency judgment against the assuming purchaser.

3. **Foreclosure:** *Foreclosure* is the process by which the mortgagee may reach the land to satisfy the mortgage debt, if the mortgagor defaults.

    a. **Judicial foreclosure:** Usually, foreclosure is *judicially supervised* — the foreclosing mortgagee must institute a lawsuit, and the actual foreclosure sale takes place under supervision of a government official (usually a sheriff).

    b. **Private foreclosure sale:** Some states allow the mortgage lender to use a document called a *"deed of trust"* rather than a "mortgage." The deed of trust allows the lender (or a third person) to hold the property as *"trustee,"* and to sell it in a *private sale* if the borrower defaults. However, the private sale must be held in a *commercially reasonable manner* so as to bring the highest price possible — if the lender does not do this, he will owe damages to the borrower in the amount that the borrower might have gotten back (representing the borrower's equity above the mortgage amount) had the sale been a commercially reasonable one.

B. **Installment contracts:** Land can be bought under an *installment contract*. The buyer makes a down payment, and pays the rest of the purchase price in installments (usually monthly). Here, the buyer does *not receive his deed* until after he has paid all (or, sometimes, a substantial portion) of the purchase price.

1. **Forfeiture:** If the installment buyer defaults, the seller does not need to go through complex foreclosure proceedings — he can just exercise his contractual right to declare the contract *forefeited* (in which case the seller theoretically gets to keep whatever has been paid on account). But modern courts often hold that if the buyer has paid a *substantial portion* of the purchase price, and the seller would be unjustly enriched by a complete forfeiture, ordinary *foreclosure proceedings* (applicable to mortgages) must be used.

III. DEEDS

A. **Nature of deed:** The *deed* is the document which acts to *pass title* from the grantor to the grantee.

1. **Merger:** Under the doctrine of *merger*, most obligations imposed by the contract of sale are *discharged* unless they are repeated in the deed. (*Example*: The contract calls for merchantable title, in the form of a warranty deed. Buyer carelessly accepts a "quitclaim" deed which makes no warranties. Buyer will not be able to sue Seller on the contractual provision if the title turns out to be defective — the contractual provisions are extinguished and replaced by whatever provisions are contained in the deed, under the merger doctrine.)

2. **Two main types of deeds:** There are two basic types of deeds: (1) the *quitclaim* deed, in which the grantor makes no covenant that his title is good (he merely passes on to the grantee whatever title he in fact has); and (2) the *warranty deed*, in which the grantor makes one or more promises about the state of the title.

B. Description of the property:

1. Types of description: There are three main ways of *describing* land in a deed. Their use varies by region and type of land:

    a. Metes and bounds: A *"metes and bounds"* description begins by establishing a starting point (usually based on a visible landmark or "monument"). Then a series of "calls and distances" is given, each of which represents a line going in a certain direction for a certain distance.

    Example: "From the southwest corner of East and Main Street, then running north 50 degrees 26 minutes for 273 feet, then west 59 degrees 8 minutes for 100 feet," etc.

    b. Government survey: In many rural areas, especially west of the Mississippi, the description method uses the U.S. *government survey*. Land is divided into six-mile-square tracts called "townships"; each township is divided into 36 one-mile-square tracts called "sections"; each section contains 640 acres, each of which can be directly referred to.

    c. Plat: The *"plat"* method relies on the recording of a map or "plat" of property by a developer, in which the plat shows the location of individual lots.

    Example: "Lot 2 in Block 5 in Highwood, a subdivision platted on a map filed in the Register's Office of the County of Westchester on June 13, 1910."

2. Interpretation: In interpreting the description of the land conveyed, the court attempts to ascertain the *intent* of the parties.

    a. Construction in grantee's favor: Courts tend to interpret the deed in a way which is *most favorable to the grantee* (i.e., the document is construed against the grantor, since the grantor usually drafts the deed).

C. Formalities: Deeds must meet certain *formalities*, which vary from state to state.

1. Signature: The grantor must place his *signature* on the deed. The signature of the *grantee* is generally *not* necessary.

2. Attestation or acknowledgment: In most states, statutes require the deed either to be *"attested"* to (i.e., *witnessed* by one or more persons not parties to the transaction) or to be *notarized*.

D. Delivery of deed: For a deed to be valid, it must not only be executed, but also *"delivered."* But this "delivery" requirement does not necessarily refer to physical delivery; what is required is that the grantor use words or conduct evidencing his intention to make the deed *presently operative* to vest title in the grantee.

1. Not revocable: If the delivery occurs, title passes immediately to the *grantee*. Thereafter, return of the deed to the grantor has *no effect* either to *cancel* the prior delivery or to reconvey the title to him. The only way the title can get back to the grantor is if a new, formally satisfactory, conveyance takes place.

E. Covenants for title in warranty deed: If the deed is a *"warranty"* deed (as opposed to a "quitclaim" deed, which merely conveys whatever interest the grantor has without making any promises), the grantor is held to be making various promises about the state of his ownership. These promises are called *"covenants for title."*

1. **The covenants:** The covenants fall into three basic groups:

    a. **Seisin and conveyance:** The covenants of *"seisin"* and of *"right to convey"* mean that the grantor has an *indefeasible estate* in the quality and quantity which he purports to convey.

    Example: These covenants might be breached if the grantor purported to convey a fee simple absolute, but actually only owned and conveyed a fee simple subject to condition subsequent or a fee simple subject to an executory limitation.

    b. **Against encumbrances:** The covenant *"against encumbrances"* is a promise that there are no encumbrances against the property, that is, no impediments to title which do not affect the fee simple but which diminish the value of the land.

    Examples: *Mortgages, liens, easements* and *use restrictions* are all encumbrances, so if the grantor gives a deed containing a covenant against encumbrances, the existence of any of these will constitute a breach of that covenant.

    c. **Quiet enjoyment and warranty:** The covenants of *"quiet enjoyment"* and *"warranty"* represent a *continuing contract* by the grantor that the grantee will be entitled to *continued possession* of the land in the future. (*Example*: These covenants would be breached if a third person not only asserted that he had paramount title, but commenced proceedings to *eject* the grantee.)

2. **Present vs. future covenants:** Be sure to distinguish between: (1) *present* covenants; and (2) *future* covenants.

    a. **Present covenants:** The covenants of *seisin*, *right to convey*, and *against encumbrances* are *present covenants*. They are breached, if at all, at the *moment the conveyance is made*. Thus a breach can occur *even though there is no eviction* — all the grantee needs to do to recover on the claim is to show that title was in fact defective on the date of the conveyance.

    b. **Future covenants:** By contrast, the covenants of *quiet enjoyment* and *warranty* are *future covenants*. They are breached *only when an eviction occurs*.

    Example: Grantor conveys Blackacre to Grantee under a warranty deed. Ten years later, Grantee discovers that X has a paramount title to that held by Grantor. This is a breach of the present covenants (seisin, right to convey and against encumbrances), even though there is no eviction. But it is not a breach of the future covenants (quiet enjoyment and warranty), because X has not tried to evict Grantee.

3. **Statute of limitations:** The main reason for distinguishing between present and future covenants involves the *statute of limitations*. The statute starts to run on a *present* covenant *at the time the conveyance is made*. It starts to run on a *future*

covenant only *when an eviction occurs.* Therefore, if many years pass from the time of the conveyance, and the grantee discovers that someone has paramount title, the grantee is likely to be out of luck: the time for suing on the present covenants is likely to have passed (since that clock started running at the time of the conveyance), yet there will be no breach of the future covenants if the holder of the paramount title has not attempted to eject the grantee. (Thus on the facts of the above example, Grantee is likely to be out of luck, with his present covenants time-barred and his future covenants not yet breached due to the absence of any ejectment action by X.)

4. **Enforcement by future grantee (running of covenants):** A second reason for distinguishing between the present and future covenants concerns whether the covenant *runs with the land*, i.e., whether it is *enforceable by subsequent grantees*.

    a. **Present covenants:** The present covenants usually *do not run with the land*.

    b. **Future covenants:** But the future covenants *do run with the land*.

    > **Example:** O conveys to G1 under a warranty deed. G1 conveys to G2. G2 discovers that X has always held a paramount title superior to O's. G2 cannot sue O on the present covenants (seisin, right to convey and against encumbrances), because these do not run with the land. But he may sue O for breach of the future covenants (warranty and quiet enjoyment). (But remember that these future covenants will not be breached unless X actually sues to eject G2.)

5. **Measure of damages:** If the grantor breaches any of these warranties, the grantee's recovery is generally limited to the *purchase price paid* — the grantee may *not* recover for any *appreciation* in the value of the land since the conveyance.

F. **Warranty of habitability:** Most courts today recognize an *implied warranty of habitability* on behalf of the purchaser of a *new residence* against a *professional builder* who built the house.

> **Example:** Developer, who is in the business of building homes, sells a home to P. Shortly after P moves in, he discovers that the foundation is cracked and the roof is structurally unsound. In most states, P may sue Developer for breach of the implied warranty of habitability.

1. **Used homes:** The buyer of a *used home cannot* sue the prior "amateur" owner. But the second buyer may, in most states, sue the *original builder* for breach of the implied warranty of habitability, provided that: (1) the defect was *not obvious* at the time of the second purchase, and (2) the defect occurred within a *reasonable time* after construction of the house.

    > **Example:** On the facts of the above example, if P sold the house to P1, P1 could sue Developer if the foundation and roof problems were not obvious at the time of the P-P1 sale, and occurred within a reasonable time after Developer built the house.

G. **Co-ops and condos:**

1. **Co-ops:** The term *"co-operative"* or *"co-op"* usually refers to a means of owning an apartment house. The building is owned by a co-operative *corporation*. What the lay-person thinks of as an "owner" of an individual apartment unit is really a *shareholder* in the corporation. Each shareholder is entitled to enter into a *"proprietary lease,"* in which the corporation is lessor and the shareholder is lessee. The lessee is generally required to pay his portion of the building's *mortgage* interest and principal, and various *"carrying charges"* used to defray the maintenance and operating costs of the building.

2. **Condominium:** The *condominium* or *"condo"* is a form of ownership in which each individual resident holds a *fee simple* in a certain physical space or parcel, but all the residents collectively own certain *"common areas."* In the typical "horizontal" condo structure (e.g., two-story townhouses spread over a large parcel), each individual resident might own the soil upon which his townhouse stands, but he would not own the surrounding lawns, swimming pool, etc. — these would be held by the condominium association.

CHAPTER 12

THE RECORDING SYSTEM AND TITLE ASSURANCE

I. RECORDING STATUTES

A. General function of: The main function of *recording acts*, which are in force in every jurisdiction, is to give a purchaser of land a way to check whether there has been an *earlier transaction* in the property inconsistent with his own. Even if there has been an earlier transaction, if it is not recorded the later purchaser will generally gain priority — thus the recording acts give a buyer a way to be sure that he is getting good title.

1. **Relations between original parties:** Recording acts only govern the relationship between a grantee and a subsequent purchaser of the same property. They do *not* govern the relation between the *grantor and the grantee under a particular conveyance*.

> **Example:** D conveys Blackacre to P. D then conveys it again to X, who doesn't know about the D-P conveyance. X records his deed before P can record his. Because of the recording act, X's deed takes priority over P's. P sues D for his double-dealing. P will be able to recover against D, because the recording act has no effect upon the relations between both parties to a particular deed (i.e., P and D), only the relationship between two grantees under different deeds (i.e., P and X).

B. Different types of acts: There are three basic types of recording acts: (1) *"pure race"* statutes; (2) *"pure notice"* statutes; and (3) *"race-notice"* statutes.

1. **Pure race statutes:** A *race* statute places a premium on the *race to the recorder's office*. The subsequent purchaser must *record before the earlier pur-*

chaser, but he is protected *regardless of whether he has notice* of the earlier conveyance. Very few pure race statutes remain on the books.

2. **Pure notice statute:**   A pure *notice* statute provides that an unrecorded instrument is invalid against *any* subsequent purchaser without notice, *regardless of whether the subsequent purchaser records prior to the first purchaser*.

3. **Race-notice statute:**   A *race-notice* statute protects the subsequent purchaser only if he meets *two* requirements: (1) he *records before* the earlier purchaser records; and (2) he takes *without notice* of the earlier conveyance.

> **Illustration:** In 1985, O conveys Blackacre to A. In 1986, O conveys to B. In 1987, B records. In 1988, A records. Here is how the rights of A and B to Blackacre would be resolved under various types of recording acts:
>
> > *Race:* Under a pure race statute, B wins automatically, without regard to whether he had actual notice of the earlier conveyance to A — B recorded his deed before A did, so that is the end of the matter. (Had A recorded in 1987 and B in 1988, A would have won, even though at the time B took, he had no way to find out about the earlier conveyance to A.)
> >
> > *Notice:* Under a pure notice statute, B wins. In fact, B would have won even if he never recorded at all, or recorded after A — the mere fact that B took after A, and without notice of A's interest, would be enough to give him the victory.
> >
> > *Race-notice:* Under a race-notice statute, B will win only if he took without actual notice of A's interest. Furthermore, if B had recorded after A (instead of before A, as really happened), B would have lost due to his late recording even if he took without actual notice of A's interest. So under the race-notice statute (probably the most common kind of statute), the subsequent purchaser (here, B) has two obstacles to overcome: (1) he must record first; and (2) he must take without actual notice of the earlier interest.

C. **Mechanics:**   Here is a summary of the mechanics of recording:

1. **Deposit:**   The grantee (or the grantee's title insurance company) brings the deed to the recording office (usually located in the county where the land lies). The recorder stamps the date and time of deposit, and then places a photocopy of the deed in a chronological book containing all recorded deeds.

2. **Indexing:**   Then, the deeds are *indexed*. Usually there is both a *grantor* index (enabling a searcher to find all conveyances made by a particular grantor) and a *grantee* index (permitting the searcher to find all conveyances made *to* a particular grantee).

D. **What instruments must be recorded:**   Recording acts generally allow (and in effect require) the recording of *every instrument by which an interest in land*, whether legal or equitable, is *created* or *modified*. Thus not only fee simple conveyances, but also *life estates*, *mortgages*, *restrictive covenants*, and *tax liens*, are all required to be recorded.

1. **Not recordable:** Some types of interests are usually *not recordable:*

    a. **Adverse possession:** Thus titles based upon *adverse possession* are usually not recordable (since there is no instrument to record).

    b. **Some easements:** Similarly, an *easement* by *implication or necessity* usually does not have to be recorded (since it does not give rise to a recordable document). (But in some instances, a conveyance of the property to a bona fide purchaser who takes without notice of the easement may cut the easement off.) On the other hand, an *express* easement is recordable.

    c. **Short leases:** In many states, a *short term lease* (e.g., less than three years) may not be recorded. If so, that lease will be valid against a subsequent bona fide purchaser.

    d. **Contracts:** Similarly, some states do not allow executory *contracts of sale* to be recorded. (But the vendee's rights will be subordinate to that of a subsequent claimant who actually buys the property.)

E. **Parties protected:** The subsequent grantee, to get the protection of the recording act against a prior grantee, must either be: (1) a *"purchaser for value"* or (2) a *creditor* meeting certain standards.

1. **Purchaser for value:** In most states, a grantee gets the benefit of the recording act (i.e., he takes priority over an earlier unrecorded conveyance) only if he *gives value* for his interest.

    a. **Donee:** Thus a *donee* is usually *not protected* by the recording act. (*Example*: O conveys to A. O then purports to give the property, for no consideration, to B. B records, A never does. Under most statutes, B still loses to A, because B — although he is a subsequent grantee who recorded first — did not give valuable consideration.)

    b. **Less than market value:** Although consideration is required, it does *not* have to be an amount *equal to the market value of the property* (but it must be more than *nominal* consideration). (*Example*: On the facts of the above example, if B had paid half the market value of the property, he would probably have prevailed against A; but if he only paid $1, he would not.)

    c. **Purchase from or through grantee:** One who purchases for valuable consideration from the record owner is of course protected. But also, one who buys from the *heirs or devisees* of the record owner will also be protected.

        Example: O conveys to A. O then conveys to B for value. B records, A does not. B then bequeaths the property to C. C conveys to D. D will prevail against A — even though B in one sense took "nothing," his right to prevail under the recording act against a prior unrecorded deed is itself devisable.

2. **Creditors:** A landowner's *creditors* may also receive the protection of the recording act.

    a. **Mortgage:** If a creditor receives a *mortgage* from the landowner, he is treated as a "purchaser," and he must generally meet the consideration requirement. This means that if he is giving something of *new value* (e.g., cancelling part of the debt in return for the mortgage, or extending the owner's time to pay), he will probably be deemed to have given consideration, and will thus be protected against a prior unrecorded conveyance. But if he merely retains the same rights he always had (to be paid the full amount of his debt, at the time promised), then he is not giving new value, and his mortgage will not be protected against a prior unrecorded conveyance.

   b.   Judgment and execution creditors: A creditor who obtains a *judgment*, or who is allowed to *attach* his debtor's property at the beginning of the lawsuit, gets a *lien* against the debtor's property. This lien may or may not be protected under the recording act against a prior unrecorded purchase, depending on how the statute is drafted. (If the statute only protects "purchasers," the lien creditor probably does not get protection against the prior unrecorded deed.)

3.   Eligible to be recorded: The subsequent purchaser who wants the protection of the recording act must record his own deed, and that deed must be one which is in fact *eligible to be recorded*. If it is not, the purchaser will not be protected even if the recording clerk makes a mistake and accepts the document.

   a.   Must record whole chain: Also, the subsequent grantee must see to it that his *entire chain of title* is recorded. (Thus if one of the subsequent grantee's predecessors in interest submitted, say, an improperly-notarized document that was therefore not eligible for recording, the subsequent grantee would lose.)

F.   Notice to subsequent claimants: In virtually all jurisdictions (that is, jurisdictions having notice or race-notice statutes, but not those very few having pure race statutes) the subsequent purchaser will lose if he was on *notice* of the earlier deed. A purchaser can be on notice in three ways: (1) *actual notice*; (2) *record notice*; and (3) *"inquiry"* notice.

1.   Actual notice: If the subsequent purchaser is shown to have had *actual* notice of the existence of the prior unrecorded interest, he will not gain the protection of the recording act in a notice or notice-race jurisdiction.

2.   Record notice: The subsequent grantee is deemed to have *"record"* notice if the prior interest is *adequately recorded*. However, the mere fact that a deed is recorded somewhere in the public records does not mean that the recording is "adequate" — the document must be recorded in a way that a reasonable searcher would *find* it.

   a.   Defective document: A document which is *not entitled to be recorded* will not give record notice, even if it is mistakenly accepted for recording. (*Example*: If the jurisdiction requires the deed to be *notarized*, and it is not, it will not give record notice. However, states often treat certain formal defects in deeds as being "cured" after the passage of a certain amount of time.)

   b.   Imputed knowledge: If proper recording of the earlier document took place, subsequent purchasers are on "record notice" even if they *never actually see* the document that has been filed. That is, the court *imputes* to the subsequent purchaser the knowledge which he *would have obtained* had he conducted a diligent title search.

    c. **"Chain of title":** Therefore, the recording of an instrument gives record notice to a subsequent searcher only if that searcher *would have found the document* using generally-accepted searching principles (use of the grantor and grantee indexes). A recorded instrument which would not be found by these principles is said to be outside the searcher's "chain of title," and prevents the giving of record notice.

> **Example:** O conveys to A; A never records. A then conveys to B; B records. O conveys the same property to C; C records. Assume that C has no knowledge of the O-to-A or A-to-B conveyances. C will have priority over B, even though B's interest is recorded. This is because C, when searching title, has no way to know of the A-to-B deed — C would never find the original O-to-A conveyance, and thus cannot know to look under A's name in the grantor index to discover whether he ever conveyed to anyone else. (Nor would C have any way to know to look for B's name in the grantee index.) The A-to-B deed is said to be "outside C's chain of title"; C is therefore not on record notice of the A-to-B deed, and will take priority over B.

3. **Inquiry notice:** Even if a purchaser has neither record notice nor actual notice of a prior unrecorded conveyance, he may be found to have been on *"inquiry" notice* of it. Inquiry notice exists where a purchaser is in *possession of facts which would lead a reasonable person in his position* to make an *investigation*, which would in turn advise him of the existence of the prior unrecorded right. Such a person is on inquiry notice even if he does not in fact make the investigation. (But the purchaser is responsible only for those facts which the investigation would have disclosed.)

    a. **Possession:** Thus if the parcel is *possessed* by a person who is *not the record owner*, this will place a subsequent purchaser on inquiry notice. That is, the purchaser must: (1) *view* the property, to see whether it is in the possession of someone other than the record owner; and (2) if there is such a possessor, he must inquire as to the source of the possessor's rights in the property.

> **Example:** Same facts as above example. C had a duty to inspect the property — if inspection would have disclosed that B (or someone claiming under B) was in possession of the property, C would be held to be on "inquiry notice" of B's interest. Since C could then have learned B's name, he could have checked back in the records to find the A-to-B deed, and perhaps might have discovered the O-to-A unrecorded deed. If a judge decided that this investigation would have enabled C to trace B's interest all the way back to O, C would lose in a contest with B because of the inquiry notice principle.

4. **Timing of notice:** In order for a subsequent purchaser to be protected by the recording act, she must have made *substantial payments* before being on notice of the prior conveyance.

    a. **Installment contract:** Where the subsequent purchaser is buying under an *installment contract*, if she receives *record notice* (but not actual notice), she is protected as to payments she makes.

Example: O conveys to A, who does not record. O conveys to B under an installment contract. After B has started making payments, A records. B doesn't learn of the recording, and keeps making payments. Most courts hold that B is protected as a b.f.p. as to payments made before and after A's recording, as long as the payments are made before B received *actual* notice of the prior conveyance to A.

5. **Purchaser from one without notice:** If a purchaser who takes without notice of a prior unrecorded instrument *resells* the property, the *new* purchaser is treated as one who may claim the benefit of the recording act, even if *he* buys *with* actual notice. This is done to protect the earlier (innocent) purchaser's market for the property.

II. TITLE REGISTRATION (THE TORRENS SYSTEM)

A. **How the system works:** In some parts of the U.S., the *"title registration"* system or *"Torrens"* system is available as an *option*. This system enables the owner of a parcel to obtain a *certificate of title*, similar to an automobile certificate of title. When the holder of the certificate wishes to sell, his prospective purchaser merely has to inspect the certificate itself (on which nearly all encumbrances must be noted) — a lengthy title examination is unnecessary.

1. **How it works:** The registration process begins with an *application* by a person claiming ownership of a parcel to have it registered. Notice is given to anyone shown on the ordinary land records as having an interest in the property. Then, a court hears any claims regarding the property, and if satisfied that the applicant indeed has good title, orders a certificate of title to be issued.

B. **Where used:** The Torrens system is never required, but is available as an option in 11 states. In only a few areas does the system account for a significant portion of the land area (e.g., Hawaii, Boston, parts of Minnesota and parts of Ohio.)

III. TITLE ASSURANCE

A. **Examination by lawyer:** One way the purchaser sometimes assures himself that he is getting valid title is to have a title examination performed by his *lawyer*. Usually, the lawyer does not directly search the records; instead, he orders an *"abstract"* of title from an abstract company and reviews that abstract. The lawyer then gives his client a written opinion as to the state of the title. The lawyer is liable for his own negligence in rendering an opinion on the title as presented in the abstract (but not liable for any mistake in the abstract itself — here, the abstract company might be liable).

B. **Title insurance:** The leading means by which a buyer of property can assure himself of a good title is *title insurance*.

1. **Covers matters not shown in title search:** Title insurance will protect the buyer against many risks that would *not* be disclosed even by the most careful title search. For instance, the buyer would be covered if title turns out to be bad because of forgery of an instrument in the chain, fraudulent misrepresentation of marital status by a grantor (so that the spouse's inchoate right of dower persevered), defects in a prior grant due to lack of delivery, etc. Also, the policy usually

covers the insured's *litigation costs* in defending his title even if the defense is successful.

2.Scope: But title policies usually contain a number of *exceptions*, including the following:

    a.   Facts which survey would show: Policies usually exclude facts which an *accurate survey* of the property would disclose. Thus *encroachments* (either by the insured onto adjacent property or vice versa) and violations of set-back rules are generally not covered.

    b.   Adverse possession: Also, the title policy does not protect against a claim of *adverse possession*, at least if the physical possession exists at the time the policy is written. Therefore, the buyer must still *inspect* the property.

Chapter 13

RIGHTS INCIDENT TO LAND

I.   NUISANCE

A. Defined: A landowner may sue another person for *"private nuisance."* Private nuisance is an interference with a landowner's *use and enjoyment of his land*.

    1.   Substantial interference: The interference with the plaintiff's use and enjoyment must be *substantial*. Thus if P's damage consists of his being *inconvenienced* or subjected to unpleasant smells, noises, etc., this will be "substantial" damage only if a person of *normal sensitivity* would be seriously bothered.

    2.   Defendant's mental state: There is *no* rule of *"strict liability"* in nuisance. P must show that D's conduct was *negligent*, *intentional* or *abnormally dangerous*.

        a.   Intentional: If P wants to show that D's conduct was "intentional," P does not have to show that D *desired* to interfere with P's use and enjoyment of his land. P merely has to show that D *knew with substantial certainty* that such interference would occur.

        Example: D, a factory owner, knows that his plant is spewing pollutants and smoke into the air over P's property. P can sue D for "intentional" nuisance so long as P can show that D was on notice of what was happening, even if D did not "desire" this result to occur.

    3.   Unreasonableness: Even if D's conduct is intentional, P will not win in nuisance unless he shows that D's actions were *"unreasonable."* In determining what is reasonable, the *nature of the neighborhood* is likely to be quite significant.

        Example: A steel mill located in an otherwise completely residential area is much more likely to be found an "unreasonable" interference than is a steel mill in the middle of an industrial park.

B. Remedies: P has a chance at either or both of the following remedies:

    1.   Damages: If the harm has already occurred, P can recover *compensatory damages*.

2. **Injunction:** If P can show that damages would not be a sufficient remedy, he may be entitled to an *injunction* against continuation of the nuisance. To get an injunction, P must show that the harm to him actually *outweighs* the social utility of D's conduct.

> **Example:** D operates a large cement plant employing hundreds of people. The Ps sue D for nuisance because of dirt, smoke and vibrations, which interfere with their nearby property. A court might not issue an injunction even though nuisance occurred, because the harm to the Ps may be found not to outweigh the job-creation and other economic utility of D's plant. But in that event, D would still have to pay money damages for the harm, no matter how socially useful D's conduct.

II.   LATERAL AND SUBJACENT SUPPORT

A. Generally: Every landowner is entitled to have his land receive the necessary *physical support* from adjacent and underlying soil. The right to support from adjoining soil is called the right of *"lateral"* support. The right to support from underneath the surface is known as the right to *"subjacent"* support.

B. Lateral support: The right to *lateral* support is *absolute*. That is, once support has been withdrawn and injury occurs, the responsible person is liable *even if he used utmost care* in his operation.

> **Example:** A and B are adjoining landowners. A very carefully constructs a large excavation extending almost to the edge of his property. This causes B's soil to run into A's excavation, impairing the surface of B's property. B's right to lateral support has been violated, and he may recover damages.

1. **Building:** But the absolute right to lateral support exists only with respect to land in its *natural state*. If the owner has constructed a *building*, and the soil under the building subsides in part due to the adjacent owner's acts, but also in part because of the weight of the building itself, the adjacent owner is *not liable* unless he has been *negligent*. (If P's building is damaged, and he can show that his land would have been damaged even with no building on it, courts are split as to whether D is liable in the absence of negligence.)

C. Subjacent support: The right to *subjacent* support arises only where sub-surface rights (i.e., *mineral rights*) are *severed* from the surface rights. When such a severance has taken place, the owner of the surface interest has the right not to have the surface subside or otherwise be damaged by the carrying out of the mining.

1. **Structures existing:** The surface owner has the absolute right to support, not only of the unimproved land, but also support of *all structures existing* on the date when the severance took place.

III. WATER RIGHTS

A. Drainage: Courts are split as to the rights of an owner to *drain surface water* from his property onto the property of others. In general, courts seem to be moving to a rule that an owner may do this only if his conduct is *"reasonable"* under all the circum-stances.

B. Streams and lakes: States are sharply split as to when and how a landowner may make use of waterfront *streams and lakes* that abut his property.

   1. Common law approach: In all parts of the country except for about 17 western states, courts apply the common-law *"riparian rights"* theory. Under this theory, *no advantage is gained by priority of use*. Instead, each riparian owner is entitled to only so much of the water as he can put to *beneficial use* upon his land, with due regard for the equal rights of the other riparian owners, and without regard to how long the owner has been using the water.

   > **Example:** A and B each own property that abuts a river. A is upstream from B. Under the common-law "riparian rights" theory, A may make "reasonable use" of the water — for instance, to irrigate his crops — but reasonableness will be determined by reference to B's reasonable needs as well as A's. The fact that A has been using the river for a particular use longer than B, or vice versa, is irrelevant.

   a. Riparian only: *Only riparian owners* are entitled to make use of the water, under this doctrine. That is, the owner's land must *abut* the stream or lake, at least in part. So one whose land is not contiguous with the water may not carry the water by pipe or ditch to his property.

   2. Prior appropriation doctrine: Seventeen *arid* states (all west of the Missis-sippi) adopt a completely different theory, called the *prior appropriation* doctrine. In many of these states (e.g., California), an owner must apply for a *permit* to use the water; if the application is accepted by the government, the user's priority dates from the time of the application.

   a. Riparian ownership not required: Under the prior appropriation system, water may be appropriated by a *non-riparian owner*.

C. Ground water: In most American states, an owner may make only *"reasonable use"* of *ground water* drawn from under his property. For instance, he may generally use as much of the water as he wishes for applications on the parcel which sits on top of the pool, but he may *not divert* the water to other properties which he may own.

IV. AIR RIGHTS

A. Airplane flights:

   1. Direct overflights: If an airport permits flights to occur *directly over* an owner's property, and within the *"immediate reaches"* of his land, the landowner may sue in *trespass*. But flights beyond a certain height are not deemed to be in the "imme-diate reaches," so no trespass suit may be brought.

   2. Adjacent areas: If flights occur at low altitude on property *adjacent* to P's prop-erty, some states may permit him to bring a suit for *nuisance* if the flights are low enough, frequent enough and noisy enough to substantially interfere with his use and enjoyment of his land. Also, a court may let such an owner bring a suit in "inverse condemnation," to establish that the interference is so great that it amounts to a "taking" for which compensation must be given under the U.S. Constitution.

B. Other air-rights issues:

1. **Tall buildings:** An owner generally has the right to build as *high a building as he wishes* (assuming that it satisfies all applicable zoning requirements and building restrictions). Thus if two owners are adjacent to each other, one cannot object to the other's tall building on the grounds, say, that it ruins the quality of radio and television signals.

2. **Right to sunlight:** Generally, a landowner has *no right to sunlight*. For instance, an owner almost never acquires an easement of "light and air" by implication or even by necessity. So if A and B are adjoining owners, B can, without liability, build in such a way that A's sunlight is blocked. (But if A uses sunlight as a source of *solar energy*, it is possible that he might have a claim — perhaps in nuisance — against B for blocking that energy source by a tall building.)

EXAM TIPS

SUMMARY OF CONTENTS
of EXAM TIPS

EXAM TIPS

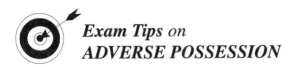

Exam Tips on
ADVERSE POSSESSION

Whenever it appears that a person has *encroached on another's property*, check to see whether the encroacher may have taken title by adverse possession. Adverse possession questions are favorites of profs, in part because an adverse possession issue can be well-hidden inside an essay fact pattern involving other topics.

Note: In the examples in this section, we assume a 20-year adverse-possession statute unless otherwise noted.

Adverse possession generally

Remember to list and discuss *all* the requisite elements even if they are obvious. In your analysis, discuss in greater detail the elements that are less clear. Also, note the *state statutory period*. If one isn't mentioned, write that you're assuming the occupation has occurred for the requisite length of time.

☛ **Hostility requirement:** Make sure the occupation is *hostile*. If the rightful owner *assents* to the occupation (e.g., by giving *verbal permission* to the occupier, or by *accepting rent* from the occupier, then this requirement has *not* been met).

   ☞ **Owner's knowledge:** The rightful owner's *knowledge of the encroachment,* coupled with his *lack of response* to it, will likely be viewed as **assent**.

   Example: The occupier, AP, tells the rightful owner, O, that AP knows he is encroaching and he will remove the encroachment if O so requests. O remains silent. O's silence will be construed as permission. Therefore, AP is not holding with the required hostility, and his holding won't count toward the statutory period.

   ☞ **Co-tenancy:** If the contest is between two co-tenants (call them A and B), and A claims to have taken sole title by adverse possession, look for clear actions indicating the *ouster* of B, the other cotenant. If there's no ouster — no sign that A kept B from the premises — A won't take B's share by adverse possession.

Example: A and B inherit Blackacre as co-tenants. A decides to live on the property; B continues to live far away. A pays all taxes and insurance, and makes all repairs on the property. A pays nothing to B for imputed rent. At the end of the statutory period, has A taken B's one-half interest by adverse possession? No. If there is no evidence that A prevented B from using the premises and thus ousted her, the court will presume that B consented to the arrangement. Therefore, A won't take B's interest by adverse possession.

☛ **Physical requirements:** Look in your fact pattern for, and note in your answer, the *physical actions* that would reasonably *give notice* to a rightful owner that her land is being hostilely occupied. (*Examples:* AP builds a fence around O's property, or plants and harvests crops, or pays property taxes — any of these would put O on notice that AP is occupying the property.)

☛ **Continuity requirement:** Remember that the claimant must possess the property *continuously* for the statutory period. Be careful to note when the occupier's possession is interrupted.

  ☞ **Exception:** But if the interruptions are *consistent* with the appropriate use of the property, then the occupier's claim is *not* affected. (*Example:* A summer cabin need only be occupied during the summer months.)

☛ **Requirement of actual possession:** The occupier must *"actually possess"* the property. But possession does not necessarily require that the occupier be physically present on the property.

  ☞ **Lease:** For instance, if the occupier *leases* her interest to another, the lessee's time on the premises will count toward the occupier's holding period.

    Example: AP moves onto Blackacre, which belongs to O. AP remains there for 10 years, then purports to lease his interest to T. T remains for another 10 years. At the end (assuming a 20-year statute), AP owns by adverse possession — the time T was in possession under claim of right from T will be credited to AP. (But these 10 years won't count towards any claim of adverse possession by *T* against either AP or O, because T is there with AP's permission.)

  ☞ **Possession under color of title:** Also, look for a situation where a party receives a *defective deed* and is therefore not in legal possession of the property. In that situation, she is entering the property under *color of title* (which meets the "hostility" requirement in most states), and she will be deemed to have gained possession of the *entire area* *described in the deed,* even if she *does not use part of the described land.*

> *Example:* AP purchases realty at a foreclosure sale, unaware of the fact that O purchased it six months earlier and has not defaulted on any payments. AP records her deed, constructs a house on part of the property, and encloses the house and a small area around it with a fence, but does not use any of the other land around it. At the end of the requisite period of time, AP can claim title by adverse possession of the *entire plot* that is described in the deed.

☛ **Future interest:** Be on the lookout for a possessor who is claiming against the holder of a *future interest* in the property — profs love to test this, because it's tricky. You have to check whether the future interest existed at the moment the adverse possession began, because the solution depends on this.

   ☞ **Interest exists when possession starts:** If the future interest *already exists* at the time the adverse possessor enters, the statutory period does *not* begin to run against the holder of the future interest until the future interest *becomes possessory.*

> *Example:* Z makes a will leaving Blackacre "to B for twenty years; the remainder to C. However, if C is not alive at the termination of B's estate, C's oldest child at the death of Z shall take the remainder." When Z dies, in 1975, B and C are alive and D, a minor, is C's oldest child alive. AP moves on to the property in 1976 and C dies in 1984. Twenty years after Z's death (in 1995) D discovers that AP has been in possession of the realty for 19 years. However, D attempts to have AP ejected from the realty only after two more years have passed (in 1997), at a time when AP has been in possession for 21 years. Nonetheless, D will succeed in his action because the statute of limitations began to run against him only two years previously — since D's future interest existed at the time AP began his possession, AP's possession began to count against D only when D's interest became possessory (at the termination of B's 20-year interest, in 1995), so only two years had elapsed by the time D brought his ejectment suit.

   ☞ **Successor in interest:** But don't confuse the above situation with a situation where there is a *successor in interest* to the property (i.e. where the owner conveys his interest to another after the adverse possession has already begun). In that case, *tacking* is *allowed.* In other words, the time against the first owner gets added to the time against the subsequent owner.

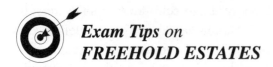

Exam Tips *on*
FREEHOLD ESTATES

Defeasible fees

This is a frequently tested area. Your success in tackling this subject will depend heavily on your ability to dissect the language used.

☛ **Key phrases:** When analyzing a fee simple defeasible to determine whether it is determinable or subject to a condition subsequent, look for key words.

    ☞ **Determinable phrases:** "So long as," "during," "until" indicate that it is *determinable* and ends *automatically* upon the occurrence of the event.

    ☞ **Condition-subsequent phrases:** When a fee simple is subject to a *condition subsequent,* the grant will usually contain a phrase like "upon condition that," "but if," or "provided that," and also a clause providing for *re-entry* when the condition is broken.

☛ **Restraints on alienation disliked:** Remember that courts *dislike restraints on alienation*. This attitude manifests itself in several ways:

    ☞ **Defeasible vs. absolute:** If there is a doubt whether a defeasible fee or a fee simple absolute is indicated, courts will *prefer* finding that a grant is a *fee simple absolute*.

    Example: A deed contains the following provision: "To have and to hold the described tract of land in fee simple, subject to the understanding that within one year from the date of the instrument said grantee shall construct and thereafter maintain and operate on said premises a public health center." Because the language "subject to the understanding that" does not clearly indicate a defeasible fee, a court would probably interpret the conveyance as a *fee simple absolute* with the imposition of a *personal contractual obligation* on the grantee. (So if the grantee fails to construct, the grantor gets damages but doesn't get back the property.)

    ☞ **Condition subsequent vs. determinable:** If there is a doubt, courts will *usually*, but not always, interpret a defeasible fee as *subject to a condition subsequent* rather than determinable, because courts disfavor forfeitures.

☞ **Automatic end:** But if the language indicates that the estate is to come to an end *automatically* on the happening of the stated event (i.e., *without any action* by the grantor or his heirs), this will make the grant a fee *determinable*, even if there is some other ambiguity in the language.

Example: O's grant provides: "To A and B, exclusively, as joint tenants, with right of survivorship, to be used as a parking lot, but if said premises should ever be used for a different purpose, then this conveyance shall immediately become void." Because of the clear language indicating that the estate is to end *immediately* (without action by O or his heirs), a court would probably determine that this grant is determinable despite use of the "but if" language (which would otherwise usually suggest a condition subsequent).

☞ **Minor deviation:** But even if a defeasible fee is clearly indicated, courts will require that the occurrence of the triggering event be *clearly established* — if there's ambiguity about whether that trigger occurred, courts will lean towards a finding that it didn't.

Example: As in the above example, O grants land to A and B for use as a parking lot, with the estate to end if the property is "ever used for a different purpose." A and B build a storage facility on a portion comprising 20% of the land, with the remainder still used for parking. Probably A and B can successfully argue that the estate ends only if the land is used *exclusively* or *primarily* for another purpose, which it wasn't.

☞ **Waiver:** Where the grant is subject to a condition subsequent (needs action by grantor to terminate) rather than being determinable (ends automatically), courts will often find that the grantor (or his heirs) has *waived the right to terminate* the fee simple subject to condition subsequent.

Example: In the above fact pattern regarding a storage facility constructed on the parking lot, suppose O parked in the lot three times while the storage facility was being erected and did not object to it at the time. Suppose further that the grantees A and B, in reliance on O's apparent acquiescence, incurred substantial expenses in expanding and adding on to the storage facility. O then changed his mind and sued to have the estate terminated. It's likely that a court would find that O waived his right of re-entry.

Fee tails

☛ **Fee tail generally:** Look for the language *"and the heirs of his body."* This language of course always indicates that at common law, the grant was a fee tail (could only pass to the grantee's direct line, and would revert to the grantor if the grantee's line ran out).

    ☞ **Note modern consequences:** But if your fact pattern does not tell you to assume that common-law rules are in effect, you should say in your analysis that although this would be a fee tail at common law, modern statutes may change its effects — you might want to note, for instance, that in a slight majority of states a fee tail is converted by statute to a fee simple absolute.

    ☞ **"If A dies without issue...":** Sometimes the fee tail is accompanied by language stating what happens if the grantee *dies without issue.* If so, note in your answer that in some states (though just a minority), the fee tail is treated as a fee simple subject to executory limitation, with the remainder passing in fee simple.

    Example: O grants "to A and the heirs of his body, but if A dies without issue, then to B." Note that while in a slight majority of states A gets a fee simple absolute, in some states A gets a fee simple subject to an executory limitation — in that event, if A dies without issue, B gets the property in fee simple absolute.

Life estates

☛ **Duties of tenant and remainderman:** Questions regarding the life tenancy most frequently involve distinguishing between the *duties* of the *life tenant* and the duties of the *remainderman*.

    ☞ **Duties:** Remember that the *life tenant* is required to pay *real estate taxes* that become due during the life tenancy. The life tenant is also responsible for mortgage *interest* to the extent that it does not exceed the reasonable rental value of the realty. However, the *remainderman* is responsible for payment of *principal*.

        ☞ **Trick:** Don't be tricked by a fact pattern that indicates that the reasonable rental value of the realty exceeds the sum necessary to pay *both* the principal and the interest on a loan. The life tenant's responsibility still will not extend to payment of principal.

☛ **Waste:** Profs love to test for *waste.* Look for a fact pattern where the life tenant does an affirmative act that causes *unreasonable, permanent damage* to the holder of the future interest.

    ☞ **Cutting timber:** Questions often involve the *cutting of timber.* If the life tenant is making reasonable use of the wood for the purpose of *maintaining* the realty (e.g., to repair the fences surrounding livestock pastures), then she will not be liable for waste. But if she's cutting the timber to sell it, and timber cultivation is not the sole reasonable use of the property, then the cutting *will* usually be waste.

☞ **Earth and minerals:** The life tenant may not *remove minerals* unless: (i) the property was used for mining prior to the commencement of the life estate ("open mines" doctrine) or (ii) mining is the only way of accomplishing the purpose of the lease (because mining is the only use for which the property is suitable or because mining is necessary for the agricultural use of the property that was intended).

Example: X dies, leaving his farm to his son Y for life, remainder to Z charity. Y tries farming the land for awhile because his father was a farmer, but he loses interest. Instead, he finds that mining gravel from the land is very lucrative. Y is liable to Z for voluntary waste because gravel was never removed from the land previously and the property was fit for farming, its intended purpose.

☛ **Conveyance:** A life tenant can *convey* the interest which she holds, but may not convey one that is larger.

Example: X conveys a parcel of realty "to Y for Y's life, and the remainder to my children." Y may convey his estate to Z, but only one that terminates on Y's death.

Exam Tips on *FUTURE INTERESTS*

Spend a lot of time reviewing the material in this chapter, especially the Rule against Perpetuities (RAP); and read the complex fact patterns carefully. On an exam, allocate a lot of time to solve a Future Interests or RAP problem — they take a lot of analysis.

Grantor's Interests

☛ **Grantor's interests, generally:** Always identify what type of interest the grantor retains, if she retains something. Memorize the following pairings (all assume that the grantor starts with a fee simple absolute):

❑ If grantee gets a *life estate* or an *estate for years* (and grantor keeps the rest), then grantor retains a *"reversion"*;

❑ If grantee's interest is *determinable* (i.e., is to *terminate automatically* on the stated event), then grantor has a ***"possibility of reverter"***;

❑ If grantee's interest is **subject to condition subsequent** (i.e., interest won't terminate automatically, but needs some action by grantor), then grantor has a ***"right of re-entry"***.

Remainders

Remember that a remainder is an interest that is: (1) created in one other than the grantor, and (2) follows an estate (created by the same instrument) that is certain to terminate.

> *Example:* O conveys "to A for life, then to B and his heirs." B has a remainder in fee simple (a type of vested remainder).

☛ **Distinguishing between vested and contingent:** Read the language of the conveyance or bequest carefully to distinguish between the two main types of remainders (***vested*** and ***contingent***). This will be vital to solve Rule against Perpetuities problems.

☞ **Contingent:** A remainder will be contingent if it meets either of two conditions: (1) it won't become ***possessory until the fulfillment of a condition; or (2) it's in favor of an unborn or unascertained*** person.

> *Example:* M has a son, A. A has one child, B, who has no children. M conveys realty "to A for life, with the remainder to B's children." At the time of the conveyance, B's children, because they are not yet born, have a contingent remainder.

☞ **Alternative contingent remainders:** Where a condition precedent involves survivorship, it is likely you will find an alternate party who is to take if the condition is not met. In such a fact pattern, you will have "alternative contingent remainders."

> *Example:* T's will bequeaths her realty "to my nephew, A for twenty years, remainder to my niece B if she is living at that time; but if B is not living at the termination of A's estate, to the oldest child of B at the time of my death." T dies, survived by A, B and B's two children, E, age 14 and F, age 7. B and E have alternative contingent remainders.

☞ **Vested:** If there are no conditions precedent to a person's taking, then the remainder is vested. Don't get misled by conditional language in another part of the grant.

> *Example:* O conveys realty "to A for life, but if A should ever use liquor on the premises to B for life; then to C." C's remainder is vested, since he will take either on the death of A or on the death of B, events that are certain to occur. The "liquor" contingency is a "red her-

ring" when it comes to C's interest.

☞ **Vested subject to divestment:** If a condition exists which could destroy the interest *after* it has vested (and maybe even after it has become possessory), the interest is "vested *subject to divestment.*" It is easy to confuse a vested remainder subject to divestment with a contingent remainder. A clue to the former is language granting an unconditional grant followed by a "but if" clause.

Example: Testator's will devises realty "to A for life; and upon the death of A: a one-third interest to the children of A, a one-third interest to the children of B, and a one-third interest to the children of C, but if any of C's children should fail to survive to the age of 25 years, then the interest of such child or children of C shall pass to all grandchildren of C equally, share and share alike." Several years after Testator dies, while A is still alive, C gives birth to Z. After Z's birth, Z's interest is a vested remainder subject to divestment — that's so because: (1) it's vested, because if A were to die today, Z would take, but (2) it's subject to being divested if C should die at an age of less than 25 while A was still alive.

☞ **Vested subject to open:** Some remainders are "vested *subject to open*." Look for a situation where a holder of a vested interest may have to *share the interest* with others in his class who do not yet have vested interests. The most common example of this is a remainder to the children of a living person.

Example: T's will devises realty "to B for life, remainder to be divided equally among B's children, share and share alike." At T's death, B is still alive, and has one child, X. X has a "vested remainder subject to open," since he may have to share his interest with others if B has any more children.

Executory interests

☛ **Executory interests generally:** An interest that follows an estate which may, but will *not necessarily* terminate, is an executory interest. The most commonly tested is the shifting executory interest, a subsequent estate which can possibly cut off a prior estate.

Example: T bargains and sells realty: "to my children, but if my friend F is still alive 30 years after this conveyance, to F." The children's estate may be cut off if F lives another thirty years. Therefore, the children have a fee simple determinable, and F has a shifting executory interest.

☞ **Perpetuities problem:** If your problem has an executory interest, always be on the lookout for a violation of the ***Rule against Perpetuities*** — such violations are common in exam questions containing executory interests.

> *Example:* O devises realty "to my niece A and her heirs for as long as the property is not used for the sale of alcohol; but if the property is ever used for the sale of alcohol, to the National Cancer Association." The Association's interest is a void executory interest because its interest will not vest until alcohol is sold on the property, an event which might occur outside of the perpetuities period.

Rule against Perpetuities (RAP)

Remember the core statement of the rule: ***"No interest is good unless it must vest, if at all, not later than 21 years after some life in being at the creation of the interest."***

> *Example:* O conveys: "to A, her heirs and assigns, so long as the premises are used as a working farm, then to B and his heirs." A and her heirs have a fee simple determinable. Notice that the property might be used for residential purposes for 200 years, longer than any life in being at the time of the conveyance. Then, if the property stopped being used as a farm, the shifting executory interest to B and his heirs would vest. Since that vesting would be more than 21 years after any life in being at the time of the conveyance, the vesting would not be within the Perpetuities period. Therefore, the interest in B is deemed invalid from the beginning (even though it might in fact vest while, say, A or B was still alive — the mere *possibility* of a too-late vesting ruins the interest, at common law).

Concentrate on the following issues concerning the RAP:

☛ **Step 1 — Does the RAP apply:** First, check to see whether the RAP applies. There are several important ***exceptions***:

   ☞ **Shifting executory interest:** The RAP normally applies to shifting executory interests (as in the above example), but ***not*** where the shifting interest is in favor of a ***charity***, and follows a valid interest in favor of a ***different charity***. This is a frequently-tested point.

   > *Example:* A devise provides: "To Senior Center, for so long as the realty shall be used as a home for the elderly, but if racial discrimination is practiced in the admission of residents to said home, to Senior Life for as long as the realty shall be used as a home for the elderly." The fact pattern indicates that Senior Center and Senior Life are both charitable institutions. The devise to Senior Life is a

valid executory interest and not void under the RAP, because it follows a prior interest that was also held by a charity.

☞ **Vested remainder:** The Rule doesn't apply to an interest that is *vested*. Don't mistake a vested remainder *subject to a condition subsequent* (not subject to the Rule) for a *contingent remainder* (subject to the Rule). (This is the main reason you have to determine whether a remainder is vested or contingent.)

> *Example:* T's will devises realty "to A for life; and upon the death of A: a one-third interest to the children of A, a one-third interest to the children of B, and a one-third interest to the children of C, but if any of C's children should fail to survive to the age of 25 years, then the interest of such child or children of C shall pass to all grandchildren of C equally, share and share alike." Several years after T dies, C gives birth to Z. Z's interest is a vested remainder subject to divestment on account of a condition subsequent (survival). Therefore, it is not subject to the Rule.

☞ **Grantor's interests:** The Rule does not apply to interests maintained by the grantor. Thus it doesn't apply to *reversions*, *possibilities of reverter* and *rights of re-entry*. That's true even though these might be held by a descendant of the grantor by the time they take effect, several generations in the future.

But the RAP *does* apply to some interests where you might not think it does.

☞ **Options:** For instance, the Rule applies to *options to purchase realty* unless they are *attached to a lease* or other interest in the realty. This is one that profs like to test, because it's tricky.

> *Example 1:* X and Y enter into an option agreement whereby Y pays for the right to purchase realty at a fixed price thirty years from the date of the agreement. One year later, X sells the land to Z. Y protests that the sale to Z violated the option. Y will lose, because Y's option agreement is void under the Rule.

> *Example 2:* Same basic facts. Now, however, assume that Y *leases* the property from X for 99 years, and the option to buy is only to be effective while the lease is in force. Now, the option will *not* be void under the Rule, because it's appurtenant to a lease or other interest in the real estate (so the Rule doesn't apply at all).

☞ **Step 2 — Measuring each interest:** Once you have determined that the Rule applies, measure *each* of the interests to determine their validity.

☞ **Life in being:** Always identify (and note in your answer) the life (or lives) in being. Don't skip this step. And be careful to resist the temptation to classify the interest merely based on the number of years mentioned in the grant.

> *Example:* X conveys realty "to Y, his heirs and assigns; but if Z shall be living thirty years from the date of this deed, then to Z, his heirs and assigns." Z is the relevant life in being, and the 30-year condition is irrelevant. Z's and Z's heirs' interests are valid because the interests will vest or fail within Z's lifetime. (If Z lives another 30 years it will vest; if he dies before 30 years it will fail).

☞ **Bequest v. *inter vivos* gift:** Remember to measure the interests at the time they are effective. Remember that in the case of a *will*, the interests are considered created from the date of the testator's death.

☞ **Gift to grandchildren:** Be on the lookout for gifts to unborn *grandchildren*: the validity of the gift will frequently turn on whether it was created in a will or a conveyance. If it is an *inter vivos* gift, there is always the chance of the conveyor having children after the conveyance has been made. These after-born children cannot be lives in being. Therefore, their own children's interests could possibly vest outside the perpetuities period, even if the gift must vest before that child turns 21. However, if the gift is a *bequest*, then each of the children of the devisor can serve as the "life in being" for their respective children (the testator's grand-children), and the gift to them will be valid as long as they take effect before the child turns 21.

> *Example:* By will, X devises realty "to such of my grandchildren who shall reach the age of 21; and by this provision I intend to include all grandchildren whenever born." At the time of his death, X has three children and two grandchildren. At X's death all his children are lives in being, since he can't have more children once he's dead. Thus, X can't have grandchildren who can turn 21 more than 21 years after the measuring lives, and the gift to those grandchildren is valid.

☞ *Must* **vest if at all:** Determine whether it is *possible* for the interest to vest outside of the perpetuities period. If it is, the interest is *void*. Don't be misled by a fact pattern that indicates that an interest *did in fact vest* within the period — this won't save the bequest, under the common-law approach. (But many states today have "wait and see" statutes which change this result.)

> *Example:* X leaves Blackacre in his will "to my wife for life, remainder to those of my children who achieve the age of twenty-one years. If any child of mine shall predecease me, or if any child

of mine shall survive me but shall die before achieving the age of twenty-one years, that child's share shall be distributed equally among any of that child's children who shall marry..." At his death, X has three children, A, B, and C, ages 18, 19, and 22. Two years after X's death, A gives birth to Z, and dies one week later at the age of twenty. Z marries at the age of eighteen. Since Z's marriage *might* have taken place more than 21 years after the deaths of X's three children (the lives in being), her interest *might* have vested outside of the perpetuities period. Therefore, the gift to Z is void at common law; it is irrelevant that Z in fact married within the period of lives in being + 21 years. (But the gift to Z would be valid under a "wait and see" statute, since it in fact vested within a life in being at X's death + 21 years.)

☞ **Class gifts:** Generally, a *class* must *close within the perpetuities period* and all conditions precedent for every member of the class must be satisfied, if at all, within the period.

☞ **Per capita gift:** When there is a gift of a *fixed sum* to each class member, the amount of the gift is not dependent upon the number of children or grandchildren who fulfill the condition of survival. Each gift is tested separately under the Rule, and some may be valid while others are invalid.

Example: G's will provides: "I further direct that my realty be sold, and that the proceeds of such sale be given to a charity..., provided, however, that out of said proceeds two thousand dollars shall first be given to each of my children and grandchildren who survive to the age of twenty-two years." At the time of G's death, his children A, B, and C are 18, 19, and 22 years old, respectively. Two years after G's death A gives birth to Z. A dies a week later at the age of 20. After the property is sold, C demands payment of two thousand dollars from the executor. Because the disposition provided that the members of the class must survive to age 22, the Rule is violated as to some possible bequests (e.g., as to Z), because it is possible that interests of certain members of the class will vest outside of the perpetuities period. However, since the gift was a per capita disposition, C's interest vested immediately upon G's death and is valid.

☞ **Partially void grant:** Separately evaluate *each clause* of a grant. Just because one part is void under the Rule does not mean that all other interests are void. In your answer, say which parts are void and which are valid.

Example 1: C conveys a parcel of land "to D and his heirs until the U.S. goes to war with the Republic of Z. In that event the land is to go to E." E's interest is void under the Rule because his interest might vest hundreds of years after the conveyance. However, D's interest is a valid fee simple determinable because it vested immediately.

☞ **Consequences of void grant:** Be prepared to figure out and explain the *consequences* of a grant that's void because of the RAP — you'll want to explain who took the interest(s) that remained after the failure.

Example: O conveys Blackacre by deed: "to A and his heirs as long as it is used exclusively for residential purposes, but if it is ever used for other than residential purposes, to the American Red Cross." Several years later, O dies, leaving a will by which he devises all his real estate to his brother, B. Several years after O's death A contracts to sell Blackacre to X in fee simple. X refuses to perform because he claims that A cannot give good title.

A will lose if he sues to have the contract specifically performed. Explanation: Because the shifting executory interest to the American Red Cross was void under the Rule, A retained a fee simple determinable and O retained a possibility of reverter, which he devised to B in his will. Therefore, B must join in any conveyance of the property.

Exam Tips *on*
CONCURRENT OWNERSHIP

Joint Tenancy

☞ **Joint tenancy vs. tenancy in common:** Generally, a tenancy in common, *not* a joint tenancy, is presumed unless there is a *clear intent* to establish a joint tenancy.

   ☞ **Identify interest:** First look at the grantor's language. A joint tenancy is clearly indicated by a grant which provides: "To A and B as joint tenants with right of survivorship."

      ☞ **Ambiguity:** Watch for language that does *not* clearly indicate a joint tenancy; when this happens, lean in favor of a tenancy in common.

      Example: O grants realty "to A and B, to be held by them jointly."

Most courts would find a tenancy in common because of the ambiguous language. However, in your answer, analyze the surrounding circumstances which may influence a court to decide differently. For instance, if A and B are related to each other and to O, and the property is a single-family residence, you can argue that O intended to keep the property in the family and that he would not have created a situation where one cotenant might possibly be forced to share a home with a stranger (which could happen with a tenancy in common).

☞ **Survivorship:** Remember that the unique characteristic of a joint tenancy is that upon a cotenant's death, her share *passes to the surviving cotenants in equal shares*; the remaining cotenants are then in joint tenancy with each other.

> *Example:* A, B and C are in joint tenancy with each other. Each holds an undivided one-third interest in the property. If A dies, her interest passes to the other two. Therefore, B and C will each hold an undivided one-half interest in the property, as joint tenants.

☞ **Severance:** The most frequently-tested issue regarding a joint tenancy is the issue of *severance*. Often fact patterns will be complicated, with several transfers having occurred, and you will be asked to determine the rights of the various parties to the property; to do this, you'll have to recognize where severance of the joint tenancy has occurred.

> ☞ **Sale or other conveyance:** Look for a *conveyance* by one cotenant to another party. This *effects a severance* as to that interest but *not* as to the interests of the other joint tenants.
>
> *Example:* A, B, and C are joint tenants in a parcel of land. B sells her share to Z. The result is that A and C hold equal shares of a two-thirds interest in the land as joint tenants with each other, and Z holds a one-third interest in the land as a tenant in common vis a vis the other two.

> ☞ **Devise:** Don't be fooled when a cotenant devises her share of a joint tenancy in her *will*. This does *not* effect a severance, nor does it pass the share on to the devisee. The decedent's share automatically passes to the other cotenant(s).
>
> *Example 1:* O conveys realty "to my brothers A and B, their heirs and assigns as joint tenants with right of survivorship." A dies, devising his interest to his only child, "C for life, and then to C's son, S, for life, and then to S's children, their heirs and assigns." B dies and devises his interest "to my friend, F, his heirs and

assigns." F later conveys by quitclaim deed "to P, his heirs and assigns."

P owns the realty in fee simple because: (1) A's interest went to B when A died (despite the fact that A tried to devise it by will), leaving the whole parcel in B; (2) B devised the whole parcel to F; and (3) F conveyed the whole parcel to P.

Example 2: A, B, and C are joint tenants of a parcel. A conveys her interest to D, her daughter. Later, B dies, with a will leaving all B's real estate to S, his son.

When A conveyed her interest to D, D became a tenant in common with a one-third interest, while B and C continued to be joint tenants as to the remaining two-thirds. B's attempted devise to S was ineffective and C received B's interest, leaving C with an undivided two-thirds interest and D with an undivided one-third interest as tenants in common.

☞ **Mortgage:** If a joint tenant mortgages his interest in a state that treats a mortgage as a transfer of *title,* then the joint tenancy is *severed.* However, in a state where a mortgage is treated as merely a *lien* to secure repayment, the tenancy is *not severed.*

☞ **Partition:** Another method of severance that appears in fact patterns is *partition*: the dividing up and distributing of the land or the sale of the land and distribution of the proceeds, which can be done either by agreement of the parties, or by court order at the request of one party. Partition effects a severance — each cotenant is given a share equal in value. If the estate can't be divided equally, the cotenant who receives the land of greater value may be required to make a cash payment to the other cotenant.

Tenancy in common

☛ **T/C generally:** A conveyance to two or more people is presumed to be a tenancy in common unless a contrary intention is shown.

Tenancy by the entirety

☛ **Tenancy by the entirety generally:** In jurisdictions which recognize tenancy by the entirety, a conveyance *to a husband and wife* is *presumed* to create a tenancy by the entirety. But the presumption operates only if there's no indication that the parties had a contrary intention.

Example: Bride and Groom receive a wedding gift of a parcel of realty. The deed states: "to Bride and Groom, husband and wife, as joint tenants." Several years later Bride and Groom separate and Bride moves in with another man, Mon. At Mon's request, Bride executes a quitclaim deed conveying her interest in the realty to Mon.

The "as joint tenants" language rebutted the presumption of a tenancy by an entirety, and instead created in Bride and Groom a joint tenancy with right of survivorship. When Bride conveyed to Mon, the joint tenancy was severed, and Groom and Mon became tenants in common.

Ouster

☛ **Ouster generally:** Look for a fact pattern which indicates that a tenant not in possession of the land has attempted to physically occupy the land and the occupying tenant has refused to allow access. When this occurs, point out that the cotenant who has ousted the other cotenant or prevented her from occupying the premises may be required to *account to the other cotenant for rent.* (Each co-tenant normally has a right of *equal access* to the property.)

Exam Tips on *LANDLORD AND TENANT*

Tenancies — their creation and operation

This is a frequently tested area. Issues to watch for:

☛ **Distinguish:** Distinguish among the various types of tenancies, and be sure to state in your answer which kind is involved. Here are two special kinds (in addition to the ordinary tenancy for a term of years):

☞   **Tenancy at will:** This is a tenancy with no fixed duration. It can therefore be terminated *at any time* by either party.

☞   **Periodic tenancy:** This tenancy continues for a stated period, and *automatically renews* for repeated similar periods unless proper notice of termination is given by either party.

☛ **Tenant's right of possession and enjoyment:** Questions sometimes involve a tenant who is *not given possession* of the premises on time.

☞   **Holdover tenant:** Usually the problem involves a *holdover tenant*, H, who is making it impossible for the new tenant, T, to gain possession of the leased premises. The issue is either: (1) whether T owes rent for the time when T can't get into the premises; or (2) whether T can terminate the lease and recover damages on account of his inability to get entry.

☞ **Contrast two rules:** Be prepared to explain that the result on both issues depends on whether the *"American" view* (where the landlord has the duty to deliver *only legal possession*) or the *"English" view* (where the landlord has the duty to deliver *actual possession*) applies. If "American" applies, T owes rent, and can't terminate or recover; if "English" applies, T doesn't owe rent, can terminate, and can recover for breach.

☞ **Frustration of purpose:** You'll also sometimes be given a fact pattern in which it's impractical for the tenant to use the premises for the purpose she planned on. Here, remember that the doctrine of *"frustration of purpose"* will often come to the tenant's rescue.

Example: A written five-year lease between T and L contains a restriction that the premises shall be used "as a dance studio and for no other purpose." T operates a dance studio there. One year later, a dance student falls through a floor board. Upon repair of the floorboard, it is discovered that the floor is not strong enough to support a dance studio. T is likely to be relieved of his obligations regarding the lease, under the doctrine of frustration of purpose. (But if L hadn't known, at the time the lease was signed, that the premises were to be used as a dance studio, the frustration doctrine probably would *not* apply.)

☞ **Condition of premises:** If the premises become *physically damaged* during the course of the tenancy, consider the following:

☞ **Express warranty:** First, consider whether L has made an *express warranty* about the condition of the premises. If so, consider whether that warranty has been breached. Often, the fact pattern will be set up so that there is probably no breach of the express warranty even though there has been some deterioration in, or problem with, the premises.

Example: A one-year lease between L and T contains a clause allowing T "to give up possession and terminate liability for rent if the premises, through no fault on T's part, are destroyed or damaged so as to be uninhabitable." Several months after coming into possession of the apartment for a monthly rental of $900 a month, T surrenders possession and moves out because of a leaky roof (which leaked from the very beginning). L refuses to accept the surrender, but offers to attempt to re-let the premises on T's account. T declines. T can argue that L has breached his express warranty of habitability. But L has a good argument that (1) the warranty does not cover *deterioration* of the premises due to some latent defect (but only damage by some sudden external force); and (2) the leaky roof did not cause the premises to become completely *uninhabitable*, the only situation covered by the warranty.

☞ **Implied warranty of habitability:** Remember that most states now impose some sort of *implied warranty on landlords* regarding the condition of premises, especially residential ones such as apartments. So if a fact pattern does not indicate whether the common law or statutory law applies, contrast the modern-law implied warranty with the common-law rule (under which L has no duty of repair, and under which because of the independence of covenants even a breach by L would not relieve T of her duty to pay rent). When you talk about the modern implied warranty of habitability, pay attention to these issues:

   ☞ **Damage by third person:** Courts are split about whether L is liable to repair *damage caused by a third person*; probably most would agree with the Restatement that the warranty does *not* apply in this situation.

   Example: Children playing baseball break a windowpane, rain comes in through the broken pane and the living room floor gets warped. L would probably prevail in his argument that because the damage was caused by third persons, L was not required to make the repair.

   ☞ **Notice:** Make sure that T has *notified* L of the condition which he claims makes the apartment uninhabitable, and has given L a *reasonable amount of time* to make the repair before T has, say, cancelled the lease and moved out.

   ☞ **Time of departure:** Also, if T has cancelled and moved out, make sure that T did not wait to leave until *after* the condition about which she is complaining no longer exists — if so, T's cancellation is wrongful.

   ☞ **Substantial impairment required:** Also, remember that there must have been a *substantial* impairment in the use or enjoyment of the property; minor problems won't suffice.

   Example: T claims that the apartment is "noisy" because of fights and parties by other tenants. This may not be a sufficiently substantial interference with T's use and enjoyment — it depends on degree. (Also, a given amount of noise may be less damaging if it occurs in daytime or early-evening than if late at night.)

☞ **Commercial vs. residential:** Note that the implied warranty is more likely to apply to a *residential* lease than a *commercial* one. Note in your answer what kind of lease is indicated by the fact pattern.

Fixtures

☛ **Fixtures generally:** Be alert for issues about *fixtures*, whenever a fact pattern indicates that a tenant wishes to remove an item of personal property (originally owned by the tenant) that has somehow become *attached* to the premises. The two main rules to remember about when fixtures may be removed are:

☞ **Damage:** If there will be damage to the real estate from the removal, that cuts in favor of not allowing removal.

☞ **Trade fixtures:** If the fixture is a *"trade fixture"* (i.e., used in the tenant's trade or business), this cuts in favor of allowing removal.

Examples involving fixtures:

(1) If T operates a retail store and puts a prefabricated aluminum structure on the parking lot to be used as an inventory storage shed, this will probably be removable, because it is prefabricated and related to T's business.

(2) Plumbing installed in walls by T would probably be considered permanent and not removable, due to the need to break open the walls to remove it.

(3) Air conditioning units installed by T on the roof of the premises would be probably be removable, because they are easily removed without damage to the premises.

L's remedies if T abandons premises

☛ **Landlord's remedies, generally:** Look for a scenario where T *abandons* the premises. The main question to address: Do L's actions indicate the *intent to accept* the surrender? If "yes," then the surrender is deemed accepted and T is off the hook; if "no," then T is still liable for the unpaid balance.

☞ **Intent:** So look for particular facts supporting or disputing the finding of intent by L to accept surrender.

Examples:

(1) L's silent acceptance of keys from T is probably ***not*** enough to show intent to accept surrender.

(2) If L occupies the premises for her own purposes (e.g., for use as a management office for the building) it is probable that a court *would* deem her actions as acceptance of surrender;

(3) If L re-lets the premises but does not notify T that the re-letting is being done for T's benefit, intent to accept the surrender will be presumed, and L's actions will not be understood as a mere attempt to mitigate damages.

☛ **Duty to mitigate:** Profs sometimes test L's duty to mitigate (by finding an alternative tenant). Distinguish between residential and commercial leases: although an increasing number of courts are imposing upon landlords the duty to try to find a new tenant in the case of residential leases, this is usually *not* the case in ***commercial leases***.

Transfer

A number of issues can be tested where there is an ***assignment*** of a lease.

☛ **Lease prohibits assignment:** Check to see whether the lease itself prohibits assignment. If so, remember that restraints on alienation of estates in land are ***strictly construed***. Therefore:

☞ **Ban on subletting doesn't ban assignment:** If the lease contains a clause prohibiting ***subletting*** (where *part* of the remaining leasehold is transferred) then an ***assignment*** (where there is a transfer of the *entire* remaining interest) would ***not*** be construed as being prohibited.

☞ **Watch for waiver:** Where a landlord reserves the right to terminate a lease in the event of violation of the covenant not to assign, the assignment is ***not*** automatically void, but merely voidable at the landlord's election. And, according to the "Rule in Dumpor's Case," the landlord's consent to *one* assignment bars him from objecting to *any subsequent transfer* by the assignee.

☞ **Co-tenant's objection:** Notice *who* is objecting to the assignment — a ***co-tenant*** who objects to an assignment cannot enforce an anti-assignment clause. Such a clause is ***for the benefit of the landlord only***.

☛ **Who is liable for unpaid rent:** Assuming that there has been a valid assignment, a common issue is ***who is liable*** if the assignee does not pay rent.

☞ **Original lessee still liable:** The original tenant ***always remains liable*** on the lease because she is in *privity of contract* with the landlord (unless she has been released from the obligations of the lease). This point is very frequently tested.

☞ **Assignee is liable on lease only for period of possession:** Generally, the *assignee* of the original lessee can be held liable only for the rent due *during the period of time he was actually in possession* and not for breaches by the original lessee or subsequent assignees.

> *Example:* L enters into a 10-year lease to rent office space to T at $1,000 per month. T occupies the premises for two years and pays rent as it became due. T then assigned the balance of the lease to U, who agrees to be personally liable to L for all obligations under the lease. U assigns the balance of the leasehold to V with several months on the lease remaining. V does not personally assume the obligations of the lease. V takes occupancy for two months but does not pay any rent. V assigns the balance of the lease to W, who does not pay any rent and who abandons the premises at the expiration of the lease five months later. Under these circumstances, V is responsible to L for $2,000 — that is, V is liable for just the amount of rent which was unpaid during his two-month occupancy, not the rent that accrued during W's subsequent five-month occupancy.

☞ **Assignee's assumption is exception:** But there's an important exception to this general rule that the assignee is only liable for rent accruing during her time of occupancy: When the assignee promises the assignor that the assignee will *personally assume the obligations* of a lease there is *privity of contract* between the assignee and the landlord. Therefore, the assignee becomes liable for rent accrued before the assignment went into effect or after it terminates.

> *Example:* After two years of paying rent to L on a five-year lease, T assigns her lease to X, who in the assignment document personally assumes all obligations of the lease. (By this assignment, X will be deemed to be in privity of contract with L.) X, after paying rent for six months, assigns the balance of the lease to Y, who pays rent for two months and then stops paying rent and abandons the premises. X is liable for all rent which

accrued during the duration of the lease, including the time when the premises were occupied by Y.

Exam Tips on
EASEMENTS AND PROMISES CONCERNING LAND

Easements and covenants regarding land are tested more frequently than you might think. Probably that's because it's easy to draft complex questions that have an objectively-correct answer. So you have to study the technical rules in detail and master them — you can't safely rely on your ability to "argue the pros and cons" without technical knowledge.

Easements, generally

☛ **Type of easement:** Identify the *type* of easement and how it was created. Issues that arise:

☞ **Easement by implication:** When an easement is not expressly created, you may argue that an easement has been created by *implication*. For an easement by implication, you must find that *all* of the following conditions are met:

[1] the servient estate was *used* for the purpose for which the easement is now being claimed *before the severance* of the dominant and servient estates;

[2] the use was *reasonably apparent and continuous* at the time of the severance, and

[3] the easement is *reasonably necessary* to the enjoyment of the dominant estate.

Example: B purchases Lot 1 from O. Lot 1 is a plot with a house on it located adjacent to O's Lot 2, which also contains a house. O then sells Lot 2 to C. B razes the house on Lot 1 and discovers on her lot a sewer pipe connecting Lot 2's house with the public sewer. The pipe runs beneath the surface of the land outside where the Lot 1 house was, and then runs above the surface in an accessible crawl space located beneath the first floor of the now-razed house. B demands that C remove the pipe from B's land; C does not want to do this because of the expense of getting a substitute sewer hookup.

C can plausibly argue that he has an easement by implication for the pipe across Lot 1. Requirement [1] is clearly satisfied, because Lot 1 was used for the pipe before ownership of Lot 1 was severed from Lot 2. Requirement [2] is more debatable: C can argue that the part of the pipe that was in the crawl space was visible to the owner of Lot 1 at all times, so that the easement was "reasonably apparent and continuous" before the severance (but B can argue the converse, that this use was not apparent because the owner of Lot 1 would be unlikely to have noticed it). Requirement [3] is easily satisfied, since the owner of Lot 2 has reasonable need for a sewer hookup. Therefore, C will be found to have an easement by implication if he can persuade a court that the use of the pipe was reasonably apparent to O at the time O sold Lot 1.

☞ **Easement for "light and air" (i.e., view):** A fact pattern will often indicate that construction on a parcel is *blocking the view* from an adjoining lot. Remember that an easement for an unobstructed view — sometimes called an easement of *"light and air"* — generally *cannot be created by implication.* So unless such an easement is created by express grant, you should say that no easement exists.

Example: O owns Lots 1 and 2. Lot 2 is adjacent to the shoreline, and that lot lies between the shore and Lot 1. There is a house on Lot 1, and nothing on Lot 2. O sells Lot 1 to A, and Lot 2 to B. The sale documents for both transactions say nothing about whether B can build on Lot 2. B begins to build a large house on Lot 2, which when completed would have the effect of blocking A from seeing the shoreline from Lot 1. A tries to enjoin the construction, arguing that Lot 1 has an easement of light and air over Lot 2. In most states A will lose, because the easement could only have come into existence by implication (there was no express grant of easement), and in most states there can be no easement of light and air created by implication.

☞ **Easement by necessity:** The requirements for an *easement by necessity* are different from those for an easement by implication. For the easement-by-necessity, two requirements must be met:

[1] The servient and dominant parcels must have been under *common ownership* at one time (this requirement is the same as for easement-by-implication); and

[2] The use must be *"strictly necessary"* (rather than just "reasonably

necessary," the standard for easement-by-implication).

But there is *no requirement* that the easement have been in *actual use* prior to severance.

Here are some examples that would probably qualify as easements by necessity (always assuming that Lot 1 and Lot 2 were once under common ownership):

❑ Lot 2 is inaccessible to the public road except via a right-of-way over Lot 1. (The easement-by-necessity will exist even if the road, and therefore the right-of-way, didn't come into existence until after the two lots were severed.)

❑ Lot 2 has a sewer line that passes through Lot 1 on its way to the public sewer, and relocating the line so it doesn't pass beneath Lot 1 would be prohibitively expensive. (In other words, on the facts of the above sewer example on p. 129, C would probably win on easement-by-necessity even if he lost on easement-by-implication).

☞ **Easement by prescription:** Finally, remember that there can be an *easement by prescription* — that is, an easement can come into existence by operation of the *adverse possession* statute.

    ☞ **Use must be adverse:** Be sure to identify in your answer all the requirements for this kind of easement: that it be (1) *adverse* to the owner of the servient estate; (2) *"open and notorious"*; and (3) *"continuous and uninterrupted"* for the full statutory period.

    Pay closest attention to the requirement that the use be *adverse* to the rights of the owner of the servient parcel. That is, look at whether the servient owner has *granted permission* to the dominant owner to use the piece of the servient's land that is in dispute — if permission has been granted, then the use is not adverse.

☞ **Express easement:** An *express* easement is one created by the express agreement of the parties. Most important: an express easement must *satisfy the Statute of Frauds* (i.e., be in writing), and must be *recorded* in the same way as any other interest in land. If a right to use land is oral, it therefore cannot be an express easement (and will usually be just a revocable "license" — see below).

Scope and use of easement

☛ **Scope, generally:** Once you've concluded that an easement exists, look for a change in the *use* of the easement from the time it was created. If the new use arises from the normal, *foreseeable*, development of the dominant estate without imposing an ***unreasonable burden*** on the servient estate, it is permissible. Be especially skeptical of expansions of the scope of express easements (as opposed to easements by implication or prescription).

> *Example:* X buys Lot 1 from A and receives a deed reserving a 30-foot ingress-and-egress easement for the benefit of adjoining Lot 2 (currently owned by A). Y later purchases Lot 2 from A and receives a deed which mentions the easement. Y then executes a deed to an electric company granting it the right to erect power poles and string wires over the right-of-way for the purpose of bringing power to Lot 2. X would probably be successful in an injunction action preventing the erection of the poles, because the scope of the easement only covered ingress and egress, and construction on the easement would be beyond this scope. (Courts are especially unwilling to allow much expansion of the scope of *express* easements, on the theory that the documents drafted by the parties should control.)

☞ **Interference by servient owner:** Also look for ***interference by the owner of the servient estate*** — the servient owner does not have the right to ***unreasonably interfere*** with the dominant owner's use of the easement.

> *Example:* X holds an easement for a four-foot-wide strip of land on Z's property for an underground sewer line. Z later connects his own sewer line to X's line. This causes X's sewer line to overload and to occasionally back up waste onto X's property. Z's hookup would be considered an ***unreasonable interference*** with the servient estate.

Transfer of easement

☞ **Transfer of appurtenant easements:** An appurtenant easement is ordinarily ***automatically transferred*** along with a conveyance of the dominant estate.

☞ **Transfer of easement in gross:** Commercial easements ***in gross*** are ***freely alienable*** as long as alienation does not increase the burden on the servient estate.

> *Example:* O, the owner of Blackacre, gives an easement in gross to Telephone Co. for the erection of poles and wires on Blackacre, so Telephone Co. can provide Blackacre and other nearby owners with telephone service. Cable Co., a cable TV company, then contracts with Telephone Co. to be able to transmit cable television signals through the wires. The wear and tear on the wires is not increased as a result, and the burden on

the servient estate is not increased. Therefore, the partial transfer of the easement by Telephone Co. to Cable Co. is valid.

☞ **Recording:** If alienable easements are ***recorded***, subsequent grantees of the servient estate take the servient estate subject to the easement.

> *Example:* Same facts as prior example. If Telephone Co. records the easement over Blackacre, and A then buys Blackacre from O, A will be bound by the easement.

Termination of easement

☞ **Abandonment and non-use of express easement:** Fact patterns will often indicate that the easement is ***no longer being used.*** This is usually a trick: it's true that an easement can be extinguished by abandonment, but abandonment will be found only if the easement-holder has a ***clear intent to abandon***, as shown by her ***actions*** (not just her words). Most importantly, the fact that the easement is ***no longer needed*** ***won't*** by itself show abandonment, at least where the easement is express (rather than by necessity or implication, both of which require that the easement continue to be necessary).

> *Example:* X owns six acres of land, which he divides into three lots. He sells two of them and retains ownership of the middle lot, Lot 2. In his deed to A, the new owner of Lot 1, X reserves for himself an easement over a dirt roadway located on that lot which is necessary for ingress and egress to the main road. After five years, a new road is constructed, making X's use of the dirt roadway unnecessary, although X continues to maintain it. If A brings an action to enjoin X from using the dirt roadway, A will fail because X did not show an intent to abandon the easement, and the fact that the easement is no longer necessary will not extinguish it (given that the easement is an express one).

☞ **Merger:** Remember that an easement can be destroyed by ***"merger."*** Read carefully to determine whether at any time after creation of the easement the dominant and servient estates come to be ***owned by the same person*** — if so, the easement is ***destroyed and must be re-created*** in order to be enforceable.

> *Example:* X owns six acres of land, which he divides into three lots. He sells two of them and retains ownership of the middle lot, Lot 2. In his deed to Y, the new owner of Lot 3, X reserves for himself an easement for access to a lake. Two years later, Y sells Lot 3 back to X. One month later, X sells Lot 3 to A by a

deed which does not mention the easement. X then sells his Lot 2 to B by a deed granting a right-of-way over Lot 3 for access to the lake. However, A refuses to allow B access over the right-of-way when B attempts to go to the lake.

If B tries to enforce the easement against A, B will lose. The easement was destroyed when the dominant and servient estates came under common ownership, i.e., when Lot 3 was sold back to X. It was not automatically revived later by X's sale of Lot 3 to A, because the X-to-A deed did not mention an easement. And X's sale of Lot 2 to B with a purported reservation of the easement did not re-create the easement, because at that point X had no interest in Lot 3, and thus no power to create an easement over it.

Profits

☛ **Profits generally:** Occasionally, a landowner will give another person a right to go onto the owner's land and remove the soil or a product of it, such as sand, gravel and stone or minerals. When this happens, call the right a *"profit,"* but treat it *as if it were an easement* (since in the U.S. the rules for profits are the same as for easements).

  ☞ **Right to do what's necessary to exploit:** The holder of the easement has the right to *use and modify* the property in any way reasonably required to exploit the right.

    Example: O gives A the right to mine ore from Blackacre, an undeveloped parcel. The property has no roads over it. The only commercially-feasible way for A to mine the ore is for A to build a dirt road to the mine head. A's profit will be interpreted to permit A to build this road at A's expense.

Licenses

☛ **License generally:** A *"license"* is merely a personal privilege to enter upon another's land which is *revocable* and is not an interest in land. If you see a permission that's given *orally*, assume that it's a license, and that it's therefore revocable at the licensor's will.

    Example: O owns a lakefront property with a dock. O orally says to A (owner of a land-locked parcel 2 miles away), "Whenever you want, you may launch your boat from my dock." 6 months later, O changes his mind, and refuses to allow A access.

    O's grant cannot be an easement, because it's not in writing. Therefore, it's a license. Since it's a license, it's revocable at O's discretion at any time.

Covenants and Equitable Servitudes

The most tested area in this section is the *equitable servitude.* But first, some tips on *covenants*.

☛ **Covenants generally:** Make sure all the requirements are present for the running of the benefit and the burden.

   ☞ **Intent to run:** Check to make sure that the parties intended that the benefit or burden (whichever is in issue on your facts) run with the land.

      ☞ **"Assigns" as clue:** Look for the word *"assigns"* — if present, that will virtually guarantee an intent to have the benefit (or burden) run.

      Example: "The parties hereto hereby covenant for themselves, their heirs, successors, and assigns..." The reference to "assigns" of both parties means that the benefit and burden will both run.

      ☞ **Surrounding circumstances:** But remember, intent to have burden/benefit run may be found from the *surrounding circumstances* as well.

   ☞ **Privity:** In your answer, note whether there is both horizontal and vertical privity. In general, *both must exist* if the burden and benefit are to run.

      ☞ **Horizontal privity:** The most important and frequently-tested type of privity is *horizontal*. Assume as a general rule that there *must be horizontal privity for either the benefit or burden to run.* In other words, make sure that at the time of the covenant, between the promisor and promisee there's either a *landlord/tenant* relationship or a *conveyance* from one to the other. Two *"strangers to title"* don't have horizontal privity, and they therefore can't create a covenant whose burden or whose benefit will run.

      Example: A owns Lot 1 and B owns Lot 2. There is a strip of land 10 feet by 100 feet which lies half on Lot 1 and half on Lot 2. A and B both want to use the strip of land as a driveway. They exchange covenants, under which each agrees to keep the driveway unbuilt-upon, and to pay half the costs of keeping it paved and cleared of snow. A then sells Lot 1 to C, and B sells Lot 2 to D. Neither C nor D can sue the other for damages for breach of the covenant. That's so because at the time of the covenant, A and B did not have horizontal privity — they were "strangers to title" — so neither the benefit nor burden of the covenant could run with the land after a sale.

☞ **Touches and concerns land:** Remember that the benefit will run only if that benefit *"touches and concerns"* the promisee's land; similarly, the burden will run only if it touches and concerns the promisor's land. (But the benefit can run even if the burden is "in gross," i.e., doesn't touch the promisor's land.)

   ☞ **Test:** When you analyze whether a burden touches and concerns the land, look for a burden that *affects the value of land* by diminishing or limiting the promisor's and his successor's use or enjoyment of it. That's a sure clue that the touch-and-concern requirement is met (on the burden side).

   ☞ **Homeowner's association fees:** Watch for *homeowner's association fees* to *maintain common areas.* This is a commonly-tested type of real covenant. Even though the obligation is to pay money, it *is* considered to touch and concern the promisor's land.

   Example: Developer, who has developed condos that abut a golf course, puts in the deed to each unit that the owner will pay annually to an Association of home owners a pro rata share of the fees needed to maintain the course. A buys Unit 1, then sells to B, whose deed is silent about the association-fee promise. The fee promise will be deemed to touch and concern Unit 1. Therefore, the Association will be permitted to bring suit against B to recover the fees (i.e., the burden will be found to run).

   ☞ **Utility purchases:** However, a mere agreement to *purchase utilities* or other services typically will *not* be deemed to touch and concern the promisee's land.

   Example: Same facts as above example. Now, however, assume that Developer also inserts into each deed a requirement that the owner buy all electricity from Electric Co., a particular utility. A again sells Unit 1 to B, with this promise omitted from B's deed. Now, Electric Co. won't be able to enforce the promise against B, because the promise won't be deemed to touch and concern the land of the promisee (A), preventing the burden from running.

☛ **Equitable servitude:** On exams, most covenants must be analyzed as equitable servitudes. That is, in the typical exam setting the promise is a negative one — "I won't use the land in a particular way" — and the plaintiff seeks an injunction, not damages for monetary loss.

☞ **General rules:** Generally, the *burden must touch and concern the land* in order to run with the land. Although the benefit need not always touch and concern the land, the original parties must be fairly specific as to who may enforce the promise. And successors will be bound only if they had *notice*.

☞ **Who may enforce promise:** When the words used do not clearly indicate an intent to bind subsequent transferees, look at the surrounding circumstances. If there's no clear evidence of an intent to let, say, the benefit run, it won't run.

> *Example:* An agreement is entered into by A and B, two neighbors, permitting A, a scientist conducting an experiment, to let his wolves wander freely over B's property. C, a scientist working with A, buys A's land and tries to enforce the promise. A court will probably hold that there was no intent that the benefit of the promise will run with the land because the promise was given specifically to A for the purpose of permitting *him* to complete *his* experiment.

☞ **Subdivision plan:** Where a *developer* records a *subdivision plan* with a description of restrictions, this filing will generally accomplish two things: (1) it will indicate that the *burden and benefit* of the restrictions is intended to *run* with the land; and (2) it gives *constructive notice* to subsequent takers (so the requirement of notice is satisfied).

☞ **Zoning laws:** Don't be fooled when a fact pattern indicates that a deed restriction is *more restrictive* than the applicable *zoning* laws. That is permissible.

☞ **Termination due to changes in the neighborhood:** An equitable servitude may be terminated if changes in the neighborhood make it no longer *substantially* possible to secure the benefits which the restrictions were intended to create. However, this is an argument that usually fails.

> *Example:* O owns Lot 1 and Lot 2, adjacent to each other. O sells Lot 1 to A; in the deed, A promises, on behalf on his successors and assigns, that Lot 1 will continue to be used as a single-family house forever. (At the time of the conveyance, Lots 1 and 2, and all nearby lots, are single-family houses, and zoning laws require them to be so). 20 years go by. The zoning is

changed to allow multiple-family houses, and there are some in the neighborhood. A conveys Lot 1 to B. B proposes to tear down the house on the lot and put up an apartment building. O sues for an injunction. Although B can argue that the nature of the neighborhood has changed enough to make the restriction no longer sensible, he will probably lose (since there is still some benefit to O from not having an apartment building on that particular lot next to his own).

☞ **Implied reciprocal servitude:** Where a large tract of land has been subdivided into lots, watch for a subsequent property owner whose deed does not contain a restriction and a prior grantee who wishes to bind him to restrictions found in his own deed. As long as the court can find that (1) there was a general plan of restrictions for the subdivision; and (2) that the owner whose deed doesn't have the restriction had at least constructive notice of the general plan, the court will probably find that an *"implied reciprocal servitude"* came into existence, and will grant the injunction. This type of fact pattern is surprisingly-often tested.

Example: Developer has a large parcel, which he subdivides into 300 lots. Developer advertises all 300 lots by saying, "Part of a carefully controlled 300-lot residential community, which will forevermore consist solely of single-family houses." For each of the first 140 lots, Developer sells the lot with a deed that says, "Grantee agrees, for his successors and assigns, that the land will never be used for any building other than a single-family house." Each of these deeds is duly recorded. One of them, Lot 10, is bought by A. The market then enters a downturn, and Developer decides that the remaining 160 lots will sell better if they are sold without restrictions. He therefore issues deeds without any restriction, and advertises that the lots may be used "for any purpose valid under local zoning laws." B buys one of these later lots, Lot 182, without any actual knowledge that the first 140 lots were sold with restrictions. He then starts to build an apartment building (valid under zoning laws) on the lot.

A can probably get an injunction against B under an "implied reciprocal servitude" theory. That is, A can argue that Developer enacted a general plan of restrictions for the entire subdivision, by advertising the restrictions and recording restrictions for the first 140 units. He can further argue that when A burdened his own lot, Developer (then the owner of lot

182) impliedly promised to burden all of his remaining lots with the same restriction. Since B had constructive notice of the restriction (a check of the land records for any of the first 140 homes in the division would have turned up the restriction), the court will probably find that an equitable servitude was, as A argues, created against Lot 182 in favor of all prior and subsequent owners. If so, A would receive his injunction.

Exam Tips *on* LAND-USE CONTROLS

The topics in this chapter are not very likely to be treated as the major issues in an exam question, but will nevertheless appear as sub-issues. Common topics include:

☛ **Aesthetic zoning:** Remember that most courts will not allow *aesthetic considerations* to be the *sole factor* supporting the zoning ordinance. Therefore, look for another factor justifying the municipality's decision, and if there isn't one, argue that the decision may well be invalid.

> *Example:* A zoning ordinance prohibits free-standing signs more than fifteen feet high. The owner of a parcel of land wants to erect a fifty-foot sign on her property for commercial reasons. The municipality can argue that, aside from aesthetics, the ordinance is a safety measure because it will reduce the risk of vehicular accidents caused by distracted drivers.

☛ **Spot zoning:** When like parcels are treated differently under an *amendment* to a zoning scheme, discuss the issue of "*spot zoning*." Point out that if the court believes that one or a few small parcels have been singled out for treatment favorable to the owner(s), the court may conclude that this constitutes illegal spot zoning, in which case the amendment will be struck down.

> *Example:* A zoning ordinance is enacted designating Lots numbered 1-12 as Single Family Residential. At the time, a nightclub is located on Lot 6 (and is grandfathered in as a nonconforming use). Fifteen months later Lot 6 is rezoned as Commercial, the County Commissioners stating that it is a likely site for a shopping center. The other landowners attack the reclassification of Lot 6. There is a good chance that the court will hold that singling out Lot 6 for special favorable treatment constituted illegal spot zoning.

☞ **Abandonment of "non-conforming uses":** Fact patterns will sometimes involve an owner who has a pre-existing *non-conforming use* (i.e., a use that predates the zoning ordinance that makes it non-conforming, but that is permitted to continue for some length of time as a *"grandfathered"* use). When this happens, look for the possibility that the use has been *abandoned* by that owner — if so, it *can't be restarted* under the grandfathering clause.

☞ **Mere cessation not enough:** But mere *cessation* of the use for some period of time does *not* constitute abandonment — the owner must be shown to have had an *intent* to abandon the use, plus to have made an *overt act* demonstrating that intent.

> *Example:* O operates a tavern. A zoning ordinance is then adopted restricting use of property on the street to single-family dwellings and providing: "No non-conforming use, once abandoned, shall be reinstated. For the purpose of this section, 'abandoned' is defined as cessation of the non-conforming use for six or more consecutive months." Several years later, O conveys the tavern to B, who operates the tavern for a year-and-a-half and then closes it for nine months because his liquor license is suspended. As soon as his license is restored, he tries to re-open, but the city says that he has abandoned his non-conforming use and may not reinstate it.
>
> If B challenges the city's "can't reinstate" ruling, B will probably win. B's closing of the tavern during the nine months that his liquor license was suspended would probably not be considered abandonment because it was not voluntary.

☞ **Taking:** An owner will sometimes argue that land-use regulation of her parcel is so extensive that it amounts to a *"taking"* which, under the Fifth and Fourteenth Amendments, may not occur without compensation. However, no taking will occur unless the restriction fails to *"substantially advance"* a legitimate governmental objective. In the case of zoning, as long as the owner is left with some *economically viable use of his land*, there will be no taking unless the regulation is completely arbitrary (an extremely hard-to-satisfy requirement). So you should lean heavily against a conclusion that a particular zoning restriction constitutes a taking.

> *Example:* A zoning ordinance prohibits free-standing signs more than fifteen feet high. This prevents O from effectively operating a service station on his land near a highway, since he won't be able to signal his existence to motorists. However, since parcel can be used for other economically-viable purposes (e.g., a small shopping center), and since the regulation substan-

tially advances a legitimate governmental objective (fighting visual blight), a court will almost certainly find that there has been no taking.

Exam Tips *on*
LAND-SALE CONTRACTS, MORTGAGES & DEEDS

The topics in this chapter tend to be very heavily tested.

Land sale contracts

Within the area of contracts for the sale of land, here are the most frequently-tested issues:

☛ **Statute of Frauds:** When a fact pattern indicates that a contract was made *orally*, make sure you discuss the Statute of Frauds issue. Be on the lookout for exceptions to the general requirement of a writing for any transfer of an interest in land.

  ☞ **Reliance:** The most important exception is that where the purchaser takes action in *reasonable reliance* on the contract's existence, the court will generally grant at least limited enforcement at equity.

    ☞ **Actions showing reliance:** Common actions showing reliance are *building a structure*, *fencing in*, paying *taxes*, and making other improvements on the land. Remember that in some courts, the reliance or detriment must be *substantial*, so note the cost and extent of the actions.

    ☞ **"Unequivocally referable":** Don't forget that in most courts, the supposed reliance actions must be shown to have been taken *clearly in response* to the oral contract, and not otherwise explainable. This is the *"unequivocally referable"* requirement (the reliance must be "unequivocally referable" to the alleged oral contract).

      Example 1: B leases and operates a gas station owned by O. After the lease period ends, O and B enter into a oral agreement for the sale of the premises to B and they agree that no further lease payments are required. Then B installs new equipment on the premises at a cost of $18,000. Since it would otherwise be illogical for B to make improvements on the premises after expiration of the lease period, his actions will probably found to be unequivocally referable to the alleged oral a ment of purchase. That agreement will therefore be enforceable although oral.

Example 2: O orally says to his daughter, D, "I'm giving you the house and lot." D takes possession of the house, makes substantial and expensive improvements and lives in it for six years (without paying anything to O) until she relocates for business purposes. O and D then have a falling out, and O claims that the house still belongs to him. If D was an only child, O can plausibly argue that D's actions were not unequivocally referable to O's transfer of the property to her because she could have been preparing for her likely inheritance of the land and her actions are therefore otherwise explainable. If the court agrees that this explanation is plausible (the court does not even have to believe that the explanation is probably the correct one), the oral agreement will be without effect.

☛ **Equitable conversion:** The issue of equitable conversion arises frequently in the case where property is destroyed and it must be determined who bears the risk of loss.

   ☞   **Common scenario:** A contract is entered into for the sale of realty. Then a fire partially destroys the realty. Remember that most courts apply the equitable conversion doctrine here: the signing of the contract is deemed to have shifted equitable title to the buyer, so the risk of loss passes to the buyer at that moment.

       Example: In May, O and B contract for the sale of O's home, title to close in July. B is to move into the house in June and to pay rent until the closing. In June, after B moves in, he falls asleep while smoking in bed and causes damage to the house. B attempts to collect on an insurance policy he purchased in May. In a jurisdiction recognizing equitable conversion, B would be deemed to have an insurable interest as of the time of closing, and he could therefore collect on the policy. (On the other hand, B won't be able to void the sale contract, or lessen the purchase price, on account of the fire, because the risk of loss will be deemed to have passed to him on the signing of the contract in May.)

   ☞   **Exceptions:** But remember that even in courts applying equitable conversion, there are some *exceptions*. Most important: if (1) the damage is due to the *vendor's negligence*, or (2) the vendor did not have, and probably wouldn't have been able to get, *marketable* *title*, the doctrine doesn't apply.

☞ **Parties' right to allocate:** Also, remember that parties can agree as to when risk of loss passes regardless of the rule in their jurisdiction.

☞ **Death:** If the fact pattern mentions the *death* of one of the parties to the contract after the contract has been entered into, apply the doctrine of equitable conversion in enforcing the contract. If the seller dies, the devisees of his personal property collect the proceeds of the sale. And, if the buyer dies, the buyer's estate may specifically enforce the contract against the seller (and vice versa).

☛ **Marketable title:** Generally, a seller must convey *marketable title,* i.e., a title that a reasonable buyer, fully informed of the facts and their legal significance, would be willing to accept. Look for an impending sale of property where there is an ambiguity about title.

☞ **Common scenario:** You'll sometimes see an earlier series of grants and/or devises which do not validly transfer the property because true title to the parcel lies in a different party. In general, these earlier ineffective grants *won't* impair the marketable title of the person who in fact has good title.

> *Example:* O conveys Blackacre to "my sisters S and T as joint tenants." S dies and devises "all my interest in Blackacre to my daughter, D, for life, then to D's daughters, A and B for life, then to all the children of A and B whenever they are born." T dies, and devises "all my interest in Blackacre to my friend, F." F then quitclaims the parcel to Y for $20,000. Y contracts to sell the parcel to Z, promising to convey marketable title. Z claims that the devise to D renders Y's title unmarketable.
>
> Z will lose. When S died, T received S's interest as the surviving joint tenant, rendering S's attempt to devise her property invalid. Therefore, F received an unclouded title from S and transferred an unclouded title to Y, who can transfer an unclouded title to Z.

☞ **Encumbrances:** Because a reasonably prudent purchaser would not be willing to buy a lawsuit, *encumbrances* on the property requiring litigation to clear them up would render title unmarketable and are also considered to be a breach of warranty. (See also the section on deeds, p. 145 below.) Look for these possible encumbrances:

☞ **Zoning ordinance**: Any deviation from an applicable zoning ordinance, however slight, should be considered an encumbrance, because it would present the reasonable buyer with fear of litigation.

Examples of zoning violations that would probably render title unmarketable:

❑ Violation of a setback rule, even if only by a fraction of a foot;

❑ Proposed sale of a business and property located in an area zoned exclusively for residential use, even though authorities have never tried to shut the business down.

☞ **Adverse possession:** Seller's title based on *adverse possession*, unless there has been a judicial determination, is *insufficient* — the buyer shouldn't be required to litigate whether the requirements for adverse possession have been satisfied.

Example: AP has been in possession of Blackacre for 21 years (the statutory period is 20 years), has never paid any rent to O (the record owner), and has never made any agreement with O. O lives in another city. AP now contracts to sell Blackacre to B. B declines to close on the ground that AP does not have marketable title.

B will almost certainly win — a title founded upon adverse possession is not marketable, unless there has been an adjudication that the title has passed to the adverse possessor.

☞ **Mortgage**: An outstanding mortgage may be satisfied by the seller — i.e., paid off — at the *closing*, out of the sale proceeds, thereby avoiding a breach of covenant. So the fact that there is a mortgage prior to closing does not mean that the seller has violated the promise to convey marketable title. (But if the mortgage was for more than the proposed selling price, then the mere existence of the mortgage might make title prospectively unmarketable, since the seller wouldn't be able to satisfy the mortgage out of the sale proceeds.)

☞ **Implied:** If the contract is silent about whether there is an obligation to convey marketable title, the requirement of marketable title will be *presumed*.

☞ **Death of either party:** Remember that the *death* of the seller does not prevent the title from being deemed marketable — the seller's estate can make the sale.

Mortgages

☞ **Mortgage assumption:** Pay attention to whether a party takes *"subject to"* a mortgage or *"assumes"* a mortgage. A party who assumes a mortgage agrees to be personally liable for payments on the mortgage note, whereas one who takes subject to the mortgage does not.

☞ **Forever liable:** Don't be misled by a fact pattern where there is a series of subsequent sales and the different buyers assume and/or take subject to the mortgage. *All* of the parties who assume the mortgage remain liable on the note and can be sued.

Example: O sells to A; A assumes the mortgage to Bank. A then sells to B; B assumes the mortgage. A is still personally liable to Bank, even though B has assumed.

Deeds

☛ **Deeds generally:** Concentrate on these issues:

☞ **Merger:** Remember that if there is a disagreement between the contract and the deed, *the terms of the deed prevail.*

Example: O owns two adjacent parcels, Whiteacre (where O lives) and Blackacre, a vacant parcel. O and B sign a contract under which O agrees to convey Blackacre to B. As O knows, B plans to use the property for a factory. The contract is silent about any restrictions on how Blackacre is to be used. At the closing, O hands B a deed in which B agrees, on behalf of his successors and assigns, to use the property only for residential purposes. B reads the deed, pays the sale price, but refuses O's request that B sign the deed. O records the deed.

A court will probably hold that B (and his successors) may not use the property for non-residential purposes, because in the case of a conflict the deed controls over the contract. (And the fact that B refused to sign the deed is irrelevant, because although the Statute of Frauds requires a writing for a land transfer, the recipient's signature on the writing is not considered necessary to satisfy the statute.)

☞ **Identification of property:** Make sure the deed contains an *adequate description* of the realty so that it can be identified.

☞ **Non-traditional descriptions ok:** Don't rule out a description that is not in the traditional form of metes and bounds, markers, or property address as long as the parcel *can be identified with reasonable effort.* (*Example:* Land covered by a grant of "all my land in the state of X…" is easily identifiable, so the grant is adequate.)

☞ **Error in size:** Also, don't void a description that is sufficient to identify the realty, but makes an error as to the *size* of the parcel. (*Example:* X grants "All of my property located on Barrett Road, consisting of four acres of undeveloped land." Even though the realty is a three-acre parcel, the description is adequate.)

☞ **Identification of parties:** Make sure that the parties are adequately described. (*Example:* A deed cannot be made out to "bearer.")

☞ **Error:** Again, though, a less-than-perfect description is not necessarily void — all that's required is that the intended parties be readily identifiable.

Example: A grant of "all my land in the state of X to my niece and nephew Paula and Mark as joint owners." The first names are sufficient if the parties can be accurately identified, i.e., if there are only one niece and one nephew of the grantor with those names.

☛ **Consideration:** Remember that a conveyance can be a gift, so that there is *no* requirement that a deed be *supported by consideration*.

☛ **Delivery**: Delivery issues are the most frequently-tested aspect of deeds.

☞ **Intent to have deed take present effect:** Remember that a deed isn't effective to complete a transfer unless the grantor *intends that the deed be effective immediately.* Therefore, looks for facts showing the grantor's intent to have immediate effect. These may be *words of present intent* (e.g., "I now give..."). Alternatively, present effectiveness may be shown by the fact that the grantor *gives up control over the deed* so that revocation is not possible. It doesn't matter that later on the grantor acts in such a way as to attempt to revoke the grant (by giving a deed to another party).

☞ **Physical delivery to grantee:** *Physical delivery* is a common way of effecting a present transfer. Tricks to watch out for:

☞ **Delivered to cotenant:** Watch for a fact pattern where the deed grants realty in cotenancy and the deed is handed to only one of the tenants. Delivery to one cotenant is usually viewed as *delivery to all cotenants.* Argue that there has been delivery.

☞ **Oral conditions:** Watch for a grantor who imposes an oral *condition* to the effectiveness of the deed. As long as the grantor intends the transfer to be immediately effective, the fact that the grantor has imposed some condition or delay to the effectiveness of the estate in land being transferred won't invalidate the transfer.

Example: G, a landowner, drafts a deed purporting to grant an undivided one-quarter interest in the parcel to C, grantor's chauffeur. G hands C the deed, and says, "Because you have been a good and faithful chauffeur, I'm giving you this deed. But you don't get your interest in the property until I die."

The transfer is likely to be construed as a present transfer of a future interest to become possessory on the grantor's death. In that event, the delivery is valid, despite the condition. Alternatively, however, a court might construe the condition as making the deed itself ineffective until G's death; in that event, the transfer would be completely invalid unless it satisfied the requirements for a will (e.g., notarized and witnessed).

☞ **Remains in the grantor's control:** Look for facts showing that the grantor still has *control over the deed* and is *free to change his mind.* This would mean that delivery did not occur.

☞ **Agent of grantor:** This can happen in fact patterns where the grantor enlists an *agent* to take transfer the deed — while the deed is still in the agent's possession, it probably hasn't been "delivered" yet, since the grantor still has power to terminate the agency and get the deed back.

Example: G gives a deed to her chauffeur, C, and says, "I want you to give this deed to my niece, N. I also want you to go to the bank and the grocery store. Be sure and call me before you come home." C goes to the bank and the grocery store, then checks in with G to find out whether there is anything else she wants him to do. He is told that G died shortly after he left the house. Since C was G's employee, G retained the right and power to change her mind. Consequently, there was no delivery of the deed. The property will instead pass according to G's will.

☞ **Ready to be mailed:** Similarly, a fact pattern may indicate that a deed is ready to be mailed (e.g., it has been placed on the dining room table and the grantor intends to mail it the next morning). If the grantor dies before it is mailed, there has been no delivery.

☞ **Escrow agent:** A grantor who deposits a deed with an *escrow agent* no longer has control over the deed. In this situation, the deed is to be delivered to the grantee upon the happening of a condition outside the grantor's control, and title will pass automatically upon the happening of the specified condition. Consequently, if the grantor dies (or tries to revoke) after the escrow deposit, the transfer will still be *effective*.

☞ **Acceptance:** *"Acceptance"* of the deed is also required. But remember that if a conveyance is beneficial, it is *presumed* to be accepted

     ☞ **Returned for safekeeping:** Watch for a fact pattern where the grantee *returns the deed* to the grantor. If the return is just for safekeeping, this will not equal a lack of acceptance.

     Example: G gives Z a deed. Z examines the deed, thanks G, and hands the deed back to G, asking that G hold it for safekeeping. The deed has been accepted by Z, and is thus effective.

☛ **Interest conveyed:** A deed that is silent as to the *type of interest* conveyed, but is otherwise complete, is presumed to convey *whatever interest the grantor holds* at the time of conveyance.

     ☞ **Quitclaim:** Likewise, a *quitclaim deed* conveys only the interest which the grantor holds at the time of its execution. The most important thing about a quitclaim deed is that it includes *no implied warranties* of title.

     ☞ **Estoppel by deed:** Look for a fact pattern where a party attempts to convey an estate which he does not have but *subsequently acquires* title to. The *estoppel-by-deed* doctrine causes the after-acquired title to *pass directly to the grantee.*

       Example: O purports to sell realty to A, who immediately records the deed. O's grandmother is the true owner of the realty. Later, O's grandmother dies, devising the realty to O. Then O deeds the realty to C for full satisfaction of a debt owed to C by O.

       In a contest between A and C, A will win. Under the doctrine of estoppel by deed, title to the realty passed to A immediately upon O's grandmother's death, so there was nothing for O to deed to C.

Covenants of title

Covenants of title are not tested very often. A couple of things to look for:

☛ **Breach of covenants as to title, generally:** Most covenant problems relate to the *"present"* covenants (covenants of *seisin*, right to convey and against encumbrances). These are representations that the grantor has a right to convey the title which he purports to convey. The present covenants are breached *only at the time the deed is delivered*, and only the *grantee* can bring an action for damages.

> *Example:* G grants a fee simple absolute to O, under a warranty deed. O then grants a fee simple to A. It turns out that X, not G, had title to the property. A may not bring an action against O for breach of warranty, because only the grantee may sue for breach of the covenant of seisin. Same result if the breach was because X had an undisclosed easement over the property (breach of covenant against encumbrances).

☞ **Easement**: Sometimes you'll have to know whether the presence of an *easement* in favor of a third party constitutes a breach of the seller's covenant against *encumbrances*.

    ☞ **Buyer unaware:** If the buyer was *unaware* of the easement at the time she took the deed, clearly the easement's existence is a breach of the covenant.

    ☞ **Buyer aware:** If the buyer was aware of the easement at the time she took the deed, courts are split, but many recognize a breach of the covenant here, too.

Exam Tips on
THE RECORDING SYSTEM & TITLE ASSURANCE

The most important things to remember in this area:

☞ **Types of statutes:** You must recognize and identify the applicable statute, and be able to analyze how it works.

    ☞ **Recognition:** Be aware of the standard verbal formulations for each of the three main types of statutes. Your exam question usually *won't* say, "The jurisdiction has a race-notice statute." Instead, the question will typically contain *actual statutory language*, and it's *up to you to recognize* the language as constituting, say, a race-notice statute.

    ☞ **Typical formulations:** For each of the three main types of statute, here's a typical chunk of statutory language that you'll have to identify:

        ❑ **Pure notice:** "No conveyance of real property is effective against a subsequent purchaser for value and without notice unless the same be recorded." (Notice that there's nothing requiring the first purchaser to record first in order to get protection; that's why it's not a race-*notice* statute.)

        ❑ **Pure race:** "In determining the priority of conflicting interests in land, the first such interest to have been recorded shall have priority." (Observe that there's no requirement that the second purchaser take without notice in order to get protection; that's what it's not a *race*-notice statute.)

❑ **Race-notice:** "Every conveyance of real estate is void as against any subsequent purchaser who takes without notice and for value whose conveyance is first duly recorded." (Notice that the second purchaser won't win unless she *both* takes without notice and records first.)

☞ **Discuss all possible outcomes:** Many times a fact pattern will not mention what type of recording statute is in effect, and the question asks you to analyze the rights of various parties to a parcel. If this happens, discuss the differing outcomes that would result based on the application of the three main types of statutes.

> *Example:* O hands to her employee, E, a deed to property, but later discharges E and deeds the land to another employee, F, in the presence of another employee, G. Later, O discharges F and informs G that she has revoked the deeds to E and F. Then, O conveys the property to G for valuable consideration. G records the deed immediately. O dies. E records his deed one day later and F records her deed one day after that. At O's funeral, E and F inform G of their recordations. G then mortgages the property to Mortgage Co., which records it the same day.
>
> Under a pure race statute G (and Mortgage Co.) would prevail, because G was the first to record. Under a pure notice statute E would prevail, because F was on constructive notice of E's recordation and G had actual notice (or at least was on inquiry notice) of E's and F's interests. Under a race-notice statute E would prevail, because G had actual or inquiry notice of the other interests and E recorded before F.

☞ **Purchaser for value:** Make sure to notice whether the statute requires that a purchaser give *value* for his interest (a/k/a *"consideration"*). If so, check the fact pattern to see whether there is any indication of value being given. Often, the pattern will not say "there was no consideration given in return," but will indicate a gift by circumstantial evidence (as in the above example, where the facts tell you that O "hands" the deed to her employee).

☞ **Release of debt:** Sometimes, property is transferred in return for the *cancellation of a preexisting debt* (a loan from grantee to grantor). In that instance, the grantee is generally deemed to have given consideration.

☞ **Notice:** The question of whether a subsequent purchaser has been put on *notice* of the earlier deed is one you'll commonly need to answer. If a party does not have *actual* notice then look for:

☞ **Record notice:** The recording of an instrument gives *"record notice"* to a subsequent purchaser, but only if that searcher *would have* found the document using generally-accepted searching principles. A conveyance *outside the chain of title* is treated as an unrecorded conveyance. Make sure every grantor appears as a grantee in the land records to reflect when he received the property, and then as a grantor when he conveys it away.

> *Example of **unrecorded** link:* O conveys realty to A. A does not record the O-to-A deed, and immediately sells to B. B records the A-to-B deed and sells to C, who immediately records his deed. O then purports to convey to Z, who immediately records his deed (and who did not have actual knowledge of the prior conveyances by O, A or B). Assume the jurisdiction maintains grantor-grantee indices. Since A never recorded his deed, A's conveyance to B was recorded outside O's chain of title, and there was no way for a searcher working for Z to connect O's parcel and O's conveyance to A with the subsequent conveyances. Therefore, in a pure-notice or race-notice jurisdiction, the deeds from A to B and B to C would not be effective against Z, who will be deemed to have purchased without notice.

☞ **Wild deed:** Where a party gets a deed from a person whose own deed was never recorded (a *"wild deed"*), make sure the new grantee records her *whole chain* of title. If that subsequent grantee does *not* record her whole chain, she'll probably forfeit the protection of the statute as against a prior unrecorded (or late-recorded) deed.

> *Example:* The jurisdiction has a race-notice statute. A conveys a parcel to B. Several months later, A conveys the same parcel to C, who does not record the deed. C then conveys to D, who records immediately. (D does not know about the A-to-B deed). B then records. D discovers that C's deed from A is unrecorded, so she obtains it from him and records it. Since D had a "wild deed," and did not record her whole chain of title before B recorded her deed, B will probably have priority to the realty. That is, in a race or race-notice jurisdiction, D will not be deemed to have "recorded" prior to B, and will lose the protection given to a subsequent good-faith purchaser who records

first.

☞ **Inquiry notice:** Look for facts which would cause a reasonable person to conduct an *investigation* which, if taken, would had led her to discover the existence of the prior unrecorded deed. In this situation, the person is said to be on "inquiry notice."

> *Example:* O conveys to A. A doesn't record, but takes possession. O then conveys to B, making no mention of any tenant on the property. B will be probably be deemed to be on "inquiry notice" of A's deed — B had a duty to inspect the property, and at least to ask the possessor about the source of his possession; had B done this, B would almost certainly have learned from A about the O-to-A deed.

☞ **Quitclaim deed:** In some jurisdictions, the fact that the grantee is being given a *quitclaim deed* places her on inquiry notice.

☞ **What a reasonable inspection would show:** Before you conclude that a grantee is on inquiry notice, make sure that a *reasonable inspection* of the property and *questioning* of the grantor would have led to discovery of the prior interest. For instance, if the land is vacant and there is no other way of finding out about the prior deed, then there is no inquiry notice.

☛ **Common law rule:** When a recording statute does not cover a situation, apply the common law rule, i.e., *first in time, first in right.*

☞ **Tip:** This will generally occur when a grantee receives the property as a *gift*, since the recording statute usually protects only a subsequent purchaser "for value."

> *Example:* O borrows money from L and executes a note secured by a mortgage on his realty. O later deeds the realty to his son, S, as a birthday present. S records his deed; L then records his mortgage. The statute gives protection to a subsequent grantee against a prior unrecorded interest only if the grantee is a "purchaser for value."
>
> Since S was not a purchaser for value, S does not get the protection of the recording act. Therefore, the common-law rule — first in time, first in right — applies, making L's interest, received first, superior.

Exam Tips *on*
RIGHTS INCIDENT TO LAND

When this subject appears on an exam, it will generally be as a sub-issue, not a major issue. Things to keep in mind:

☛ **Water rights:** Most courts follow the *"reasonable use"* approach to riparian rights. Look for an indication that consumption by a riparian owner is more than what is reasonably necessary. Make sure that the reasonable use does not significantly interfere with a similar or more beneficial use of the water: domestic use is "higher" than agricultural use.

☛ **Nuisance:** Remember that for a nuisance to occur, there has to be a *substantial* interference with the plaintiff's use and enjoyment of his property.

Examples of interferences great enough to be "substantial":

❑ D hooks up a sewer to a sewer line passing through P's property, causing the sewer line to be overloaded and to back up onto P's land;

❑ D, angry that P has refused to comply with deed restrictions regarding house style, puts up a 20-foot-high brick wall adjacent to and parallel to the entire boundary with P's lot, paints the side of the wall facing P's lot black and coats it with a foul-smelling preservative.

☞ **Coming to the nuisance:** The fact that the condition existed before the plaintiff came into possession of the property (*"coming to the nuisance"*) is a factor making nuisance more likely, but it is not dispositive of the issue. The issue is always whether the interference is "unreasonable" (as well as substantial), and a condition that existed before P moved in can still be unreasonable.

☞ **Nature of neighborhood:** Also, remember that the *nature of the neighborhood* counts in determining reasonableness.

> *Example:* An odorous pig farm is more likely to be "unreasonable" (and thus a nuisance) in a primarily-residential neighborhood than in a neighborhood dominated by farms or factories.

SHORT-ANSWER QUESTIONS

CHAPTER 2

POSSESSION AND TRANSFER OF PERSONAL PROPERTY

1. Oscar was the owner of a very valuable painting, "Rosewood." In 1970, Rosewood was stolen from Oscar's home. Oscar reported the theft to the police, collected insurance proceeds, and made no further efforts to locate the painting. (For example, he did not report the theft to a national information bank that lists stolen paintings, nor did he notify local art dealers.) In 1973, unbeknownst to Oscar, Anita, an art collector, "bought" Rosewood from a private gallery for $10,000. (This price was approximately the fair market value of the painting at the time, on the assumption that there was clear title.) The galley showed Anita documents indicating that the gallery had the right to sell the painting, and Anita had no reason to believe the painting to be stolen.

Anita proudly displayed the painting at her house for the next 17 years. Even though Anita and Oscar lived in the same town, Oscar did not learn of Anita's possession of the painting until 1990, when a friend happened to mention it to him. The local statute of limitations on actions to recover personal property is 10 years. Assuming that the state follows the "modern" rule regarding when the statute of limitations on stolen personal property begins to run, if Oscar sues Anita in 1990, may he recover the painting from her?_____

2. Olivia's 1989 Suburu was stolen one day while parked on the street in front of her house. Six months later, Arnold purchased from Dealer a used 1989 Suburu to which Dealer appeared to have good title. Arnold paid the full fair market value for the car. In fact, the car was the one which had been stolen from Olivia, though there was no way Arnold could reasonably have known that the car was stolen property. Through a random check of Vehicle Identification Numbers by local police, the police discovered that the car being driven by Arnold was stolen property, and so notified Olivia. Olivia has now sued Arnold in 1990 for return of the car. Arnold defends on the grounds that he is a bona fide purchaser for fair value. Assume that there are no relevant statutes. May Olivia recover the car?_____

3. In 1980, Sidney, a wealthy industrialist, said to his son Norman, "I am hereby giving you my valuable Monet painting, 'Ballerinas.'!" Sidney did not, however, at any time give Norman possession of the painting, nor did he give him any document indicating any transfer. The painting continued to hang on Sidney's wall for the next 10 years. In 1990, Sidney died. His will bequeathed all of his personal property to his daughter, Denise. Who owns the painting, Norman or Denise?_____

4. Albert, an elderly widower, placed $100,000 in a bank savings account bearing the designation, "Albert in trust for Bertha." Bertha was Albert's girlfriend. During the next two years, Albert made no withdrawals, nor did Bertha. Albert then died, leaving all of his personal property by will to his son Steven. Steven and Bertha each now claim the proceeds of the bank account. Neither produces any evidence of Albert's intent in creating the bank account. What part, if any, of the proceeds should be awarded to Bertha?_____

CHAPTER 3

ADVERSE POSSESSION

5. In 1960, Beck purchased valid title to Blackacre, located in Ames. That same year, Warren purchased valid title to Whiteacre, the adjoining parcel. Both parties reasonably but mistakenly believed that the boundary line b*etween Blackacre and Whiteacre was a large oak tree, so in 1961 both fenced their property accordingly. In reality, the proper boundary between the two parcels is 30 yards to the south of the oak tree, so that the existing fencing has been depriving Warren of the use of land which belongs to him. In 1990, Warren discovered the error, and has brought an action to recover the 30-yard strip. May Warren recover the strip?_____

6. In 1950, Osmond, the owner of Blackacre, left the property "to my son Steve and my daughter Deborah in equal shares." Steve moved onto the property and lived there for the next 40 years. Deborah never liked the property, and made no attempt to live there at any time. In 1989, Deborah died, leaving all of her personal and real property to her son Frank. If Frank now seeks a judicial declaration that he is the owner of a one-half interest in Blackacre, will he succeed?_____

7. Orlando acquired Blackacre in 1950. In 1960, Alice acquired Whiteacre, the adjacent parcel. Alice built a fence on what she thought was the border between the two properties. In fact, her fence encroached 40 yards into Orlando's property. Alice actively, openly and continuously occupied this 40-yard strip for the next 25 years. In 1985, Orlando discovered the error, and informed Alice that she had been using his property. Alice said, "O.K., I now recognize that this strip is your property." She also moved the fence. Shortly thereafter, Alice died, leaving Whiteacre to her son Stokes. Who owns the strip, Stokes or Orlando?_____

CHAPTER 4

FREEHOLD ESTATES

8. O'Malley was the owner in fee simple of Blackacre. As a gift, O'Malley delivered to Abel a deed to Blackacre; the deed read, "to Abel and his heirs." Abel recorded the deed as required by local statutes. Abel then delivered a deed to Blackacre to Barbara, who recorded it. Abel then died, leaving as his sole heir his son, Callaway. Who owns Blackacre?_____

9. In the State of Ames, there is a one-year statute of limitations on actions to enforce a right of entry for condition broken. Ames also has a statute barring any possibility of reverter 50 years following the creation of a fee simple determinable. In Ames, O held a fee simple absolute in Blackacre. Because O had watched his daughter's marital prospects be ruined by her early involvement as a pornography star, O sold Blackacre to A, a nightclub operator, under a conveyance, "To A and his heirs so long as the premises are not used for topless or erotic dancing, and if they are so used, then the premises shall revert to O." This conveyance took place in 1960. A complied with this restriction. In 1968, O died, leaving all his real and personal property to his son S. In 1970, A conveyed, "To B and his heirs, in fee simple absolute." That same year, B began to use the premises as a topless bar, and continued doing so for the next 10 years. In 1980, S asks the court for a determination that the property now belongs to him because of B's operation of the topless club. Should the court grant S's request?_____

10. Same facts as the prior question. Now, however, assume that the deed from O to A stated, "To A and his heirs, provided that no topless or other obscene dancing ever takes place on the premises. If such dancing does take place, Grantor or his heirs may re-enter the property." All other facts remain the same, except that in 1980, S files suit for a decree authorizing him to re-enter the property. Should the court grant S's request?_____

11. O conveyed Blackacre "to A for life, remainder to B." One year later, A quitclaimed all of his interest in Blackacre to C. After this quitclaim deed, what is the state of title?_____

CHAPTER 5

FUTURE INTERESTS

12. O held a fee simple absolute in Blackacre. He conveyed "to A for life." After this conveyance, what interest, if any, does O hold in Blackacre?_____

13. O conveyed Blackacre "to A for life, then to B and his heirs." Immediately after the conveyance, what interest, if any, does B have in Blackacre?_____

14. O conveyed Blackacre "to A for life, then to B's children and their heirs." At the time of this conveyance, B had one child, C. Immediately following the conveyance, what interest, if any, does C have in Blackacre?_____

15. O conveyed Blackacre "to A for life, then to B and his heirs. However, if B dies without issue, then to C and his heirs." Immediately following this conveyance, what interest, if any, does B have in Blackacre?_____

16. O conveyed Blackacre "to A for life, then, if B is living at A's death, to B in fee simple." Immediately after this conveyance, what interest, if any, does B have in Blackacre?_____

17. O conveyed Blackacre "to A for life, then to B and his heirs, but if B dies before A, to O and his heirs." Immediately after this conveyance, what interest, if any, does B have in Blackacre?_____

18. O conveyed Blackacre "to A for life, remainder to the first daughter of A who produces a child while married." A then died. At A's death, he has one daughter, D, who has not yet married or had a child. O is still alive. Immediately after A's death, what is the state of title to Blackacre? Assume that all common-law doctrines are in force without statutory modification._____

19. O conveyed Blackacre "to A for life, remainder to A's oldest daughter for life if she has a child while married, remainder to B and his heirs." At a time when A's oldest daughter, D, had not yet married, A conveyed his life estate to B. After that conveyance, what is the state of title? Assume that all common-law doctrines are in force without statutory modification._____

20. O, in his will, left Blackacre "to A for life, remainder to A's heirs." A then issued a quitclaim deed (giving whatever interest A had, without specifying or warranting what that interest was) to B. Two years later, A died, leaving as his sole heir at law S, a son. What is the state of title to Blackacre?_____

21. In a state with no statutes modifying the relevant common-law rules, O conveyed Blackacre "to A for life, remainder to O's heirs." Shortly thereafter, O quitclaimed any interest he might have in Blackacre to B. O then died, leaving as his sole heir a son, S. A then died. What is the state of title?_____

22. The same facts as the prior question. Now, however, assume that all transactions occurred in the late 20th century, in a state that follows the usual 20th-century approach to conveyances of the ones described in the question. Assume further that in O's initial conveyance to A, he added the sentence, "I mean for this gift to take effect in exactly the manner that I have expressed." What is the probable state of title?_____

23. O owned Blackacre in fee simple. He bargained and sold it "to A and his heirs, but if liquor is ever served on the premises, then to B and his heirs." Immediately after this conveyance, what is the state of title?_____

24. O conveyed Blackacre "to A for life." At the time of the conveyance, Blackacre had always been used as farm land, and O knew that A was a farmer. However, the parties made no agreement concerning the use to which A would put the property. A took possession, and began farming. Shortly thereafter, oil was discovered on an adjacent parcel. A immediately drilled an oil well on the property, and struck a gusher. A sold the resulting oil and put the proceeds of the sale in his bank account. Has A's conduct violated O's rights?_____

For questions 25-30, assume that the common-law Rule Against Perpetuities is in effect.

25. O conveys "to A for life, remainder to A's oldest son who survives A for life, remainder to B and his heirs." A and B are alive at the time of the conveyance, but A does not yet have a son. Is the remainder to B and his heirs valid?_____

26. In 1960, O conveys "to A for life, remainder in fee simple to the first son of A who has a child while married." At the time of this conveyance, A has no son who has had a child while married, but does have an unmarried childless son, B. In 1965, B has a child while married. In 1970, A dies. Is the remainder to B valid?_____

27. In 1960, O, the owner of Greenacre, gave to A Corporation (in return for a payment of $20,000) the following document: "I, O, hereby grant to A Corp. an option to purchase Greenacre at any time during the next 30 years for a price equal to $100,000 plus an additional sum equal to the compounded interest, at 10%, on $100,000 from the date of this option." O died in 1970, leaving all his real and personal property to B. In 1988, A Corp. seeks to exercise its option. Does it have a right to do so?_____

28. In 1980, O bequeathed Blackacre "to A for life, then to A's widow." At the time of this bequest, A was not yet married. In 1982, A married B, a 30-year-old woman. A died in 1988. Does B get Blackacre?_____

29. In 1960, O bequeathed Whiteacre "to A for life, then in equal shares to those of A's children who survive him, but only when each attains the age of 30. I want to be sure that children born to A after my death are included in this bequest." In 1960, A had one child, B, who was 10. In 1985, A died, without ever having had any other children, and with B still alive. Does B take the property?_____

30. Same facts as prior question. In a state following the most common statutory modification to the Rule Against Perpetuities, would the gift to B be valid?_____

CHAPTER 6

MARITAL ESTATES

31. In 1960, O conveyed Blueacre, a 900-acre farm, to H. In 1965, H married W. In 1970, H, in return for reasonable consideration, delivered to A a deed in fee simple for Blueacre. In 1980, H died. What is the state of title in Blueacre? (Assume that the common law is in force in all relevant particulars.)_____

32. H and W live in a community property state. If H and W are divorced, which of the following items will be community property? (Assume that H and W's divorce is no-fault.)_____

(A) Blackacre, which W bought before the marriage, and which has remained in her name before the divorce._____

(B) Whiteacre, which W inherited from her father after the marriage, and which has remained in her name until the divorce._____

(C) $20,000 in a bank account entitled "H and W jointly," representing net rental proceeds paid by a tenant of Whiteacre; all of these payments were made after W inherited the property as described in (b) above._____

(D) $100,000 in a bank account in H's name alone; this represents money earned by H from his salary during the years following the marriage, while working for ABC Corp., a large company.

(E) Stock in ABC Corp. held in H's name, which he received as part of ABC Corp.'s stock ownership plan._____

(F) A summer home purchased by H, in his own name, from which the down payment and all subsequent mortgage payments have been made out of H's earnings._____

CHAPTER 7

CONCURRENT OWNERSHIP

33. O conveyed Blackacre "to A and B as co-tenants." A then died, bequeathing all of his real and personal property to his son, S. B is still alive. What is the state of title to Blackacre?_____

34. O conveyed Blackacre "to A and B as joint tenants." B then conveyed to C, by a quitclaim deed (conveying whatever interest B had in the property). Subsequently, A died, bequeathing all of his real and personal property to his son, S. What is the state of title?_____

35. O, the fee simple owner of Whiteacre, died, leaving the property by will to his three children, A, B, and C, "as tenants in common." A purchased C's interest. The property is a single-family home. A moved in, and used the property as his principal residence. B, a bachelor, has now demanded to live in the home as well. If A refuses, will a judge order A to share the house with B?_____

36. Henry and Wanda were husband and wife. Using funds supplied entirely by Henry, the two purchased Blackacre from Oscar. (The deed from Oscar to Henry and Wanda read, "To Henry and Wanda in fee simple," without further elaboration.) Shortly thereafter, Henry became infatuated with a younger woman, Georgia. To celebrate the six-month anniversary of their affair, Henry conveyed to Georgia his interest in Blackacre. (Assume that the land is located in a state that permits such a conveyance.) For the next five years, Henry continued to be married to Wanda, but carried on his affair with Georgia. Then, Wanda died, leaving all of her real and personal property to her and Henry's daughter, Denise. Shortly thereafter, Henry died. What is the state of title? (Assume that the common-law approach to all relevant matters is in force, unmodified by statute or case law.)_____

37. Herb and Wendy, husband and wife, were the owners of Blackacre, which they held by tenancy of the entirety. In 1989, Herb and Wendy were divorced. They intended to sell the property, but before they could do so, Herb died suddenly. Herb's will leaves all his real and personal property to his son by a prior marriage, Stan. What is the state of the title to Blackacre?_____

38. Arthur and Bertha, after inheriting Blackacre from their father, held it as tenants in common. Originally, Arthur lived in the premises, and Bertha had no interest in doing so. After a few years, Arthur moved out, and sent Bertha the following letter: "I am moving out of Blackacre. You have the right to live on the property. If you do not do so, I will rent it out." Bertha made no response. Arthur, after advertising for a tenant, rented the property to Xavier, who responded to the ad. Xavier paid $20,000 of rent during the first year. (Xavier paid all operating costs, such as utilities.) At the end of the first year of this rental, Bertha learned of the arrangement and sent Arthur a letter stating, "You owe me one-half of the rents paid by Xavier." Is Bertha correct?_____

39. Omar, the owner of Whiteacre, left the property to his daughter Carol and his son Dan, in equal parts. The will said nothing about who should occupy the property. The property was a single-family home. Dan already had a home of his own, suitable for his family. Carol did not. Therefore, Carol moved into the house, and has since occupied it. The estimated fair market rental value of the house is $18,000 per year. Dan has demanded that Carol pay him one-half of this amount, to compensate for her use of the premises. Carol has responded, "You are free to live here with me, but I'm not paying you any money for my use of the premises." If Dan sues for one-half of the fair market rent represented by Carol's occupancy of the premises, will Dan prevail?_____

40. Edward and Felicia, brother and sister, received Whiteacre as a bequest in their mother's will. Edward, who had been living on the property while his mother was still alive, continued to do so after her death. Felicia has never had any interest in living on the property. The property is presently worth approximately $800,000, and has a rental value of $50,000 per year. However, Edward has rejected all suggestions by Felicia that the property be sold or rented out to third parties (though Edward has always indicated that Felicia is welcome to live on the property with him). What sort of action, if any, may Felicia bring to accomplish her goals?_____

CHAPTER 8

LANDLORD AND TENANT

41. On July 1, 1989, L and T orally agreed that T would lease L's premises for one year, the lease to commence on August 1 of that same year and run until July 31, 1990. T gave a deposit as called for in the oral agreement. On August 1, when T tried to take possession, he discovered that L had rented the premises to someone else. Does T have a valid cause of action against L for breach of the lease?_____

42. L and T agreed that T would rent an apartment from L for $800 per month. No specific term was set. T took occupancy on July 1, and paid the rent for that month._____

(A) What type of tenancy have the parties created?_____

(B) Suppose that after approximately two years, T wants to terminate the arrangement. If T gives notice of termination on July 15, what is the date on which his termination will be effective, under the common-law view?_____

43. Leonard leased a store to Terry, for a lease term ending August 30, 1989. In July of 1989, Leonard signed a lease with Tina for the premises, to commence September 1, 1989. Leonard knew that Tina planned to operate a new retail store, and that it would be important to Tina to be selling her Fall clothing inventory starting promptly in September. When Terry's lease term ended, he refused to vacate the premises, and was still there on September 20, at which time he moved out. May Tina sue Leonard for damages for failing to make the premises available to her on September 1?_____

44. Lester, the owner of an apartment building, rented a first floor apartment to Tess. Shortly thereafter, Lester rented ground-floor space (immediately below Tess's apartment) to the proprietor of Heavy Metal Heaven, a rock and roll club. The lease between Lester and Heavy Metal provided that Heavy Metal would conduct its activities so as not to materially inconvenience any tenants of the apartment building. But Heavy Metal set its loudspeakers to the maximum level, so that every night, Tess was unable to sleep until the club closed at 2:00 a.m. Tess decided that she could no longer tolerate the noise, and moved out. She then delivered to Lester a notice stating, "I consider our lease at an end." Lester relet the premises at a lower rate. May Lester recover from Tess the difference between the rent paid by Tess and the lower rent he is now receiving?_____

45. Same facts as the prior question. Now, however, assume that it is a tight housing market, and Tess has not been able to find another apartment at the same (relatively affordable) rate she is paying to Lester. Tess has therefore remained a resident in the apartment, but has gone on a rent strike, notifying Lester that she will not pay any rent until he makes the noise stop. Assuming that Tess continues to withhold the rent, may Lester have her evicted?_____

46. Lila, a notorious slum lord, rented a one-bedroom apartment to Terence for $400 per month. The lease made no explicit warranties regarding condition of the premises. Unbeknownst to Terence at the time the lease was signed, the apartment was (and still is) infested with rats, and the toilet did not and does not work. Terence is quite poor, and cannot pay moving expenses or a security deposit to move to a different apartment. He would like to be able to withhold the rent until the rats are exterminated and the toilet fixed. In a jurisdiction following the unmodified common-law rule on relevant issues, may Terence withhold rent on the grounds that the apartment is not habitable?_____

47. Same facts as the above question. Now, assume that the jurisdiction takes an approach towards the relevant issues that is fairly typical of the way most states now approach the issues. May Terence withhold rent?_____

48. Lena is a professional landlord, who owns a number of apartment buildings in the City of Ames. She rented an apartment in one of these buildings to Troy. The lease provided for a one-year term, with no renewal options. After Troy moved in, he discovered that the heat was inadequate, that the locks did not work, and that other things were wrong. He therefore lodged a complaint with the City of Ames Housing Agency, which is in charge of seeing that landlords obey their statutory obligations concerning residential housing. At the Agency's demand, Lena reluctantly fixed the problems. At the end of the one-year lease, Lena notified Troy that she would not renew his lease. Lena customarily renews residential leases, and gave Troy no explanation of why she would not renew his, though he suspects that this is due to his complaint to the Agency. If Troy refuses to move out at the end of the lease term, and Lena sues to evict him, what defense should Troy raise? What is the likely result if he does raise it?_____

49. Lana, a homeowner, rented her home to Tully in 1989 under a one-year lease, since she was to be abroad on an academic sabbatical for that year. The lease said nothing about the parties' obligations in the event of sudden destruction of the premises. Tully agreed to pay a rent of $500 per month. (The house had a fair market rental value of $1,000 per month, but Lana charged less because she liked Tully and thought he would take good care of the house.) After Tully had occupied the house for four months, the house was struck by lightning, and its upper floor (of two) was destroyed. The house is still "habitable" in the sense that Tully could live there, but only under much less pleasant circumstances (including the lack of a formal bedroom) than he had anticipated._____

(A) May Tully terminate the lease and stop paying rent?_____

(B) May Tully recover damages from Lana for his "loss of bargain"? If so, in what amount?_____

50. Ludlum rented a suite in an office building he owns to Trotta. As part of the lease, Trotta gave Ludlum a two-month security deposit. The lease was for five years. After three years, Trotta moved out without cause, and stopped paying rent. Because the real estate market was a tight one, Ludlum almost immediately found a new tenant. Ludlum therefore sent Trotta a letter stating, "I am hereby terminating our lease because of your abandonment of the premises. You will be held responsible for all damages I suffer." Ludlum then relet the premises to the new tenant at the same monthly rent, so that his only losses are the loss of one month's rent ($1,000). Ludlum would like to be able to keep the entire security deposit until the expiration of the original five-year Ludlum-Trotta lease term. May he do so?_____

51. Same facts as the prior question. How could the party to whom your answer was unfavorable have altered the result, either by a drafting change or by subsequent conduct?_____

52. Lombard leased office space to Toland, for a two-year term. At the end of the lease term, Toland attempted to renew the lease, but Lombard refused. One week after the lease expired, Toland still had his furnishings on the premises. Summary proceedings were available to Lombard to evict Toland, but these would have taken approximately two months, and Lombard had a tenant who wanted to take occupancy immediately. Therefore, over a weekend, Lombard entered Toland's premises, moved his furniture into the hall, and changed the locks. When Toland arrived Monday morning, he found his furniture in good shape, but he was effectively out of business until he could arrange to move into new quarters; this took him two weeks, during which time he lost $10,000 worth of business. If Toland sues Lombard for $10,000 in damages, will Toland recover?_____

53. Link leased an apartment to Taylor. With two years to go on the lease (which was for $1,000 per month), Taylor moved out and sent Link a letter saying, "I don't want the premises any more." Link allowed the premises to remain vacant, and notified Taylor that he was doing so. Link made no effort to re-let the premises, though he could easily have done so for about the same $1,000 per month that Taylor had been paying. After the term expired (with 24 months of rent unpaid), Link sued Taylor for the cumulative unpaid rent. May Link recover this amount?_____

54. Lillian, the owner of an apartment building, leased an apartment to Tracey, for two years at $1,000 per month. After one year of the lease had expired, Tracey wanted to travel in Europe for 10 months. She therefore transferred to Stuart the right of occupancy for the next 10 months, reserving to herself the right to occupy the premises for the final two months of her lease with Lillian. Rent payments (at the same $1,000 per month) were to be made by Stuart to Tracey, and Tracey would pass them on to Lillian. Tracey went off on her trip, and failed to make any payments to Lillian. Lillian has now learned that Tracey has become insolvent. Meanwhile, Stuart, after occupying the premises for four months, has moved out, and is apparently not sending rent payments to Tracey. The premises are currently unoccupied. Lillian would like to sue Stuart for both the four payments he owes Tracey covering the time he actually occupied the premises, plus the six payments that became due after he left the premises. Which, if any, portion of this money may Lillian recover from Stuart?_____

Questions 55 through 61 below relate to the following fact pattern:

Lloyd, the owner of Blackacre, leased the property to Thelma for a five-year term. In this lease, Thelma promised to pay Lloyd rent of $1,000 per month. Three years into the lease, Thelma assigned her remaining interest in the lease to Tim. In the Thelma-Tim transaction, Tim did not expressly promise Thelma to perform Thelma's obligations under the master lease, but merely accepted from Thelma a document stating, "I hereby assign to you all my rights under my lease with Lloyd." Tim then moved onto the property.

55. After Tim moved in, he made the first six monthly $1,000 payments directly to Lloyd, and Lloyd made no objection. Then, Tim did not make any payments for the next three months. If Lloyd sues Thelma for the three months during which Tim did not make payments, may Lloyd recover?_____

56. Same facts as the prior question. Assume, now, that Lloyd does not sue Thelma for the missed three months, but instead sues Tim for this period. Assume further that Tim was in residence during the three months for which no rent was paid. May Lloyd recover the three months rent from Tim?_____

57. Same facts as the prior two questions. Now, assume that after missing three months of rent, Tim assigned to Theo any interest that Tim had in the premises. Tim moved out. Theo took possession, and failed to pay the next six months rent. If Lloyd sues Tim for this six-month period, may Lloyd recover?_____

58. Now, assume that at a time when Tim was in possession (having received an assignment from Thelma of Thelma's rights, but having not made any promises of his own), Lloyd sold the property (and assigned all of his rights in the property) to Leon. In the sale documents, Leon did not make any promises to Lloyd, and merely gave Lloyd the purchase price. Assume further that in the original Lloyd-Thelma lease, Lloyd promised to keep the premises in repair. During Tim's occupancy, Leon has not made required repairs. May Tim sue Leon for damages?_____

59. At a time when Tim was in possession (having taken an assignment from Thelma but not having made any promises), Lloyd sold the property to Leon, as in the prior question. Tim failed to pay rent for six months while he was in possession. Leon has sued Tim for this rent. May Leon recover from Tim?_____

60. Assume that the original Lloyd-Thelma lease stated, in a negotiated term, that Thelma would not sublet or assign without Lloyd's written consent. Also, assume that when Thelma assigned to Tim, Thelma (as required under the lease) asked Lloyd's consent, and Lloyd consented because he felt that Tim was at least as responsible a tenant as Thelma. Now, Tim seeks to assign to Theo, but Lloyd objects because he feels (reasonably) that Theo is irresponsible. If Theo takes possession, may Lloyd have Theo evicted?_____

61. Same facts as the prior question. Now, assume that the anti-assignment clause in the Lloyd-Thelma lease was continued in the fine print "boilerplate" of the standard residential lease prepared by Lloyd, and that at the time that lease was signed, the residential housing market was sufficiently tight that nearly all landlords insisted on imposing similar no-assignment provisions. Thelma now wishes to assign her remaining rights to Tim. Tim is willing to assume all of Thelma's obligations, and is a financially responsible and otherwise good tenant. Lloyd refuses to consent to the assignment, solely because he wishes to raise the rent to $2,000 per month (now the prevailing market rent for such an apartment, because of a rise in real estate prices since the Lloyd-Thelma lease was signed). May Lloyd prevent Tim from taking occupancy?_____

CHAPTER 9

EASEMENTS AND PROMISES CONCERNING LAND

62. Orin owned a large country estate, Country Oaks, which contained a trout stream. Orin's friend and neighbor Norman, owner of an adjacent parcel, fished in the stream for several years with Orin's consent. Orin decided to sell Country Oaks to Alfred, but wanted to protect Norman's fishing rights. Therefore, with Alfred's consent, Orin's deed to Alfred contained an easement granting Norman and his successors the right to fish in the stream in perpetuity, as well as the right to get to the stream by a path running through the estate. Five years later, Alfred conveyed Country Oaks to Barbara. The Alfred-to-Barbara deed did not contain any easement for fishing._____

(A) If the jurisdiction follows the traditional common-law approach to relevant issues, may Norman continue to fish in the stream?_____

(B) In a jurisdiction following a contemporary approach to the relevant issues, may Norman continue to fish in the stream?_____

63. Angela is the owner of Auburnacre. Burt is the owner of Blueacre. The two parcels are adjacent, and have never (at least as far as property records go back, which is 200 years) been under common ownership. A lake, located on public land and open to the public, borders the eastern edge of Auburnacre; the Auburnacre-Blueacre border is on the west side of Auburnacre. For many years, the lake had been useless because it was algae-infested. However, in 1985, the state redredged and reclaimed the lake, so that it is now usable for fishing. Beginning in 1985, Angela allowed Burt to cross Angela's property to get to the lake for boating. (Because the land is out in the country where few roads exist, Burt would have to drive for 25 miles in order to get to the lake if he were not permitted to cross Auburnacre.) No written agreement between Angela and Burt regarding Burt's right to cross Angela's land ever existed.

In 1989, Burt conveyed Blueacre to Carter. Shortly thereafter, Carter attempted to cross Auburnacre to get to the lake. Angela objected, and thereafter put a roadblock across the path, in the middle of Auburnacre, that Burt had formerly used. May Carter compel Angela to remove the roadblock so that Carter can cross over to use the lake?_____

64. For many years, Daphne owned a 160-acre parcel of waterfront land, known as Lakeview Farms. In 1980, Daphne sold a 10-acre portion of Lakeview Farms (the part farthest away from the water) to Frederika. Frederika then built a fashion mall on her 10-acre portion. Of the 160 original acres of Lakeview Farms, only the 10-acre parcel now owned by Frederika adjoins the public roadway. In 1982, Frederika sold her 10-acre parcel to Gil, who operates the fashion mall today. In 1985, after the fashion mall was built, Daphne built a golf course on her remaining 150 acres. After the course was opened, Daphne instructed all golf patrons to enter via a private road which cuts through Gil's property and thus joins the golf course to the public road. (Otherwise, the patrons wouldn't be able to reach the golf course by car at all.) May Daphne's patrons use this road over Gil's objections?_____

65. Astrid and Ben were adjacent landowners. Astrid's property was valuable beach front property. Ben's property adjoined Astrid's on the side away from the ocean. From 1970 to 1987, Ben and his family continually (at least once a week in nice weather) got to the beach by walking along a beaten path crossing Astrid's side yard. (They could have driven to a public beach four blocks away, but preferred walking directly to the beach area behind Astrid's house.) Astrid never gave permission to Ben to use this path in this way, but she did not voice any objection either. Then, in 1987, Astrid sold her property to Charles. Charles immediately barred the path so that Ben could no longer use it. The statute of limitations for actions to recover real property in the jurisdiction is 15 years. Does Ben have a right to continue using the path to the beach?_____

66. From Dunes Development Co., George purchased a house just off the 16th fairway of Sandy Dunes Country Club. The Club was constructed by Dunes Development Co. The deed from Dunes stated that George would have the right to free use of the Sandy Dunes Golf Course indefinitely, but was silent on whether the golf rights received by George were transferable. Two years later, George sold the house to Henry. By then, the course was no longer being operated by Dunes Development Co., but rather, by Ian, who bought it from Dunes. When Henry attempted to use the golf course for free, Ian refused. If Henry brings suit against Ian to enforce the free-golf provision of the deed, will Henry prevail?_____

67. Quince owned a limestone quarry, and a manufacturing plant in which he worked the limestone into gravestones and monuments. A parcel owned by Pierce lay between the quarry and the manufacturing plant. Therefore, Quince purchased from Pierce an easement to drive his trucks along a 10-foot-wide strip of Pierce's land, so the stone could be taken from the quarry to the manufacturing plant. Quince's business grew over the years, and in 1980, Quince shuttered the plant, and built a newer, larger plant some miles away. At the time the old plant was shuttered, Quince told Pierce by telephone, "I won't be needing the easement across your land anymore." Shortly thereafter, Quince sold the quarry, as well as the shuttered plant and the land it stood on, to Raymond. Raymond immediately started driving his trucks from the quarry to the plant. If Pierce brings suit to stop Raymond from crossing Pierce's property, will Pierce be successful?

_____

68. Abbott and Bingham were adjacent landowners, and fanatic tennis players. Abbott, the richer of the two, built a clay tennis court on his property. At the time of construction, he said to Bingham, "For as long as you own your property, you are free to use the court whenever you wish, so long as I am not playing on it." Bingham immediately sent Abbott a letter, stating, "I want to thank you for your generosity in allowing me to use your tennis court whenever I want (assuming you are not using it, of course) for as long as I stay in the house. I regard this as

significantly enhancing the value of my own property." For 10 years, the arrangement worked well. Then, Abbott discovered one day that Bingham was having an affair with Abbott's wife. Abbott angrily wrote to Bingham, "I am hereby revoking your right to use my tennis court. Never set foot on my property again, under pain of prosecution for trespass." Bingham now sues for a declaratory judgment that he is entitled to use Abbott's court. The state where the land is located has a 25-year statute of limitation on adverse possession actions._____

(A) What property interest, if any, did Abbott grant to Bingham at the time the court was constructed?

(B) Should the court hold that Bingham has the right to use Abbott's court now?_____

69. Allison and Bertrand were neighboring land owners who owned fee simples in adjacent parcels of land. The parcels were separated by a fence which lay on Allison's property. Since proper maintenance of the fence was important to Bertrand's property as well as to Allison's, both parties agreed that when the fence needed repairs and painting from time to time, Allison would cause this to be done, and Bertrand would then reimburse Allison for half the cost. The agreement also provided that if Bertrand did not pay a debt that was properly owing, Allison could get a lien on his land for the unpaid debt. The agreement was embodied in a document signed by both parties, and filed in the local real estate records indexed under both Allison's and Bertrand's names. The document did not specifically give Bertrand any right to come upon Allison's land to make the repairs if Allison declined to do so._____

Two years after this agreement, Bertrand conveyed his parcel to his daughter, Claire, in fee simple. Claire never explicitly or implicitly promised to pay for repairs to the fence. Five years after this conveyance, Allison spent $1,000 to have the fence extensively repaired and repainted. (There had been intervening repairs which occurred while Bertrand still owned his parcel, and which he paid for. The $1,000 was for work done to repair wear and tear that occurred after Claire took title.) Allison now seeks to recover $500 from either Bertrand or Claire. If both refuse to pay, will Allison's suit be successful against Claire, assuming that there is no special statute in force relevant to this question?_____

70. Same basic fact pattern as prior question. Now, assume that Bertrand never made the conveyance to Claire. Assume further that Allison, five years after her deal with Bertrand, conveyed her parcel to her brother Doug. If Doug sues Bertrand for enforcement of the promise, may Doug recover? _____

71. Same basic fact pattern as prior two questions. Now, assume that the original Allison-Bertrand document also contained a promise by Allison that she would not replace the wooden fence with a structure made of any other material (because Bertrand liked the look of natural wood). (This promise was contained in the document that was filed in the land records.) Assume that as in the prior question, Allison conveyed the property to Doug, and further assume that Bertrand conveyed his property to Claire. If Doug begins to replace the wooden fence with a

shiny   metal   one,   may   Claire   get   an   injunction   against
Doug?_____

72. Harry and Isadore were adjacent landowners in a residential area. Each believed that swimming pools were "tacky." They therefore agreed, in a writing signed by both, that neither would ever permit his property to have a swimming pool placed upon it. Three years later, Isadore sold his parcel to James. At the time of purchase, James did not have actual knowledge of the Harry-Isadore agreement. A check by James of the real estate records failed to disclose the Harry-Isadore agreement (because it had never been filed by either party). If James had asked Isadore, Isadore would have told him about the agreement, but James never asked, and Isadore never thought to mention it. James has now begun work to prepare his site to contain a swimming pool. If Harry sues to enjoin the construction by James, should the court grant Harry an injunction?_____

73. Developer, a residential real estate developer, purchased a farm and set about creating "Happy Farms," a planned residential community. Developer prepared a subdivision map (or "plat") for Happy Farms, which showed that all 36 lots on Happy Farms were to be used for residential purposes, showed where roads and sewers were to run, and contained other details indicating that the property would be a residential community. Developer then sold parcel 1 at Happy Farms to Kathy. In the deed from Developer, Kathy agreed that her parcel would be subject to the restrictions contained in the plat, which was filed in the real estate records. Developer did not state in the deed that other parcels later sold by him would be subject to similar restrictions, though Developer orally told Kathy, "Other buyers will be subject to the same limitations, so you'll be sure that you'll have a purely residential community with high standards."

Developer then sold parcel 2 to Lewis. Due to Developer's administrative negligence, the deed to Lewis omitted the restrictions contained in Kathy's deed. However, there is evidence that Lewis knew that a general residential plan had been prepared by Developer and filed in the real estate records. Several years later, Lewis attempted to open a candy store on part of his property. (This is allowed by local zoning laws, since the area is zoned mixed-use.) If Kathy sues Lewis to enjoin him from using his property for non-residential purposes, will the court grant Kathy's request?_____

CHAPTER 10

ZONING AND OTHER PUBLIC LAND-USE CONTROLS

74. For 20 years, Dexter has operated a private dump in the town of Hampshire. The dump now receives approximately 500 tons of garbage per year, about the same annual amount that it has always received. The only negative environmental effect from operation of the dump is odor, and the odors are no more serious than they have always been, i.e., a mildly disturbing garbage smell that depending on wind condition can be perceived as far as one-half mile away from the dump. As

the town has become more affluent, the citizens have become increasingly unhappy about the dump. Finally, the Hampshire Town Council recently passed a zoning ordinance providing that no dump may be operated within the town, and further providing that any existing dump must be discontinued within two years following passage of the ordinance. Because Dexter's property now has a huge pile of unsightly garbage on it, its value has declined to $200,000 (versus an approximately $1 million value as an operating dump). Dexter has brought an inverse condemnation suit against Hampshire, arguing that the ordinance amounts to a "taking" of his property and that he must therefore be compensated for the $1 million value it has (though he is willing to give the town a credit for the $200,000 that the property will be worth after it is no longer a dump). Should the court award Dexter the $800,000 relief he seeks?_____

75. Jones operates a car dealership along a highway located in the town of Nordstom. For 20 years, Jones has had a billboard on the edge of his property extolling his dealership's virtues to passersby on the highway. Then, the Nordstrom Town Council enacted a comprehensive zoning ordinance, which among other things bars all billboards anywhere in the town. The "pre-existing uses" section of the ordinance provides that any non-conforming use must be phased out within five years of the ordinance. Jones has sued to overturn the ordinance as applied to him, arguing that while Nordstrom has the right to ban billboards prospectively, it may not require him to remove an existing billboard because this constitutes a taking of his property without due process. Will Jones prevail?_____

76. The town of Twin Peaks is a long-established wealthy community whose residents include almost no blacks or other minorities, and almost no poor people. Twin Peaks never had a comprehensive zoning ordinance until 1980. That year, it enacted an ordinance which, among other aspects, provided that no home may be built on a parcel of land containing less than two acres. Prosser, a local developer, acquired a 10-acre parcel on a quiet street in Twin Peaks. He proposed to build 20 single-family residences on the parcel. Prosser realized, of course, that he would not be permitted to build the development unless he could either have the two-acre minimum removed from the ordinance, or obtain a variance for his development. The Town Council refused to do either. Prosser is reluctant to sue the town, because he does not want to alienate it.

However, Twin Peaks has been sued by Prince, a black resident of nearby Glendale, who argues that if the two-acre minimum were lifted, he would be able to afford, and would choose, to live on Prosser's development. Prince contends that Twin Peaks' refusal to lift the minimum violates his equal protection rights. At trial, Prince has been able to prove that the two-acre minimum has the effect of dramatically reducing the number of black residents in Twin Peaks, since most nearby blacks are insufficiently wealthy to afford the two acre parcels. However, neither side has produced any evidence as to whether the Town Council of Twin Peaks was motivated by a desire to keep out blacks, either at the time the ordinance was originally enacted or at the more recent time when the Council refused to lift the two-acre minimum. On these facts, should the court find that Twin

Peaks has violated Prince's equal protection rights?_____

77. Same facts as prior question.

(A) What statutory action, if any, could Prince bring that would have a good probability of success?_____

(B) Will Prince succeed with such an action?_____

78. Same facts as prior two questions. Now, however, assume that there is convincing evidence that the Town Council of Twin Peaks was *not* motivated by any racially-discriminatory intent, and that the two-acre minimum zoning rule was enacted for the purpose of maintaining the "uncrowded" and "pastoral" nature of the town. Assume that Twin Peaks is located in the state of New Jersey. No relevant statutes have been enacted.

(A) What theory might Prosser (the developer, see Question 76) use to attack the two-acre rule?_____

(B) If the court agreed with Prosser's suit, what remedy would the court be likely to award?_____

CHAPTER 11

LAND SALE CONTRACTS, MORTGAGES AND DEEDS

79. By telephone, Simon agreed to sell, and Bryant agreed to buy, Blackacre for a price of $200,000, the closing to take place on April 1. On March 15, the day after this conversation, Simon sent Bryant a letter confirming all of the relevant terms of the agreement. The letter stated, "I will assume that this letter accurately states our arrangement, and will bind us both, unless I hear from you to the contrary by March 20." Bryant received the letter, but sent no response. On April 1, Simon arrived with a marketable deed at the time and place that his letter specified for closing. Bryant did not show up at all. If Simon sues Bryant for breach of contract, may he recover damages?_____

80. Tycoon, a wealthy industrialist, has for many years owned a 100 acre parcel of undeveloped, heavily-wooded land, called Twin Oaks, in the state of Bates. Grandson, Tycoon's daughter's oldest son, wished desperately to become a farmer. Tycoon therefore orally proposed to Grandson the following arrangement: if Grandson would move onto the property, construct a permanent dwelling, and clear at least 50 of the acres, he could keep whatever crops (or their proceeds) he could grow on the property. Furthermore, if Grandson did all this and then continued to farm for at least five years, Tycoon would leave the property to Grandson in Tycoon's will. Grandson moved onto the property, built a small cabin, cleared 75 acres, and farmed them for the next seven years, keeping all proceeds as agreed. Tycoon then died, and his will made no mention of the arrangement. (Instead, the will left Twin Oaks to Tycoon's niece, Edna.) If Grandson sues Tycoon's estate for an order of specific performance directing the estate to convey Twin Oaks to Grandson, will Grandson prevail? Assume that Bates follows the majority approach to all relevant matters._____

81. Shelby, the owner of Blackacre, contracted to sell the property to Bennett. The contract document, dated March 1, provided that the closing was to take place on April 1. The contract did not contain a "time is of the essence" clause, and did not specify the consequences if either party was unable or unwilling to close on the appointed day. On March 25, Bennett said by telephone to Shelby, "My bank loan hasn't gone through yet. I won't be able to close on April 1, but I will be ready on April 10." Shelby replied, "Either close on April 1, or the contract is off." On April 1, Shelby showed up at the appointed place with a deed, but Bennett did not appear. Bennett tendered a check for the purchase price on April 10, but Shelby refused to take it. There is evidence that Shelby was trying to get out of the contract not because the delay was material in light of the surrounding circumstances, but because someone had unexpectedly come along and offered Shelby a higher price. If Bennett sues Shelby for a decree ordering Shelby to convey the property to Bennett for the contract price, will a court grant Bennett's request?_____

82. Squires contracted to sell Whiteacre to Brady, the closing to take place on June 1. The purchase price was to be $200,000, in the form of a cashier's or certified check. The contract required Squires to convey a marketable title. On June 1, both Squires and Brady turned up at the appointed place for the closing. Squires tendered a deed, together with an abstract of title showing that Squires had good title. The contract also required Squires to have a Certificate of Occupancy for a newly-constructed deck attached to the house. Brady demanded the Certificate of Occupancy, and Squires said, "I don't have it." Brady responded, "Well, I refuse to close." Squires asked Brady to show him the certified check for the purchase price. Brady said, "I don't have it. I didn't bother going through with my bank loan, because I knew you didn't have the Certificate of Occupancy." (This assertion is true.) Squires refused to return Brady's 10% deposit, paid to Squires at the time the contract was signed. (The deposit is returnable, according to the contract, only if seller is in default and buyer is not, on the closing date.) If Brady sues Squires for the return of his deposit, will Brady win?_____

83. Same basic fact pattern as prior question. Now, however, assume that the abstract of title proffered by Squires on June 1 showed that the house on the property (an important part of the overall value of the property) encroached 10 feet onto the property of Squires' easterly neighbor. If Brady sues Squires for return of his deposit, and Squires asserts the defense that Brady did not tender his own performance (because Brady did not bring a check to the closing), may Brady recover the deposit?_____

84. Sherman contracted to sell Greenacre to Bruce. The contract was signed on June 1, 1989, and called for a closing to occur on August 1, 1989. On July 1, 1989, Sherman died. His will (executed in 1988) left all of Sherman's personal property to his daughter Deirdre, and all of his real estate to his niece Nell. The closing took place as scheduled on August 1, with the sale proceeds paid to Sherman's

estate. Who should receive the sale proceeds, Deirdre or Nell?
_____

85. Spratt contracted to sell a house to Booth. After the contract was signed, but before the scheduled closing date, the house burned down. Spratt was not at fault. Neither Spratt nor Booth had any insurance in force on the property. On the closing date, is Booth obligated to pay the purchase price to Spratt, in return for a deed to the now-much-less-valuable property?_____

86. Spence sold a house and lot to Bagley under an installment sales contract. The contract provided for the $200,000 purchase price to be paid at the rate of $5,000 per month for 40 consecutive months (with interest on the unpaid balance also being payable each month). The contract further provided that if Bagley ever became more than 30 days in arrears on any payment, Spence could at his sole option declare the contract forfeited, and reclaim the property. Bagley moved in, and made the first 20 payments without incident. He then lost his job, and fell 90 days behind in the payments. The fair rental value of the property is $2,000 per month. Spence sent Bagley a letter stating, "Because you have violated the terms of our agreement, I am hereby exercising my right to declare the agreement terminated. Please vacate immediately." If Spence seeks an order declaring the contract terminated and decreeing that Bagley leave the premises, will Spence succeed?_____

87. Steel contracted to sell Greenacre to Boswell. The contract stated that Steel would convey marketable title to Boswell, and that the deed would be a warranty deed free of all easements and other encumbrances. On the appointed closing date, Steel tendered to Boswell a warranty deed which stated that the property is "subject to an easement on behalf of a parcel located to the northwest of the subject parcel, enabling the beneficiary of the easement to use the subject parcel's driveway." Boswell and Boswell's lawyer did not carefully read the deed. Instead, they accepted it, and paid the purchase price, without realizing that the deed was subject to the easement. Several days later, when Boswell's neighbor used Boswell's driveway, Boswell realized that he had been given a deed which did not conform to the contract. Boswell now sues to recover damages under the contract for breach of the representation concerning lack of easements. Assuming that Boswell shows that the property is less valuable because the easement exists, may Boswell recover under the contract?_____

88. Fred was the owner of Greyacre, located in the state of Cabot. Cabot law requires all deeds for the transfer of real property to be witnessed by two people. Fred, who was getting on in years, decided to make a gift of Greyacre to his son, Stewart. He therefore prepared a deed giving Stewart the property, signed it, and had it witnessed by two people (thus fulfilling all of the requirements for a deed in Cabot). He handed the deed to Stewart, saying, "You are now the owner of Greyacre." The next day, Fred had a change of heart, realizing that he might live another 15 years and wanting the satisfaction of knowing that he was still the owner of Greyacre. He therefore asked Stewart to return or rip up the deed. Stewart was upset, but he was also a dutiful son. He therefore ripped up the deed (first

making a photocopy, however), and told Fred that he had done so. Shortly thereafter, Fred died, leaving all of his personal and real property to his daughter, Denise. Who owns Greyacre, Stewart or Denise?_____

89. In 1970, Spitzer conveyed Blackacre to Butler, under a standard warranty deed. In 1990, as Butler was preparing to resell the property, he discovered that Spitzer's predecessor in title had lost his title through adverse possession before ever conveying to Spitzer. The present holder of title by adverse possession is Adolf, who is not in possession of the property (Butler is), and who has never actively asserted rights to the property. Butler realizes that he will not be able to convey a marketable title to any subsequent purchaser because of Adolf's superior title. Butler therefore wishes to sue Spitzer for breach of some or all of the covenants of title. The statutes of limitation on actions for breach of the covenants of seisin, right to convey and against encumbrances are all five years in the jurisdiction. The statutes of limitation on the covenants of quiet enjoyment and warranty are both three years. If Butler brings suit in 1990 against Spitzer for breach of all of these covenants, on which, if any, may he recover? For each covenant on which he may not recover, state the reason._____

90. Same facts as prior question. Now, assume that Butler, without disclosing the fact that Adolf has a superior title, conveys the property by warranty deed to Capshaw in 1990. In 1992, while Capshaw is still the record owner of the property and in possession of it, Adolf brings an action for a declaration that he is the legal owner of the property. If Capshaw immediately brings suit against Spitzer for violation by Spitzer of the covenant of quiet enjoyment, may Capshaw recover? (Assume that nothing in the Butler-to-Capshaw deed refers to any covenants made by Butler's predecessor(s) in title.)_____

91. Schneider conveyed a house and lot to Block, under a general warranty deed. The deed did not list any encumbrances or encroachments. At the time Block received (and paid for) the deed, he was aware that a garage built and belonging to Schneider's eastern neighbor, Jones, was located half on Jones' property and half on Schneider's property. (Block closed the transaction anyway, because he thought he was getting a price that was good enough to overlook this problem.) Several years later, Block decided that he had made a mistake in tolerating this state of events. He therefore instituted a suit against Schneider for breach of covenant._____

(A) For breach of which covenant should Block sue?_____

(B) Will Block be found to have waived the benefit of that covenant by agreeing to close with knowledge of the problem?_____

92. Developer was in the business of buying large parcels, subdividing them, and building new houses on each. Developer sold a newly built house and the lot on which it stood to Benjamin, a would-be homeowner. The transaction was done by warranty deed. Both the sale contract and the deed contained the following statement in capital letters: "DEVELOPER MAKES NO OTHER WARRANTIES, EXPRESS OR IMPLIED, REGARDING THE STATE OF THE LAND OR

STRUCTURES BEING TRANSFERRED." Unbeknownst to either Developer or Benjamin, Developer's employees, because of their ignorance, had failed to use the proper mix of sand and gravel in the cement employed for the building's foundation. Hairline cracks began to appear shortly after the closing, and within one year the house was structurally unsafe and unsalable.

(A) What action, if any, should Benjamin bring against Developer?_____

(B) What is the probable result of the action you advised bringing in (A)?_____

93. Same facts as prior question. Assume that during his first and only year of ownership, Benjamin did not become aware of the cracks in the foundation. At the end of a year, he sold the house to Carter, and Carter moved in. If Carter sues Benjamin on the same theory as you gave in your answer to part (a) of the prior question, will Carter succeed against Developer?_____

CHAPTER 12

THE RECORDING SYSTEM AND TITLE ASSURANCE

94. Oliver conveyed Whiteacre to Arkin in 1980; Arkin did not record at the time. Oliver then conveyed to Beacon in 1982. Beacon did not know about the deed to Arkin at the time he took. In 1983, Arkin recorded, without knowledge of the conveyance by Oliver to Beacon. In 1984, Beacon discovered the conveyance to Arkin by doing a title search, and immediately recorded. If the jurisdiction has a "race notice" statute, who has title as between Arkin and Beacon, and why?_____

95. Oliver conveyed Whiteacre to Arkin, for value, in 1980. Through negligence, Arkin did not record at the time. Oliver, who was aware of Arkin's failure to record, sold the property to Beacon in 1982. Just before the conveyance to Beacon, Oliver told Beacon, "I conveyed to Arkin in 1980, but Arkin has not recorded. As long as you record before Arkin can, you'll be safe." Beacon paid almost full value for the property, and immediately recorded (still in 1982). In 1983, Arkin suddenly realized, with panic in his heart, that he had failed to record, and that Beacon had recorded. Arkin immediately recorded. In a race-notice jurisdiction, who has priority, Arkin or Beacon, and why?_____

96. Oliver conveyed Whiteacre to Arkin in 1980. At the time, Arkin did not record. Oliver then conveyed Whiteacre to Beacon in 1982. Beacon did not record. Beacon, at the time he took, did not have actual knowledge of the conveyance to Arkin. In 1983, Arkin recorded. Beacon has never recorded. In a "pure notice" jurisdiction, who has priority, Arkin or Beacon, and why?_____

97. In 1960, Odell conveyed Blackacre to Arias. Arias did not record at the time. In 1970, Odell conveyed to Beck. At the time of the conveyance, Beck had actual notice of the earlier conveyance to Arias. Beck recorded immediately after receiving his deed. In 1980, Beck conveyed to Cabbott. Cabbott had neither actual nor constructive notice of the conveyance by Odell to Arias, and Cabbott paid Beck fair value. In 1985, Arias finally recorded. In 1987, Cabbott recorded. The jurisdiction has a race-notice statute. As between Arias and Cabbott, who has title?_____

98. In 1950, Osborn gave a gift of Whiteacre to Abrams. At the time, Abrams did not record the deed. In 1960, Osborn purported to give Whiteacre as a gift to Boone. At the time Boone received his deed, he had no knowledge of the earlier gift to Abrams. Boone immediately recorded. In 1965, Abrams recorded. The jurisdiction has a race-notice statute. As between Abrams and Boone, who has title?_____

99. In 1960, Orcini conveyed Blackacre to Arlen for value. Arlen never recorded his deed. In 1970, Arlen conveyed to Bishop. Bishop paid fair value, and promptly recorded. In 1980, Orcini conveyed Blackacre to Chavez. Chavez had no knowledge of the earlier Orcini-Arlen conveyance, or of the Arlen-Bishop conveyance. Chavez paid fair value, and immediately recorded. The jurisdiction has a race-notice statute. In a dispute between Bishop and Chavez, who has superior title to Blackacre?_____

100. In 1950, O'Neill conveyed Blackacre to Arens. At the time, this deed was not recorded. In 1960, Arens conveyed to Burrows. This deed was not recorded at the time. In 1970, O'Neill conveyed to Craft. This deed was never recorded. In 1980, Craft conveyed to Dempsey. Dempsey promptly recorded his deed from Craft. Neither Craft nor Dempsey, at the time each took his conveyance, had any actual knowledge of the O'Neill-to-Arens-to-Burrows line of conveyances. In 1985, the O'Neill-to-Arens and the Arens-to-Burrows deeds were recorded by Burrows. The jurisdiction has a race-notice statute. In a contest between Burrows and Dempsey, who has priority?_____

101. In 1975, Oakley conveyed Blackacre to Andrews for value. Andrews never recorded the deed. In 1985, Oakley conveyed the same property to Burns for value. Burns promptly recorded. At the time Burns took, Andrews was in possession of the property (as, indeed, he had been since 1975), and the property (a farm) contained a mailbox with Andrews' name prominently displayed on it. Burns lived far away from the property, and never visited it before he took. If he had visited it, he would have seen signs of Andrews' possession. If he had spoken to Andrews, Andrews would have explained that he was the owner. The jurisdiction has a pure notice statute. In a contest between Andrews and Burns, who has superior title?_____

102. In 1960, Olivia conveyed Blackacre to Albright. At the time, Albright did not record his deed. In 1970, Olivia conveyed Blackacre to Brown. Brown took without any notice (actual or record) of the earlier conveyance to Albright. Brown promptly recorded. In 1975, Albright belatedly recorded. In 1985, Brown conveyed to Crystal. Crystal bought for value. Brown, being an honest sort, disclosed to Crystal before the sale that there was an earlier conveyance by Olivia to

Albright, and that that conveyance had been subsequently recorded. (Crystal paid a somewhat lower price to reflect the possible uncertainty about title.) Crystal promptly recorded her deed. The jurisdiction has a race-notice statute. In a contest between Albright and Crystal, who wins?_____

103. Barnes contracted to purchase Blackacre from Selish. As part of the contract, Selish provided Barnes with a metes-and-bounds survey of the property, which was in fact an accurate description of the property which Selish intended to sell and Barnes intended to buy. The survey did not disclose that the garage located principally on the property encroached three feet onto the neighboring property; in fact, the survey did not show the garage structure at all. However, if Barnes (or his lawyer) had measured the distance from the house to the garage, and compared this with the distance from the house to the rear property line, they would have seen by looking at the survey that the garage must encroach on the neighbor's property. In any event, Barnes bought the property without being aware of the encroachment. At the time of the closing, Barnes purchased from Title Co. a standard title insurance policy on the property. The policy excluded any "any facts which an accurate survey of the property would disclose." The title report that accompanied the policy did not refer in any way to the fact that the garage encroached or might encroach on the neighbor's property. Three years after the purchase, Barnes was sued by the neighbor, who obtained a court order compelling Barnes to remove the encroaching garage, at a cost of $40,000. If Barnes sues Title Co. for $40,000, will Barnes recover?_____

Chapter 13

RIGHTS INCIDENT TO LAND

104. Plotnick and Duffy were adjacent property owners. Plotnick's land had a six-story building on it, built in conformity with applicable building codes (including ones governing the depth and strength of the foundation). Duffy's property was undeveloped. Duffy decided to build his own building. He was a very conservative sort. Therefore, he dug an unusually deep foundation (15 feet). Duffy dug only up to his property line. He proceeded without negligence, and in conformity with all codes dictating how to excavate and build a foundation. However, because of the geography of the land, and the unusual nature of Plotnick's foundation, Plotnick's foundation cracked and his building was severely damaged once there was no longer supporting soil on the Plotnick-Duffy border. Plotnick sued Duffy for the damage. Duffy proved at trial that if there had been no building on Plotnick's property, Plotnick's land would not have caved in. May Plotnick recover?_____

105. Phillips and Decker each own a parcel that abuts on the Bountiful River in the state of Ames. Decker is upstream from Phillips. Since 1986, Decker has operated a private hydro-electric plant. To maintain the necessary pressure, Decker has built a dam on the river, which has the effect of diverting the water through the hydro-electric plant's turbines, and then out onto a pond at the rear of Decker's property. Beginning in 1975, Phillips, a farmer, had been irrigating a five-acre parcel of his property. This worked well until Decker built his dam in 1986; since then so little water has been present in the Bountiful River by the time it reaches Phillips' property, that the pressure needed to perform useful irrigation is not present. Assuming that Ames follows the common-law approach to relevant matters, if Phillips sues Decker for improperly using the water, will Phillips prevail?_____

106. Same facts as prior question. Now, assume that Decker's use (for hydro-electric) commenced in 1986, and that Phillips did not begin trying to use his property for irrigation until 1989. Ames follows the common-law approach to relevant matters. May Phillips recover against Decker for improper use of water?_____

107. Same facts as prior question. Assume, however, that Ames is one of the 17 states that have abolished the common-law riparian rights doctrine, and that Ames has replaced that doctrine with the most common alternative. Would Phillips win in a suit against Decker for improper water use?_____

108. Pringle and Delaney are adjacent landowners. At the time Pringle bought his property in 1970, a six-story office building was already present on that lot. This building goes up nearly to the eastern property line (and does not violate any zoning rules). Delaney has owned his lot (which is to the east of Pringle's property) since 1980. The land has been vacant. Now, Delaney proposes to build a 12-story office building on the western side of his property. This building would conform with all applicable zoning laws. However, the effect of this building will be to deprive Pringle's tenants (at least those in the eastern side of the building) of nearly all of the sunlight and view which they have always had, since the two buildings will only be three feet apart. If Pringle sues Delaney to enjoin Delaney from placing the building so close to the property line that Pringle's tenants' light and view will be cut off, will the court grant Pringle's request? _____

ANSWERS TO SHORT-ANSWER QUESTIONS

1. **No.** To begin with, anyone whose chain of title includes a thief cannot prevail over the "true" owner. But the true owner's right to recover the property can become time-barred. The modern rule on the running of the statute of limitations is sometimes called the *"discovery"* rule; by that rule, the statute of limitations on an action to recover stolen property normally does not begin to run against the record owner until the owner knows, or should know, the identity of the possessor. But the rule assumes that the owner has made prompt *reasonable efforts* to find the possessor or to put the world on notice of the stolen property. Here, Oscar did not do this; for instance, he failed to list the painting in the information bank, a step that a reasonably diligent owner would normally take. Therefore, a court will probably hold that the statute began to run against him immediately. In that event, Anita became the owner by adverse possession in 1980.

2. **Yes. As a general rule,** *a seller cannot convey better title than that which he holds*. This is true of the unknown thief. Therefore, Dealer never got good title (regardless of whether he thought he did), and could not in turn give good title to Arnold. Consequently, even though Arnold paid full value and was completely innocent, he will lose the car. (Statutes in most states set up a certificate of title program, which would have protected Arnold in this situation.)

3. **Denise.** There are three requirements for the making of a valid gift: (1) delivery; (2) intent to make a gift; and (3) acceptance by the donee. Here, the delivery requirement was not satisfied, since Sidney did not give Norman either physical possession of the painting or possession of any symbolic or written instrument representing the gift.

4. **All, probably.** The account here is a "Totten Trust" (the name commonly used to describe an account of the form "A in trust for B"). Most courts, and the Uniform Probate Code, hold that where the trustee of a Totten Trust (here, Albert) dies before the beneficiary (here, Bertha), the beneficiary is *presumed* to be entitled to all funds left in the account. This presumption is rebuttable by a showing that the trustee intended a different result, but there is no such evidence here.

5. **No, probably.** Beck obtained title to the 30 yard strip by the doctrine of *adverse possession*, 20 years after he first fenced in the property (i.e., in 1981). One of the requirements for adverse possession is that the possession be *"hostile."* But most courts hold that one who possesses an adjoining landowner's land, under the mistaken belief that he has only possessed up to the boundary of his own land, meets the requirement of hostile possession. (But a minority of courts would disagree with the result, and would hold that Warren may recover possession because Beck's possession was not hostile.)

6. **Yes.** Steve and Deborah held the property as co-tenants. As a general rule, co-tenants each have equal access to the premises. If Steve had refused Deborah's attempt to live on the premises, then Steve's occupancy for the statutory period would have been "hostile," and Steve would have taken Deborah's half interest by adverse possession. But since Deborah never asked to live on the premises, and Steve never said that she couldn't, Steve's occupancy was not hostile, so he does not take her interest by adverse possession even though he was in sole occupancy for more than the statutory period. Consequently, Deborah still owned her one-half interest at the time of her death, and that interest passed to Frank.

7.   Stokes. In 1980, Alice became the owner of the strip by adverse possession. Once she gained title by adverse possession, her title was of the same quality, and subject to the same rules, as if she had gotten title by deed. Therefore, she could not convey that title to anyone else except by compliance with the Statute of Frauds. Her oral "grant" to Orlando was ineffective because it was not in writing as required by the Statute of Frauds. Therefore, Alice owned the strip at her death, and it passed to Stokes.

8.   Barbara. The gift "to Abel and his heirs" does not mean "to Abel for life then to his heirs." Instead, "to Abel and his heirs" means "to Abel in *fee simple*." Therefore, Abel had the right to do whatever he wished with the property, and his deed of it to Barbara was effective. Thus when Abel died, he had no interest in Blackacre to leave to his son and heir.

9.   Yes. The original grant from O to A was a *fee simple determinable*. We know this because of the phrase "so long as...(D3," and the word "revert." Therefore, after the conveyance, O was left with a *possibility of reverter*. When O died, his possibility of reverter passed to his son S. When A purported to convey a fee simple absolute to B, he really conveyed only a fee simple determinable subject to S's possibility of reverter. When B began using the premises for the forbidden purpose in 1970, title *automatically* reverted to S, without S taking any formal action. Therefore, S remained the owner of the property in 1980, and is entitled to a judicial decree to that effect. (If more than 50 years passed after O's original creation of the fee simple determinable, then S or his successors would lose their right to this decree, since they would be barred by the 50-year statute of limitations on possibilities of reverter.)

10.   No. Now, the O-to-A conveyance established a *fee simple subject to a condition subsequent*. (The words "upon condition that" or "provided that," when taken with a clause providing for re-entry, establish that a fee simple subject to condition subsequent, rather than a fee simple determinable, was created.) This left O (and, after his death, S) with a right of entry, not a possibility of reverter. By the statute of limitations, S was required to bring his suit for re-entry within one year of B's commencement of the illegal use, i.e., by 1971. When S did not do so, his right of entry was extinguished. So by comparing this question with the prior one, you can see the importance of distinguishing between a fee simple determinable and a fee simple subject to a condition subsequent.

11.   Life estate *per autre vie in C, remainder in fee simple in B*. After the initial conveyance by O, A was a life tenant. In all states, a life tenant may convey the interest which he holds, or a lesser one (but not a greater one). Therefore, A was capable of conveying his life estate to C; once that conveyance took place, C had a life estate *per autre vie* (life estate measured by another person's life), since C's interest would end when A died, not when C died. B continued to hold the fee simple remainder that he got when O made the initial conveyance.

12.   A reversion. When the holder of a vested estate transfers to another a smaller estate, we call the interest which remains in the grantor a "reversion." Since the estate created by O is smaller than the one he held (i.e., a life estate is smaller than a fee simple absolute), what O was left with was a reversion.

13. Indefeasibly vested remainder. A remainder is a future interest which can become possessory only upon the expiration of a prior possessory interest created by the same instrument. Since B's interest was created by the same instrument that created A's life estate, and since B's interest will become possessory when that prior life interest expires, B has a remainder. This remainder is a vested remainder, because it is not subject to any condition precedent, and an identified already-born person (B) holds the remainder. The remainder is "indefeasibly" vested because it is certain to become possessory at some future time (even if B dies before A does, the remainder will pass by will or intestacy to B's heirs, and there is certain to be somebody who will be there to take possession when A dies).

14. Vested remainder subject to open. For an explanation of why C's interest is some sort of vested remainder, see the answer to the prior question. The vested remainder is "subject to open" because if another child (let's call him D) is born to B, C's remainder "opens up" to give D a half interest in it. The remainder will stay open until either A dies (in which case only the then-living children of B will take anything), or B dies, in which case he can have no further children.

15. Vested remainder subject to divestment. B has a remainder vested subject to divestment. If A died immediately, B's interest would become possessory. But if B died without issue (either before or after A's death), B's interest would be completely defeated or "divested". (C's interest, which cuts short B's vested interest, is called an executory interest.)

16. Contingent remainder. A remainder is contingent rather than vested if it is either subject to a condition precedent, or created in favor of a person who is unborn or unascertained. Here, the remainder to B is subject to a condition precedent (the condition that B survive A in order for his remainder to become possessory). If B does survive A, his remainder will become vested at the same time it becomes possessory.

17. Vested remainder subject to divestment. Notice that the grant here is functionally indistinguishable from that in the prior question, yet the remainder here is vested (subject to divestment), whereas the one in the prior question is contingent. This relates solely to the words: here the clause creating the remainder in B does not contain any limit, and the limit is introduced by a separate clause containing the phrase, "but if." As a matter of interpretation, the separate clause beginning with "but if" indicates that the remainder is being "taken away," and this indicates a condition subsequent rather than a condition precedent (thus a remainder subject to divestment rather than a contingent remainder).

18. Fee simple in O. After the initial conveyance by O, D had a contingent remainder. But at the time A died, D did not meet the contingency (having had a child while being married). By the common law doctrine of ***destructibility of contingent remainders***, a contingent remainder was deemed "destroyed" unless it vested at or before the termination of the preceding freehold estates. Since D had not met the contingency by the time the prior estate (A's life estate) expired, D's contingent remainder was destroyed. Therefore, O's reversion became possessory, giving him a fee simple absolute. (Today, most states have, by case law or statute, abolished the doctrine of destructibility of contingent remainders.)

19.   Fee simple in B. By the doctrine of *"merger,"* whenever *successive vested estates are owned by the same person*, the smaller of the two estates is absorbed by the larger. When A conveyed his life estate to B, B then had two successive vested estates (the life estate and the previously-received vested remainder in fee simple). Consequently, the smaller estate (A's life estate) was merged into the fee simple, and disappeared. Then, by the doctrine of destructibility of contingent remainders (see prior question), the destruction-by-merger of A's life estate caused D's contingent remainder dependent upon it to also be destroyed, since that contingent remainder did not vest at or before the termination of the preceding freehold estates.

20.   Fee simple absolute in B. Under the *Rule in Shelley's Case*, if a will or conveyance creates a freehold in A, and purports to create a remainder in A's heirs, and the estates are both legal or both equitable, the remainder becomes a fee simple in A. Thus by operation of the Rule, A received both a life estate and a remainder in fee simple. Then, by the doctrine of merger, A's life estate merged into his remainder in fee simple, and A simply held a present fee simple. A's quitclaim deed to B transferred this fee simple to B. A had nothing left at the time of his death, therefore, so S took nothing.

21.   Fee simple absolute in B. The *Doctrine of Worthier Title* provides that if the owner of a fee simple attempts to create a life estate (or fee tail estate), followed by a remainder to his own heirs, the remainder is void. The grantor thus keeps a reversion. So after the initial conveyance by O, A had a life estate and O had a reversion (with the remainder to O's heirs being void). Therefore, O's quitclaim deed to B was effective to pass O's reversion to B. Once A died, the reversion held by B became a possessory fee simple absolute. Since the initial remainder to O's heirs never took effect, S (O's heir) took nothing.

22.   Fee simple absolute in S. Today, most states make the Doctrine of Worthier Title a rule of construction, rather than an absolute rule of law as it was at common law. In other words, the Doctrine applies only where the grantor's language and surrounding circumstances indicate that he intended to keep a reversion. Here, O's statement that he wants the gift to take effect exactly as written rebuts the presumption that a reversion rather than remainder was intended. Consequently, the gift will take effect as written, which means that O's quitclaim deed to B was of no effect. Consequently, O's heirs held a contingent remainder before O's death, and that remainder vested in S when O died. When A died, S's remainder became possessory.

23.   Fee simple in A subject to an executory limitation, and a shifting executory interest in fee simple in B. The bargain and sale raises a use in A in fee simple subject to condition subsequent, and a use in B. The Statute of Uses executes both of these uses. The net result is that if A or his heirs serves liquor on the property, then the gift over to B will take effect.

24.   (A) Yes. A life tenant may not normally remove earth or minerals from the property. (There are two exceptions: (1) if the property was used for mining prior to the commencement of the life estate, the tenant may continue this use; and (2) the tenant may mine if this is the only way of accomplishing the purpose of the life estate. But neither of these exceptions applies here.)

(B) Sue for waste. If the holder of the present interest substantially reduces the value of the future interest, and acts unreasonably under the circumstances, the holder of the future interest has a cause of action for waste. Here, by removing valuable oil, A has reduced the value of O's reversion. The court will certainly award damages, and might also award an injunction against future pumping.

25. Yes. The remainder to B is a vested remainder, which vested in interest (though not in possession) on the day of the original conveyance by O. Therefore, the remainder to B vested less than 21 years after some life in being at the creation of the interest (e.g., A's life).

26. No. We always analyze the Rule Against Perpetuities as of the date of the conveyance, not by reference to how things actually work out. Viewing the matter from the date of the conveyance, it is possible to imagine a situation in which B would die, an additional son — call him C — would be born to A after the conveyance, A would die, and C would marry and have a child more than 21 years after the death of A and B. Under this scenario, however unlikely it is, the remainder would vest in C more than 21 years after all named lives in being at the creation of the interest.

Because of this possibility, the gift to B (which is a contingent remainder) will fail, *even if it actually turns out that B marries and has a child*. Observe that the key difference between this question and the prior question is that here, the remainder to B is contingent (we don't know at the time of the conveyance which child, if any, of A will marry and have a child), whereas in the prior question, the gift to B and his heirs was a vested remainder. Since the contingent remainder won't vest until it becomes possessory, and this might (however unlikely) be more than 21 years after lives in being at the time of the conveyance, the gift to B fails (whereas the gift to B in the prior question succeeds because it is a vested remainder, which vests at the moment of creation).

27. No. What A Corp. has purchased here is an option "in gross." (That is, the option is not granted in connection with a present lease of the property.) An option in gross is subject to the Rule Against Perpetuities — it will be unenforceable if it could be exercised beyond the end of the Perpetuities period, even if the optionee paid real money for it in the belief that it would be exercisable. Since there is no measuring life in being at the time of the option's creation (A Corp. is a corporation, not an individual), the option violated the Rule by being scheduled to last more than 21 years. (But a judge might order B to refund A Corp.'s $20,000 option purchase price.)

28. No. As of 1980, it was possible that A would live a long time more, would marry someone born after 1980, and would then die after 2001. That person would thus be a life not yet in being at the time of O's bequest and would be taking more than "lives in being plus 21 years" after 1980. Thus the bequest to "the widow" is invalid. This is true (at least at common law) even though the person who actually takes (here, B) was someone who was in fact born by 1980. This is the *"unborn widow"* rule. (But again, a modern "wait and see statute" would cause the gift to be valid, since the recipient, B, turns out to be someone born before the date of the original conveyance.)

29. No. It was possible, viewed as of 1960, that another child (let's call him hypothetically C) would be born to A after 1960. It was also possible that A and B might also die prior to C's ninth birthday. If both of these events happened, C's interest would then vest too remotely (more than 21 years after the deaths of the measuring lives, i.e., A and B). Because of this theoretical possibility, not only was the gift invalid as to children born after 1960, but it was also invalid as to the rest of the *class* of children, i.e., B. (If O had not included the remark about specifically covering later-born children of A, then the court might have saved the bequest by viewing the class as closing at the time of O's death, or by viewing the class as referring only to those members who could take without violating the Rule Against Perpetuities. But with the bequest as written, the common-law approach would be that since there might be a member of the class who could not take without violating the Rule, no member of the class may take.)

30. No. The most common statutory modification today is the *"wait and see"* approach, by which if the interest *actually* vests within lives in being at the time of creation plus 21 years, the fact that things might have worked out differently is irrelevant. Since here, B was a life in being at the time of O's bequest, the gift to him is valid even though it might have turned out that the later-born C took later than lives in being plus 21 years.

31. Fee simple in A for 600 acres; life estate in W for 300 acres, with remainder in A. The common-law estate of *dower* entitles a widow, on her husband's death, to a life estate in one-third of the lands of which he was seised at any time during their marriage, provided that the husband's interest was inheritable by the issue of the marriage (if any). Since H was seised of Blueacre at some point during the marriage (from 1965 through 1970), W held the estate of dower inchoate. On H's death, this became the estate of dower consummate. The husband cannot, by conveying his property during his life, defeat the right of dower. If he purports to make such a conveyance, his widow may subsequently make her claim for dower against the present holder of the property. So W is entitled to have 300 acres set aside for her for life by A; after her death, A can once again take possession of them. (Observe that A's lawyer should have had W join in the deed from H before allowing A pay money for the property.)

32. (d), (e) and (f) are all community property. They are all either H's earnings during the marriage, or things purchased from those earnings. (a), (b), and (c) are separate property, because property received by a spouse before marriage, and property received by gift, inheritance or bequest after marriage, are separate, and income from separate property is separate property.

33. B and S hold as tenants in common. Today, all states establish a presumption that an ambiguous conveyance creates a tenancy in common rather than a joint tenancy. Therefore, O's ambiguous conveyance made A and B hold as tenants in common. Consequently, when A died, there was no right of survivorship on the part of B. Instead, A's undivided one-half interest in Blackacre passed to S. S and B now hold as tenants in common.

34. S and C as tenants in common. When B conveyed to C, this had the effect of *severing* the joint tenancy between A and B. Therefore, A and C held as tenants in common, not joint tenants, immediately after the conveyance by B to C. Therefore, when A died, C had no right of survivorship. S inherited A's share of the tenancy in common.

35. Yes. Each tenant in common is entitled to *possession of the whole property*, subject to the same rights in the other tenants. It does not make any difference that one of the tenants in common has a larger undivided interest than the other — the relative size of the interests matters only when the property is sold and the proceeds are allocated.

36. Fee simple absolute in Georgia. Oscar's original conveyance to Henry and Wanda created a tenancy by the entirety in them, since at common law any conveyance to two persons who are in fact husband and wife necessarily results in such a tenancy. (In fact, in the 22 states that retain tenancy by the entirety, there remains a presumption that a husband and wife who take property take it by the entirety.) When Henry conveyed his interest to Georgia, this did not have the effect of destroying the tenancy by the entirety, since such a tenancy is *indestructible* while both parties are alive and remain husband and wife. But the conveyance did have the effect of passing to Georgia whatever Henry's rights were. When Wanda died before Henry, her interest was extinguished, and there was nothing for her to pass to Denise. Since Henry would have taken the entire property had he kept his interest, Georgia steps into his shoes, and takes the entire property.

37. Wendy and Stan each have an undivided one-half interest as tenants in common. Where husband and wife are divorced, the tenancy by the entirety automatically ends. In most states, the property is then deemed to be held as tenants in common (i.e., without right of survivorship). Thus when Herb died, his undivided one-half interest as tenant in common passed to Stan.

38. Yes. Although a co-tenant is normally entitled to occupy the premises himself without accounting for their reasonable rental value, the same is not true if he leases the premises to a third person. Once he does this, and collects rents, he is required to share these rents with his co-tenant.

39. No. Each co-tenant is entitled to occupy the entire premises, subject only to the same right on the part of the other tenant. But the occupying tenant has, in general, no duty to account for the value of his exclusive possession. If Carol refused to let Dan live in the property, then Carol would be liable to pay Dan one-half of the rental value of the premises. But as long as Carol holds the premises open to Dan, she does not have to pay Dan any part of the imputed value of her own occupancy.

40. She should bring an action for partition. Any tenant in common or joint tenant (but not a tenant by the entirety) may bring an equitable action for partition. By this means, the court will either divide the property, or order it sold and the proceeds distributed. Normally, each tenant has an absolute right to partition, even over the objection of the other. Here, since the property probably cannot be readily divided, the court will order it sold. Felicia will get half of the sale proceeds.

41. Yes. The issue, of course, is whether the L-T lease must satisfy the *Statute of Frauds.* In most states, the Statute of Frauds does not cover a one-year lease, even if the lease is to commence in the future (and thus even if more than one year is to elapse between the date the lease contract is made, and the date on which the lease itself would terminate). So even though more than one year elapsed between July 1, 1989 (the date the lease was orally agreed to) and July 31, 1990 (the last day of the lease), the contract here did not need to be in writing, according to the majority view.

42. (A) Periodic tenancy. A periodic tenancy is a tenancy which continues from one period to the next automatically, unless either party terminates it at the end of a period by notice. One way a periodic tenancy is created is where the parties make a lease without setting a duration; in this situation, the period stated for rental payments is usually the period for other purposes. Since L and T stated the rent on a monthly basis, the tenancy will be a month-to-month tenancy.

(B) August 30. When a month-to-month tenancy is terminated, the last date of the lease is generally the end of a period, but not less than one period later than the notice date. Thus T was required to give L 30 days notice, and the lease terminated at the end of the period that was in progress on the 30th day (i.e., the end of the calendar month in which the 30th day after notice occurred).

43. Split of authority. Under the so-called "American" view, the landlord has a duty to deliver only "legal" possession, not actual possession. Under the so-called "English" rule, the landlord does have a duty to deliver actual possession. American jurisdictions are approximately split between the two rules. In a court following the "American" view, Tina would not be able to sue for damages (and probably would not be able to cancel the lease either). In a state following the English rule, Tina would be able to recover damages from Leonard, and would probably also be allowed to cancel the lease. (But Tina's damages would probably be limited to the difference between the amount specified in her lease and the fair market value of the space; she would probably not be able to recover profits she would have made during the holdover period, since she is establishing a new venture whose profits are speculative.)

44. Probably not. Older cases hold that the landlord generally has no duty to control the conduct of other tenants. But the modern trend is to impute the acts of other tenants to L where these acts are in violation of the relevant leases, and L could have prevented the conduct by eviction or otherwise. See Rest. 2d, §6.1, Comment d. Especially where, as here, Lester had reason to know before he made the lease with Heavy Metal that a significant chance of inconvenience to others existed, the court will probably hold against Lester.

45. Yes. Here, Tess can only claim to have been *"constructively,"* rather than "actually," evicted. Where the eviction is merely constructive, the tenant is not entitled to terminate the lease, or to stop paying rent, unless she abandons the premises. If she stays on the premises, her only remedy is to sue for damages (i.e., the amount by which the premises are worth less to her because of the breach). So even assuming that Lester had a contractual duty to prevent Heavy Metal from making excessive noise, Tess did not have the right to remain on the premises without paying rent.

46. No. At common law, the landlord was not deemed to have made any implied warranty that the premises were habitable, even in the case of residential property.

47. (A) Yes. Over 40 states now impose some sort of implied warranty of habitability on residential dwellings. In most or all of these, infestation of rats and/or non-working toilets would render the premises uninhabitable, and in nearly all, the tenant would be justified in not paying the rent (or at least in depositing the rent into a court-administered escrow fund pending the repairs).

48. The defense of retaliatory eviction, which will probably succeed. Many courts and statutes (probably a majority) hold that even where the lease term is at an end, the landlord may not refuse to renew the lease when this is done for the purpose of retaliating against a tenant who has asserted his right to habitable premises. The doctrine of retaliatory eviction is most likely to be applied where the landlord attempts to terminate the tenancy in retaliation for complaints made to a housing authority about building code violations. See Rest. 2d, §14.9, recognizing the defense on the facts of this question. See also *Edwards v. Habib*, 397 F.2d 687 (D.C.Cir. 1968). The retaliatory eviction doctrine is more likely to be applied where the landlord is a "professional" (i.e., one in the business of renting residential space) than where the landlord is an "amateur" (e.g., one who rents the second floor of his house). See Rest. 2d, §14.8(2).

49. (A) Yes. n most states, either by statute or case law, the common law rule that required the tenant to keep paying rent for premises that were no longer usable, has been reversed. Thus the tenant normally may terminate the lease and stop paying rent, if the damage to the premises is substantial.

(B) No. In most courts, termination and abatement of rent is the *sole* remedy available to the tenant where the premises are destroyed. See Rest. 2d, §5.4, Comment f.

50. No. By terminating the lease, and re-letting for his own account, Ludlum also effectively terminated his right to keep the security deposit. Therefore, he must return that deposit to Trotta (less his $1,000 damages).

51. Ludlum could have re-let for Trotta's account rather than his own. The event that caused Ludlum to have to return the security deposit was not Trotta's abandonment, but Ludlum's letter of termination and his re-letting of the premises for his own account. Instead, Ludlum should have sent a letter to Trotta stating, "I have no obligation to do so, but I will try to re-let the premises for your account, not mine. I will hold you responsible for any shortfall between what I am able to get on the re-letting and the monthly rent you will owe." By this technique, the Trotta-Ludlum lease would have remained in force, and Ludlum would remain entitled to the security deposit until the expiration of the five years.

52. Split of authority. The modern trend is to entirely prohibit a landlord from using self-help, so that the landlord must use judicial proceedings. But other courts, probably still a slight majority, permit the landlord to use at least some degree of self-help to regain the premises (e.g., changing of locks or peaceable removal of furniture, but no touching of another human being). Lombard's conduct was probably acceptable in states following the latter approach.

53. Yes, probably. The traditional view is that a landlord has *no "duty to mitigate"*, i.e., no duty to try to find a new tenant, and that he may simply let the property stay vacant, and recover rent from the tenant who has abandoned. But a growing minority of courts hold that the landlord does have a duty to mitigate (especially in residential leases).

54. None. Since Tracey transferred to Stuart only the right to occupy the premises for *part* of the time remaining on Tracey's lease with Lillian, the Tracey-Stuart transaction was a *sublease*, not an assignment. A sublease by a tenant does not establish privity of estate between the sublessee (Stuart) and the lessor (Lillian). Consequently, the sublessee here is not liable to the lessor even on covenants running with the land. Thus Stuart is liable only to Tracey, not to Lillian, and Lillian cannot recover anything from Stuart.

55. Yes. Thelma, as the original tenant, had both privity of estate and privity of contract with Lloyd. When Thelma assigned to Tim, her privity of estate ended. But her privity of contract remained. Therefore, she was still liable on the original lease. The fact that Lloyd accepted rent payments directly from Tim, without objection, was not sufficient to release Thelma from her contractual liability (even though this acceptance of rent may have constituted an acceptance by Lloyd of the validity of the assignment from Thelma to Tim).

56. Yes. Since Tim never promised either Thelma or Lloyd that he would perform Thelma's obligations, he had no contractual liability to pay rent. But by taking possession of the premises Tim entered into ***privity of estate*** with Lloyd. He was therefore liable for performances under the lease whose burden runs with the land. Since the promise to pay rent is such a "running with the land" promise, Tim was liable.

57.   No. Since Tim never assumed contractual liability for Thelma's promises (see answer to prior question), his obligation was based only on privity of estate. When Tim assigned to Theo, and left the premises, that privity of estate ended. Therefore, there was no basis on which Lloyd could hold Tim liable for the period in which Theo, not Tim, was the occupant.

58.   Yes. A promise to make repairs runs with the land both as to benefit and burden. Therefore, Tim gets the benefit of that promise, and Leon gets the burden of that promise (even though Leon never promised Lloyd that he would perform Lloyd's repair obligations, and even though Tim had no privity of contract with Thelma).

59.   Yes. Thelma's original promise to Lloyd to pay rent touched and concerned the land, and therefore ran with the land both as to benefit and burden. Tim, by taking the assignment and moving in, became in privity of estate with Lloyd, and therefore had a non-contractual duty to pay rent for the time of his occupancy (see answer to Question 56 above). Since the benefit of Thelma's promise to pay rent ran with the land, just as the burden did, Leon got the benefit of this running. Therefore, he can recover not just against Thelma, but against Tim.

60.   No, probably. Most American courts follow the rule in *Dumpor's Case*, by which a landlord's consent to one assignment destroys an anti-assignment clause completely, even though the initial consent was to a particular assignee. (Lloyd could have avoided this problem by making his consent to the original Thelma-Tim assignment "expressly conditional upon there being no further assignments.") A substantial minority of American courts have rejected the rule in *Dumpor's* case; such courts would allow Lloyd to have Theo evicted here.

61.   No, probably. Most states now hold, either by statute or case law, that even where the lease prohibits assignment or sublease without landlord's consent, the consent ***may not be unreasonably withheld***. This is especially likely to be the case where the anti-assignment provision is a boilerplate clause imposed on a tenant who has little or no bargaining power (as was the case here).

62.   (A) No. At common law, it was not possible for an owner of land (Orin) to convey that land to one person, and to establish by the same deed an easement in a third person. This was the rule against creating an easement in a ***"stranger to the deed."***

(B) Yes, probably. Most modern courts have abandoned the common-law "stranger to the deed" rule, and allow an easement to be created by a deed in a person who is neither the grantor nor the grantee. This is especially likely where the easement relates to a use that existed prior to the conveyance. Since Norman fished in the stream prior to the Orin-to-Alfred conveyance, a modern court would probably uphold the easement in the deed to Alfred. Once that easement is recognized as valid, ***it burdened the land***, and therefore is still in force even though it was omitted from the Alfred-to-Barbara deed.

63.   No, probably. Normally, an easement may be created only by compliance with the Statute of Frauds, which did not happen here. Therefore, the only kind of easement that might have come into existence is an easement "by implication." But an easement by implication will only come into existence if (among other requirements) the owner of a parcel sells part and retains part, or sells pieces simultaneously to multiple grantees (the requirement of *"severance"*). Here, neither Angela nor her predecessors ever owned what is today Blueacre and thus never sold any part of it; consequently, the requirement of "severance" is not satisfied. (Nor does an easement "by necessity" exist, because the two parcels, Auburnacre and Blueacre, were never under common ownership.) So Carter has no easement at all.

64. Yes. Normally an easement must be express and in writing in order to be valid. However, there are several exceptions to this rule. One of these exceptions is applicable here: an *"easement of necessity"* will be found where two parcels were at one time under common ownership, and an easement over one parcel is "strictly necessary" to the enjoyment of the other. Here, these two requirements are satisfied, since Daphne at one time owned both the area on which the golf course is located and the 10 acres on which the mall is now located, and access to the public road in favor of a "land locked" parcel is the most common example of a "strictly necessary" easement. The fact that the proposed use (access for a golf course) did not exist prior to the severance (i.e., prior to Daphne's transfer of the 10 acres to Frederika) is irrelevant in the case of an easement by necessity. (However, this lack of a use prior to the severance would probably be fatal to an "easement by implication.")

65. Yes. Ben has obtained an easement by *prescription*. When one property owner uses another's property for more than the statute of limitations period applicable to adverse possession actions, and does so in an adverse manner (see answer to prior question), an easement by prescription results. The requirement of "adverse" use is satisfied here by the fact that Ben never asked Astrid's permission, and Astrid never expressly consented, merely tolerated the use. The use must be reasonably continuous, which was the case here. The use need not be exclusive, since it is only an easement by prescription, not formal title, that is being granted by adverse possession. This easement by prescription, once it came into existence in 1985, became a burden on Astrid's land, so that Charles is bound even though he was not the owner while the easement was ripening.

66. Yes. The original deed from Dunes to George created an easement appurtenant, since the free-golf rights were clearly intended to benefit a purchaser of the house in his capacity as owner of a house adjacent to the course. Both the benefit and burden of an easement appurtenant pass with transfer of the property. Thus the benefit passed when George sold the dominant parcel to Henry, and the burden passed when Dunes Development sold the servient parcel to Ian. (This rule that both benefit and burden pass with the land is always subject to a contrary agreement; thus if the original deed from Dunes to George had said that George's rights were not transferable to a subsequent purchaser of a house, Henry would be out of luck. But here, no such provision was present in the deed.)

67. No. An easement is like any other estate in land, in the sense that any extinguishment of it must normally satisfy the Statute of Frauds. Therefore, Quince's oral statement, taken by itself, did not extinguish the easement, and that easement passed to Raymond when the dominant tenement (the quarry and manufacturing plant) were sold to Raymond.

68. (A) A License. A license is a right to use the licensor's land that is revocable at the will of the licensor. A license is not required to satisfy the Statute of Frauds, and thus may be created orally. This is what happened here: Abbott did not sign any writing, and Bingham's confirmatory letter did not satisfy the Statute of Frauds as is normally required for an easement (since it was not signed by Abbott, the only person who could create the easement); nonetheless, a license was created.

(B) No. The feature that distinguishes a license from an easement is that the license is *revocable at the will of the licensor*. Therefore, Abbott had the right at any time to revoke the license, regardless of his motive.

69. No. Since Claire never promised to pay for repairs, the only way Bertrand's promise could be binding on Claire is if that promise was a "covenant running with the land." In particular, Claire will only be bound if the burden of the covenant runs with the land. There are several requirements in order for the burden to run. One is that the burden "touch and concern" the land. Here, this requirement is satisfied, since non-payment would result in a lien which would touch and concern the land. But a second requirement in nearly all states is that there must be *"horizontal privity"* between promisor and promisee. In particular, it remains the rule everywhere (except in four states that have modified it by statute) that the *burden of the covenant may not run with the land where the original parties to the covenant were "strangers to title,"* i.e., had no property relationship between them at the time of the promise. Here, this rule is not satisfied: Allison and Bertrand were strangers to title, and thus could not create a covenant the burden of which would run with the land (unless Allison gave Bertrand an easement to come onto Allison's land to make repairs if she did not do so herself; the facts say that this did not happen).

70. No. The vast majority of jurisdictions apply the same horizontal privity requirement for the running of a benefit as they do for the running of a burden, whatever that rule is in the particular jurisdiction. Since the burden of the promise here would not run (see the answer to the prior question) nearly all states would refuse to allow the benefit to run either, so that Doug would not be permitted to recover.

71. Yes. Since Allison's promise not to change fences is a negative promise, and the relief sought by Claire is an injunction, the question is whether we have a valid *"equitable servitude"* (not a "covenant at law," as we had in the two prior questions). An equitable servitude is a promise (usually negative in nature) relating to land, that will be enforced by courts against an assignee of the promisor.

The promise here satisfies the requirements for equitable servitudes, which are less stringent than for covenants at law. The promise must "touch and concern" both the promisor's land and the promisee's land; that requirement is satisfied here, since Allison (the promisor) has bound herself with respect to a structure on her property, and the appearance of Bertrand's property is directly affected by the promise. Horizontal privity (privity between Allison and Bertrand, the original promisor and promisee) is *not* required for an equitable servitude; therefore, the fact that Allison and Bertrand had no pre-existing property relationship and were thus "strangers to title" does not prevent Allison's promise from being an enforceable equitable servitude, even though it prevented Bertrand's counter-promise to pay for repairs from being enforceable at law as to Bertrand's successor (see Question 69). Nor is there any vertical privity requirement for equitable servitudes, so Claire could enforce the servitude against Doug even if she only held, say, a lease on the property owned by Bertrand. Courts will not enforce an equitable servitude against an assignee of the promisor unless the assignee was on actual or constructive notice of the servitude at the time he took possession. But the fact that the Allison-Bertrand agreement was filed in the land records put Doug on such constructive notice.

72.　No.　Harry is trying to enforce an equitable servitude against Isadore's property. But equity will not enforce an agreement against a subsequent purchaser unless the purchaser had *notice* of the restriction at the time he took. This notice can be either actual or "constructive." But the facts make it clear that James did not have actual notice at the time he purchased, and the absence of any valid recordation of the agreement means that James did not have constructive notice either. Therefore, the restriction is not binding against him, and he can build the pool.

73.　Yes, probably.　Most courts will apply the doctrine of *"implied reciprocal servitude"* in this circumstance. This theory holds that if the earlier of two purchasers (here, Kathy) acquires her land in expectation that she will be entitled to the benefit of subsequently created equitable servitudes, there is immediately created an "implied reciprocal servitude" against the developer's remaining land. For this reciprocality doctrine to apply, a general development plan must be in existence at the time of the first sale, a requirement satisfied here. Courts frequently apply the doctrine even where the restrictions are not inserted in the later deed (here, the one to Lewis).

74.　No, probably.　Occasionally, a land-use control is sufficiently draconian that a court will conclude that it amounts to a "taking" for Fourteenth Amendment purposes, for which compensation must be given. But this is extremely rare, especially in the environmental regulation area. A land-use regulation is valid as long as the means chosen "substantially advance" a legitimate state interest, and do not "deny an owner economically viable use of his land." *Nollan v. California Coastal Commission*, 483 U.S. 825 (1987). Here, the town is certainly advancing its legitimate interest in not suffering the noxious odors associated with a dump. Furthermore, Dexter is not being deprived of all economically viable use of his property, but merely the most "valuable" use. So a court is extremely unlikely to hold that the ordinance constitutes a taking. See, e.g., *Goldblatt v. Hempstead*, 369 U.S. 590 (1962) (regulation preventing continued operation of a sand and gravel pit is a valid safety regulation rather than a taking).

75.　No, probably.　The vast majority of states hold that such an "amortization" provision does not violate due process or constitute a taking, as long as the amortization period is sufficiently long for the owner to recover most of his costs and to arrange an alternative use or location. Here, Jones has already had the billboard for 20 years (plus the five-year phase-out), so he has had plenty of time to recoup its costs. Also, he can continue to run his business without the billboard, so the injury to him is not extreme. (But about five states hold, either as a matter of state statutory law or federal constitutional law, that non-conforming uses must be permitted indefinitely, rather than being "amortized.")

76.　No.　Prince probably has standing to assert his claim, since he has been directly affected by the allegedly illegal zoning. However, the Supreme Court has held that a racially discriminatory *purpose*, not merely effect, needs to be shown before an ordinance will be subjected to strict equal protection scrutiny. Without strict scrutiny, the ordinance here merely has to be rationally related to a legitimate state purpose, which is almost certainly the case. So unless Prince is able to bear the burden of showing that the town's ordinance was enacted (or maintained) for racially discriminatory purposes, the fact that the ordinance has a disparate negative effect on minorities is irrelevant to the equal protection claim. See *Arlington Heights v. Metropolitan Housing Development Corp.*, 429 U.S. 252 (1977).

77. (A) A federal Fair Housing Act suit. The Fair Housing title of the 1968 Civil Rights Act makes it unlawful to "make unavailable, or deny, a dwelling to any person because of race, color, religion, sex or national origin."

(B) Yes, probably. If Prince had been able to show that Twin Peaks intentionally tried to limit access by blacks, this would be a clear violation of the Housing Act. The Supreme Court has never decided whether a discriminatory purpose (rather than mere disparate effect) must be shown for a violation of the act, but most lower federal courts have held that the plaintiff in such a suit does *not* need to show that the defendant had a discriminatory intent. Instead, plaintiff merely has to prove that the defendant's land-use controls had a disparate effect on blacks or other racial minorities. The burden then shifts to the defendant town to show that it was acting in pursuit of a legitimate governmental interest, and that there was no less-discriminatory way of achieving that same interest. Probably Twin Peaks could not meet this burden, so probably Prince would win his suit on this theory. See, e.g., *Huntington Branch NAACP v. Town of Huntington*, 844 F.2d 926 (2d Cir. 1988).

78. (A) A *Mount Laurel* "fair share" suit. In Southern Burlington County NAACP v. Township of Mount Laurel, 336 A.2d 713 (N.J. 1975), the New Jersey Supreme Court held that exclusionary zoning practices that fail to serve the general welfare of the region as a whole violate statutory law and the state constitution. The court held that a municipality may not foreclose opportunities for low- and moderate-income housing, and must allow at least that town's "fair share" of the present and prospective regional need for such housing. Since the two-acre minimum prevents even middle-class housing, let alone lower-class housing, from being constructed, the scheme would almost certainly be a Mount Laurel violation.

(B) Grant a re-zoning of the parcel. *Mount Laurel* (and a successor case, *"Mount Laurel II"*) hold that where the trial court concludes that the project sought to be built by the developer is suitable for that specific site, the court may order the municipality to rezone the particular project. This is the so-called "builder's remedy." This would permit Prosser to go ahead with his project immediately, rather than merely watch as the town meets its "fair share" obligation by other means, such as allowing an apartment complex to be built in some other part of town. (But the New Jersey legislature has subsequently put a moratorium on the builder's remedy.)

79. No. The *Statute of Frauds* is applicable in all states to any contract for the sale of land, or for the sale of any interest in land. Therefore, either the contract itself, or a memorandum of it, must be in writing. Furthermore, the contract or memorandum must be signed by the "party to be charged." On the facts here, the party to be charged is Bryant, and the contract is not enforceable against him because of the lack of signature.

80. Yes, probably. Most (but certainly not all) states recognize the *"part performance"* exception to the Statute of Frauds for land-sale contracts. Under this doctrine, a party (either buyer or seller) who has taken action in reliance on the contract may be able to gain enforcement of it at equity. In most states, if the "purchaser" (here, Grandson, in the sense that he was "purchasing" the farm in exchange for his services) takes possession, makes improvements and changes his position in reliance, this will be the sort of part performance required. Courts generally require that the part performance be "unequivocally referable" to the alleged contract, i.e., that the part performance be clearly in response to the oral contract, and not explainable by some other facet of the parties' relationship. This requirement seems to be met here, since Grandson has made permanent improvements to the property, by building the cabin and cutting down the trees, and these improvements are not readily explainable by the mere Grandfather-Grandson relationship.

81. Yes, probably. In a suit for specific performance of a land sale contract, the general rule is that time is ***not of the essence*** unless the contract expressly so provides or the surrounding circumstances indicate that it is. Thus generally, even though the contract specifies a particular closing date, either party may obtain specific performance although he is unable to close on the appointed day (as long as the defaulting party is able to perform within a reasonable time after the scheduled date). Since the surrounding circumstances do not suggest that time was of the essence from Shelby's perspective, and since Bennett was able to perform within what a court would probably find was a reasonable time of the scheduled closing date (10-day delay), the court will probably grant Bennett a decree of specific performance. (But a few courts, most notably the New York courts, hold that where the contract does not explicitly make time of the essence, either party, by a unilateral notification to the other that it will insist upon strict adherence to the contracted-for settlement date, may make time of the essence. In such a state, Shelby would win.)

82. No, probably. The key to solving this question is that where the seller's duty to deliver the deed and the buyer's duty to pay the money are ***concurrent***, then each party must be sure to ***tender his own performance***, in order to be able to hold the other party in default. Therefore, Brady could hold Squires in default (and get a return of his deposit) only if Brady tendered his own performance. Since Brady did not have the certified check with him, or even have the funds readily available, Brady did not tender his own performance. Consequently, Squires' own "breach" is irrelevant, and Squires will probably be allowed to keep the deposit. (The result might have been different if Squires' failure to comply with the contract stemmed from an incurable problem, such as complete lack of title in Squires; it also would have been different if Squires had repudiated the contract ahead of time. But neither of these events happened here.)

83. Yes, probably. The usual rule that each party must tender his own performance in order to hold the other in breach (see prior question) does not generally apply where a defendant's inability to perform is ***incurable***. On these facts, Squires' lack of marketable title (due to the encroachment) was so severe, and so impossible to cure, that Brady's failure to tender his own performance would probably be overlooked by the court, and Brady would get his money back.

84. Deirdre. Common sense" would suggest that the answer should be Nell, since Sherman died while still the technical owner of the real estate, so it would seem fair to give Nell the proceeds from the post-death sale of an asset that was earmarked for her. But instead, courts apply the doctrine of ***"equitable conversion."*** By this doctrine, the signing of the contract is deemed to vest in the purchaser equitable ownership of the land, and the vendor is treated as becoming the equitable owner of the purchase price at that time. As a result of the equitable conversion doctrine, the purchase price goes to the person to whom the personal property was bequeathed, and the person to whom the real estate was devised gets nothing.

85. Yes, probably. Most courts adopt the rule that since the vendee acquires equitable ownership of the land as soon as the contract is signed (see answer to prior question), the risk of loss immediately shifts to him. This is true even though the vendee never takes possession prior to the casualty. There is an exception if the vendor caused the loss negligently, but the facts indicate that this was not the case.

86. No, probably. When the purchaser under an installment sales contract has paid a substantial percentage of the purchase price, most courts try hard to avoid allowing the seller to make the buyer "forfeit" his rights under the contract. The court might order Spence to use statutory foreclosure proceedings before evicting Bagley. In that event, Spence would have to put the property up for sale, and would have to pay to Bagley any amount that the property sold for less the $100,000 that Bagley still owes Spence. (In other words, the installment contract would be treated as if it had been a mortgage.) Or, the court might give Bagley the right to make the payments on which he had been in arrears ($15,000), and then continue with the contract. If the $5,000 monthly payments due from Bagley were no more than a fair rental price for the property, the court would probably not use either of these methods, since the situation would be analogous to a tenant who falls behind in his rent. But here, the monthly payments are much more than fair rental value, so the court would, as stated, take steps to avoid forfeiture.

87. No, probably. Under the doctrine of *merger*, obligations imposed by the contract of sale are generally discharged unless they are repeated in the deed. There is an exception where the contract covenant is "collateral" to (i.e., not directly related to) the promise to convey land. But here, the representation in the contract that there were no easements related directly to the transfer of title, and most courts would hold that that representation was merged out of existence when Boswell accepted the deed that did not repeat the obligation. (But the Uniform Land Transactions Act, if in force in the jurisdiction, would prevent merger from happening.)

88. Stewart. If a deed is validly executed and delivered, title passes immediately to the grantee. Thereafter, return of the deed to the grantor, or even destruction of the deed, has no effect either to cancel the prior delivery or to reconvey the title to the original grantor. The only way the title can get back to the grantor is if a new, formally satisfactory, conveyance takes place. Since Stewart never executed and delivered a valid deed to Fred, title remains in him.

89. No. The covenants of seisin, right to convey and against encumbrances are all "present" covenants. That is, they are breached at the moment the conveyance is made. Therefore, a breach of these can occur even though there was no eviction. Consequently, these were violated by Spitzer at the time of the original conveyance (at least the covenants of seisin and right to convey were breached, though the covenant against encumbrances may not have been). However, Butler's problem is that these covenants are time-barred: the five year statute of limitations on each began to run at the time of conveyance, and the actions became time barred in 1975. The covenants of quiet enjoyment and warranty, by contrast, are "future" covenants. That is, they are breached only when an eviction occurs. The covenants both promise that the grantee's possession will not be challenged. An action on either of these future covenants is not time barred, since they have not yet started to run. However, there is no cause of action on these, either: until Adolf starts eviction proceedings or otherwise actively asserts that his title is superior, Butler has not even been constructively, let alone actually, evicted. Therefore, Butler will have to wait until Adolf actively asserts his title before he may sue Spitzer. To the extent that the uncertainty renders Butler unable to convey a valid title, Butler is simply out of luck.

90.   Yes. The future covenants (warranty, quiet enjoyment and further assurance) are universally held to *run with the land*. Since these covenants are not breached until there is an actual or constructive eviction, they would be rendered almost useless if a subsequent transfer of the land cut them off. Therefore, Capshaw can sue Spitzer even though he had no privity of contract with Spitzer.

91.   (A) Covenant against encumbrances. The covenant against encumbrances is a representation that there are no encumbrances against the property. The encroachment by Jones was such an encumbrance, so this covenant was violated.

(B) No, probably.   Most courts hold that even where the grantee is aware of a defect, his knowledge does not nullify the relevant covenant. See, e.g., *Jones v. Grow Investment & Mortgage Co.*, 358 P.2d 909 (Utah 1961).

92.   (a) Suit for breach of the implied warranty of habitability. Many courts today allow a home purchaser to sue a professional developer for the breach of this warranty, in a way that is analogous to the landlord-tenant implied warranty recognized in nearly all jurisdictions.

(b) Split of authority. The strong emerging trend is to recognize an action for implied warranty of habitability in sales by professional developers of new homes.

93.   No. Courts have nearly always refused to allow an implied warranty claim against one who is not in the business of building or selling homes. The consequence is that the buyer of a used home, such as Carter, cannot sue the person who sold it to him (Benjamin).

94.   Arkin, because he recorded first. Under a race-notice statute, the second grantee (Beacon) will prevail over the earlier grantee (Arkin) only if the second satisfies two requirements: (1) he records before the earlier purchaser records; and (2) he took without notice of the earlier conveyance. Here, Beacon flunked the first of these requirements. (The fact that Beacon had notice at the time he recorded is irrelevant; what counts is whether Beacon had notice at the time he received his deed, which he did not on the facts here.)

95.   Arkin. A race-notice statute requires that the subsequent purchaser record before the earlier purchaser, and take without notice of the earlier conveyance. (See answer to prior question.) Here, Beacon failed the second of these requirements, since he knew of the conveyance to Arkin at the time he, Beacon, took. Therefore, Beacon's having recorded first does not save him. (The fact that Oliver lied about the way the recording statute works should not insulate Beacon from his own failure to comply with the statute.)

96.   Beacon. Under a "pure notice" statute, the sole issue is whether the subsequent grantee had actual or constructive notice of the prior grant at the time the subsequent grantee took. At the time Beacon took in 1982, he had neither actual nor constructive notice of the grant to Arkin (the facts tell you he did not have actual notice, and the lack of recordation means that he did not have constructive notice). Therefore, the fact that Arkin later recorded, and that Beacon never recorded, is irrelevant.

97.   Cabbott, probably. Ordinarily, the second grantee under a race-notice statute must fulfill two requirements to take priority over a prior grantee: (1) he must record before the earlier grantee records; and (2) he must have taken without notice of the earlier grant. Here, Cabbott has not fulfilled the first of these requirements, since Arias recorded before he (Cabbott) did. However, most statutes requiring a race require it only where the contest is *between grantees* *from a common grantor*. Since Arias and Cabbott are claiming under different grantors, Cabbott's failure to record before Arias probably will not be fatal. Allowing Cabbott to win fulfills the goal of encouraging reliance on the public record: at the time Cabbott took from Beck, paying full value, Cabbott had no practical way to know of the earlier conveyance to Arias, so there is a strong interest in protecting him even though he was negligent by waiting to record. (Obviously, Cabbott could have protected himself fully by recording immediately, so that he would have won the race-to-record with Arias, even though he never knew of Arias' existence.) So the court will probably find for Cabbott.

98.   Abrams. Boone appears to have fulfilled the two requirements for taking priority over a prior grantee under a race-notice statute: he took without notice of the prior grant, and he recorded before the prior grantee recorded. However, in the vast majority of states, a grantee receives the benefit of the recording act (i.e., he gets to take priority over an earlier unrecorded conveyance) only if he *gives value* for his interest. Here, Boone did not give value, but rather received a gift. Therefore, he gets no benefit from the recording act, and the usual principle of "first in time, first in right" applies. This is true even though Abrams similarly received a gift and thus did not give value.

99.   Chavez.   At first, Chavez appears to violate one of the two requirements for taking ahead of a prior grantee: Chavez failed to win the "race" to record before Bishop did. But in reality, Bishop will be deemed never to have recorded at all. A grantee records only when he adequately records. The mere fact that a deed is recorded somewhere in the public records does not mean that the recording is "adequate" — the document must be recorded in such a way that a reasonable searcher would find it. Here, only if a searcher would have found the document using the grantor and grantee indexes would Bishop's deed be adequately recorded.

A searcher in Chavez's position would have started with a "root" of Orcini (or one of Orcini's predecessors in recorded title); Chevez would then never have found the Orcini-to-Arlen deed because that deed was never recorded. Thus he would not have known to look in the grantor index to find that Arlen later conveyed to Bishop, and he consequently would never have found the deed to Bishop. In other words, Bishop would be deemed to have adequately recorded only if Bishop made sure that not only was his own deed recorded, but also *the deed by which his grantor took* (the Orcini-to-Arlen deed), and so forth back in the chain at least 50 or 60 years. Since Bishop is in a position equivalent to not having recorded at all, Chavez is the first to "adequately" record, and he is thus the first grantee; it is Bishop who is the second grantee, and he loses because he did not adequately record first. See *Losey v. Simpson*, 11 N.J.Eq. 246 (1856), holding for the party in Chavez's position on similar facts.

100. Burrows.   Dempsey's fatal mistake was that although he made sure that his own conveyance (Craft-to-Dempsey) was promptly recorded, he did not make sure that his whole chain of title was recorded. That is, he failed to make sure that the O'Neill-to-Craft deed was recorded. The entire line running from O'Neill through Arens through Burrows was then recorded (in 1985) at a time when Dempsey had still not "adequately" recorded. Therefore, Dempsey, as the second grantee, has not fulfilled one of the two requirements for a subsequent grantee to take under a race-notice statute: he did not win the race to record, because one wins that race only by "adequately" recording, which Dempsey has never done. So just as Question 99 illustrates that the earlier grantee may lose the protection of the recording acts by not seeing to it that his entire chain of title is recorded, so the subsequent grantee may lose the protection of the recording acts by failing to see to it that *his* entire chain of title is recorded.

101. Andrews. Under normal principles, Burns would get the benefit of the recording act because he took without actual or record notice of the prior grant (the unrecorded deed to Andrews). But Burns loses because of the doctrine of *"inquiry"* notice. Even if the subsequent purchaser has neither record nor actual notice of a prior unrecorded conveyance, he will be found to have been on inquiry notice of it if at the time he took he was in possession of facts which would have led a reasonable person in his position to make an investigation, which would in turn have advised him of the existence of the prior unrecorded right.

Most courts hold that the subsequent grantee has a duty to *view the property*, and if it is in possession of someone other than the record owner, he must inquire as to the source of the latter's rights in the property. Here, the facts tell us that if Burns had viewed the property, he would have discovered Andrews, and that if he had discovered Andrews, Andrews would have told him that he, Andrews, had an unrecorded deed. Therefore, Burns is charged with inquiry notice of Andrews' deed, and Burns is thus a grantee "with knowledge" of that deed (thereby removing him from the protection of the notice statute).

102. Crystal. Brown, at the time he took, met the two requirements for a subsequent grantee to take priority in a race-notice jurisdiction: he won the race to record ahead of Albright, and he took without notice of Albright's deed. That being the case, not only Brown's own "ownership," but his ability to *resell* his property, is protected by courts construing the recording acts. That is, once an interest is purged by its acquisition by one without notice of the prior unrecorded document, the interest remains "clean" when resold, *even if the new purchaser has actual or record notice.*

103. Yes, probably. Title Co. will probably argue that it is exculpated by the clause in the title policy excluding facts which an accurate survey of the property would disclose. But even if Title Co. persuades the court that this exclusion covers the garage, Title Co. will probably be liable for *negligence* for not having called Barnes' attention to the encroachment. See, e.g., *Shotwell v. Transamerica Title Ins. Co.*, 558 P.2d 1359 (Ct.App.Wash. 1976), holding that the title insurer could be liable for negligence in the search even as to an item (an easement) which was excluded from coverage by the policy.

104. No, probably. Plotnick had an absolute right to *"lateral support."* However, this absolute right exists only with respect to land in its *natural state*. If the owner has constructed a building, and the soil under the building subsides in part due to the adjacent owner's acts, but also in part because of the weight of the building itself, the adjacent owner is not liable in the absence of negligence. Therefore, since Duffy's acts would not have caused Plotnick's land to cave in had the land been vacant, and Duffy behaved non-negligently, Duffy does not have to pay for damage accruing to Plotnick's structure.

105. Yes, probably. In a common-law jurisdiction, each riparian owner has an absolute right to all or any part of the water for "natural" uses (regardless of the effect on downstream owners), but an owner may take for *"artificial"* uses only after all natural uses have been satisfied, and then only in parity with other artificial users. Irrigation of small areas of farmland is generally considered "natural," whereas use for hydro-electric power is almost certainly artificial. Therefore, Phillips has priority over Decker; Phillips can recover damages, obtain an injunction, or both. (The fact that Phillips was using the water first does not matter to the result.)

106. Yes, probably. Courts following the common-law approach do not grant any advantage based on priority of use. So the fact that a riparian owner has used stream water for a certain purpose for many years does not give him any greater rights than if he were making this use for the first time. Thus the problem is solved the way it is in the prior answer (with Phillips winning because his use is "natural" and Decker's is "artificial").

107. No, probably. The 17 arid states that have abolished the common-law riparian rights doctrine have generally adopted the ***"prior appropriation"*** doctrine instead. In some of these states, a water user must apply for a permit in order to get priority; in these states, the issue would be decided based on who got a permit first (which the facts don't disclose). But in the remaining "prior appropriation" states, the right to appropriate is absolute (i.e., no permit is required) and the priority of the right dates from the time the appropriator began construction of the necessary works to take the water. In such a state, Decker, as the first user, would prevail.

108. No. Generally, courts hold that an owner may build as tall as he wants, and as close to his property line as he wants, so long as he does not violate zoning rules. In particular, courts almost never recognize an owner's right to sunlight or view. For instance, courts almost never recognize that a landowner has acquired an easement of "light and air" by implication or even by necessity. So Pringle is almost certainly out of luck. (His remedy was to build his own building far enough in from his property line that even a neighboring building later built right up to that property line would not block his own light completely.)

MULTIPLE-CHOICE QUESTIONS

Here are 26 multiple-choice questions, in a Multistate-Bar-Exam style. These questions are taken from *"The Finz Multistate Method"*, a compendium of 1100 questions in the Multistate subjects (*Contracts*, *Torts*, *Property*, *Evidence*, *Criminal Law* and *Constitutional Law*) written by Professor Steven Finz of National University School of Law, San Diego, CA, and published by us.

Questions 1-2 are based on the following fact situation.

Givers executed a deed to his realty known as Givacre, which contained the following clause:

> "To Senior Center, for so long as the realty shall be used as a home for the elderly, but if racial discrimination is practiced in the admission of residents to said home, to Senior Life for so long as the realty shall be sued as a home for the elderly."

Senior Center and Senior Life were both charitable institutions devoted to the needs of indigent elderly persons.

1. On the day after the deed was executed, Givers' interest in Givacre is best described as

   (A) a valid reversion.
   (B) a valid possibility of reverter.
   (C) a valid right of re-entry.
   (D) void under the Rule Against Perpetuities.

2. On the day after the deed was executed, Senior Life's interest in Givacre is best described as a

   (A) valid contingent remainder.
   (B) valid executory interest.
   (C) void contingent remainder.
   (D) void executory interest.

Questions 3-4 are based on the following fact situation.

On March 1, Marcel conveyed a tract of realty to her daughters Andrea and Bessie as joint tenants. On April 1, Marcel purported to sell the same tract of realty to Parton by general warranty deed. Parton paid cash for the property, and was unaware of the prior conveyance to Marcel's daughters. Andrea and Bessie recorded their deed on April 3. Parton recorded his deed on April 5. Andrea died on April 7.

3. Assume for the purpose of this question only that the jurisdiction has ONE of the following statutes:

    I. "No conveyance of real property is effective against a subsequent purchaser for value and without notice unless the same be recorded."

    II. "Every conveyance of real estate is void as against any subsequent purchaser in good faith and for value whose conveyance is first duly recorded."

    Is Bessie's right superior to Parton's on April 8?

    (A) Yes, only if the jurisdiction has Statute I.
    (B) Yes, only if the jurisdiction has Statute II.
    (C) Yes, if the jurisdiction has Statute I or Statute II.
    (D) No.

4. Assume for the purpose of this question only that the jurisdiction has a statute which provides, "In determining the priority of conflicting interests in land, the first such interest to have been recorded shall have priority." Who has priority on April 8?

    (A) Bessie, because the conveyance to Andrea and Bessie was recorded before the conveyance to Parton was recorded.
    (B) Bessie, because the realty was conveyed to Andrea and Bessie before the conveyance to Parton was recorded.
    (C) Parton, because Bessie's interest was recorded.
    (D) Parton, because Marcel conveyed to him by general warranty deed.

5. After working twenty years for the People's Trust Company, Singer was promoted from assistant manager of the Twin Oaks branch located in another state. When he learned that Bryant was moving to Twin Oaks to replace him as assistant manager, he offered to sell Bryant his home in Twin Oaks for $60,000. After inspecting the premises, Bryant accepted the offer. They entered into a written contract of sale calling for closing of title six weeks after the signing of the contract. Because their employer was eager to have them both start at their new positions as soon as possible, the contract contained a clause permitting Bryant to move into the house immediately. Bryant did so a few days after signing the contract of sale. Singer kept the fire insurance policy on the house in effect, planning to cancel it upon conveying title to Bryant. In addition, Bryant purchased a policy of fire insurance on the house immediately after contracting for purchase of the house. Two weeks after Bryant moved in, a fire of unknown origin partially destroyed a portion of the roof, the entire kitchen, and parts of the exterior of the house. Bryant immediately notified Singer that he was unwilling to complete the transaction at the price originally agreed upon, but

that he would be willing to renegotiate to determine a new price based on the diminished value of the real estate as the result of the fire.

If Singer sues for damages based upon Bryant's anticipatory repudiation of the contract of sale, the court should find for

(A) Singer, since the risk of loss passed to Bryant when he took possession of the premises pursuant to the contract.
(B) Singer, since Bryant purchased a policy of fire insurance covering the premises prior to the contract.
(C) Bryant, since Singer had a policy of insurance insuring him against fire damage to the house.
(D) Bryant, since the risk of loss never passed to Bryant.

Questions 6-8 are based on the following fact situation.

Several years ago, the Johnson Chemical Company developed a plan to use underground pipes for the purpose of transporting non-poisonous chemical wastes to a waste storage center located several miles away from its plant. At that time, it began negotiating for the right to lay an underground pipeline for that purpose across several tracts of realty. In return for a cash payment, the owner of Westacre executed a right-of-way deed for the installation and maintenance of the pipeline across his land. The right-of-way deed to Johnson Chemical Company was properly recorded. Westacre passed through several intermediate conveyances until it was conveyed to Sofield about fifteen years after the recording of the right-of-way deed. All of the intermediate deeds were recorded, but none mentioned the right-of-way.

Two years later, Sofield agreed to sell Westacre to Belden, by a written contract in which, among other things, Sofield agreed to furnish Belden with an abstract company, to prepare the abstract. Titleco prepared an abstract and delivered it to Sofield. The abstract omitted any mention of the right-of-way deed. Sofield delivered the abstract of title to Belden. After examining the abstract, Beldon paid the full purchase price to Sofield who conveyed Westacre to Belden by a deed which included covenants of general warranty and against encumbrances. At the time of closing, Sofield, Belden, and Titleco were all unaware of the existence of the right-of-way deed. After possessing Westacre for nearly a year, Belden was notified by the Johnson Chemical Company that it planned to begin installation of an underground pipeline on its right-of-way across Westacre.

6. Assume for the purpose of this question only that Belden subsequently asserted a claim against Titleco for damages which Belden sustained as a result of the existence of the right-of-way. The court should find for

(A) Titleco, because it was unaware of the existence of the right-of-way deed.
(B) Titleco, because the right-of-way deed was outside the chain of title.
(C) Belden, because Belden was a third party beneficiary of the contract between Sofield and Titleco.

(D) Belden, because the deed executed by Sofield contained a covenant against encumbrances.

7. If Belden sues Sofield because of the presence of the right-of-way, the most likely result will be a decision for

(A) Sofield, because Belden relied on the abstract of title prepared by Titleco in purchasing Westacre.

(B) Sofield, because Sofield was without knowledge of any defects in the title to Westacre.

(C) Belden, because the covenants in Sofield's deed to Belden were breached.

(D) Belden, because Sofield negligently misrepresented the condition of title to Westacre.

8. Assume for the purpose of this question only that Belden sued for an injunction prohibiting the installation of the underground pipeline across Westacre. Which one of the following additional facts or inferences, if it was the only one true, which would be most likely to lead the court to issue the injunction?

(A) The Johnson Chemical Company sold its entire business to another company which was planning to continue operating the business exactly as Johnson had operated it, and it was the new company which was attempting to install the underground pipeline.

(B) The Johnson Chemical Company's operation had changed since the conveyance of the right-of-way, and it was now planning to use the pipeline for the transportation of poisonous wastes.

(C) No use of the right-of-way has been made since the conveyance eighteen years ago, and the law of the jurisdiction sets a ten year period for acquiring title by adverse possession or acquiring an easement by prescription.

(D) In purchasing Westacre Belden detrimentally relied on the absence of any visible encumbrances, and the installation of an underground pipeline will result in substantial reduction in the value of the realty.

9. Lance Industries completed construction of a new office building and rented the entire ground floor to Tollup, an attorney, under a three year lease which fixed rent at six hundred dollars per month. Lance was unable to obtain a tenant to rent any other space in the building. Six months later, Tollup vacated the premises. In a claim by Lance against Tollup for rent for the balance of the term, which one of the following additional facts if it were the only one true, would be most likely to result in a judgment for Tollup?

(A) The day after Tollup vacated, Lance rented the ground floor to another attorney on a month-to-month basis at a rent of five hundred dollars per month.

(B) The day after Tollup vacated, Lance began using the ground floor as a management office for the building.

(C) The reason Tollup vacated was that the building was located in a part of town not easily accessible by public transportation, and as a result many of Tollup's client refused to travel to see him there.

(D) The reason Tollup vacated was that he had been disbarred and was disqualified from the practice of law.

10. Lardner rented a warehouse to Torrelson pursuant to a lease which fixed the rent at five hundred dollars payable at the beginning of each month. The lease contained a provision stating that in the event Torrelson failed to pay rent as agreed, Lardner had the right to terminate the tenancy and re-enter the premises. After Torrelson missed two rent payments, Lardner threatened to institute an eviction proceeding unless the unpaid rent was paid immediately. The following day, Torrelson moved out, sending Lardner a check for one thousand dollars in payment of rent already owing. Also enclosed was a letter which stated that it was Torrelson's intention to surrender the premises immediately, and an additional check for five hundred dollars in payment of the following month's rent. Lardner made no attempt to re-rent the warehouse, and it remained vacant for the balance of the term of Torrelson's lease. Upon its expiration, Lardner asserted a claim against Torrelson for unpaid rent from the date Torrelson vacated until the end of the lease term.

In deciding Lardner's claim against Torrelson, the court should find for

(A) Lardner, since Torrelson failed to pay the rent as agreed.
(B) Lardner, since the lease reserved a right of re-entry.
(C) Torrelson, since the lease reserved Lardner's right of re-entry.
(D) Torrelson, since, in effect, he gave Lardner a month's notice of his intention to vacate.

11. The City of Hampshire owned land known as Hampshire Heights which was located outside the city limits, east of the city itself. Because the Hampshire River ran along the western edge of Hampshire Heights, the City of Hampshire built a bridge across the river more than fifty years ago. The eastern part of Hampshire Heights had once been used as a storage yard for city maintenance equipment, and was surrounded by an eight foot chain link fence. The part of Hampshire Heights between the fenced yard and the bridge had been used primarily as a dirt road connecting the bridge to the storage yard.

Due to periodic flooding of the Hampshire River, the City of Hampshire stopped using the Hampshire Heights storage yard and bridge thirty years ago. At that time, Adpo built a wooden shack on that portion of Hampshire Heights which had formerly been used as a dirt road between the storage yard and the bridge. Since then, Adpo has been living in the shack, and has been raising donkeys on the land formerly used as a dirt road. In addition, he planted a vegetable garden which produced food for himself and his donkeys.

Earlier this year, the City of Hampshire decided to begin using the Hampshire Heights storage yard again, and demanded that Adpo remove himself and his possessions. Adpo refused, asserting that by adverse possession he had become the owner of the land which he occupied. A statute in the jurisdiction conditions ownership by adverse possession on twenty years' continuous, hostile, open and notorious possession.

If the City of Hampshire institutes a proceeding to eject Adpo from Hampshire Heights, the outcome is most likely to turn on whether

(A) the City of Hampshire had knowledge that Adpo was in possession of part of Hampshire Heights.
(B) the jurisdiction permits the acquisition of city property by adverse possession.
(C) Adpo paid taxes on the land which he occupied.
(D) Adpo occupied Hampshire Heights under color of title.

12. Soon after Harold and Wilhemina married, they became interested in the purchase of a home with a price of $75,000. Because neither of them had been employed for very long, they were unable to find a bank to lend them money for the purchase. The seller indicated that he would be willing to accept a note for part of the purchase price if Harold and Wilhemina could obtain an acceptable co-signor.

Wilhemina's mother Marion said that she would give them the money for the down payment and co-sign the note if Wilhemina and Harold promised to make all payments on the note as they came due, and if the three of them took title to the property as joint tenants. All agreed. On the day title closed, Marion paid $25,000 cash to the seller, and she, Harold, and Wilhemina all signed a note promising to pay the balance, secured by a mortgage on the realty which they all executed. The seller executed a deed conveying the realty to Harold, Wilhemina, and Marion as joint tenants.

Harold and Wilhemina moved into the house, but Marion never did. The following year Marion died, leaving a will purporting to devise her interest in the realty to her husband Allan. The year after that, Wilhemina and Harold were divorced. Wilhemina subsequently executed a deed purporting to convey her interest in the realty to Bernard. Harold subsequently executed a deed purporting to convey his interest in the realty to Charles.

Which of the following best describes the interests of Allan, Bernard, and Charles in the realty?

(A) Allan, Bernard, and Charles are tenants in common, each holding a one-third interest.
(B) Bernard and Charles are tenants in common, each holding a one-half interest.
(C) Bernard and Charles are joint tenants as to a two-thirds interest, and tenants in common as to a one-third interest.
(D) Allan, Bernard and Charles are joint tenants, each holding a one-third interest.

13. In 1970, Altman moved onto Odette's realty and constructed a dwelling without Odette's permission. Since then, she has lived there continuously, openly, and notoriously. In 1977, Odette died, leaving the realty to his 2-year-old son Stephen. At that time Grayson was appointed as Stephen's legal guardian. In 1980, Grayson became aware that Altman was in possession of the realty which Stephen had inherited from Odette. In 1986, after Altman had been in possession of the realty for 16 years, Grayson sued on Stephen's behalf to eject Altman. In her defense, Altman asserted that she had become the owner of the realty by adverse possession.

Has Altman become the owner of the realty by adverse possession?

(A) No, because the statutory period will not begin to run against Stephen until he achieves majority at the age of 18 years.

(B) No, because the statutory period began to run against Stephen when he inherited the realty in 1977.

(C) No, because the statutory period began to run against Stephen when Grayson became aware that Altman was in possession of the realty in 1980.

(D) Yes.

14. Larrick executed a document purporting to lease a parcel of real estate to Teeter for fifty years at an annual rent of $1,000. Twenty years before the scheduled expiration of the lease, the entire parcel was taken by the state for the construction of a reservoir. At a condemnation proceeding, the trier of the facts found that the balance of Teeter's leasehold was valued at $30,000. Of the total condemnation award, Teeter should receive

(A) $30,000, but Teeter will be required to pay Larrick a sum equivalent to the rent for the balance of the lease term.

(B) nothing, because Teeter's interest violates the Rule Against Perpetuities.

(C) $30,000, and Teeter will have no further obligation to Larrick.

(D) $30,000 minus a sum equivalent to the rent for the balance of the lease term, and Teeter will have no further obligation to Larrick.

Questions 15-16 are based on the following fact situation.

Upton is the owner of a hillside parcel of realty known as Slopeacre, on which he grows apples for sale to a company which makes juice from them. For several years, Upton has been irrigating his apple trees with water from a stream which flows across Slopeacre. After flowing across Slopeacre, the stream flows through Flatacre, a parcel of realty located in the valley below Slopeacre. Downey, who owns Flatacre, lives there with his family. Downey's family uses water from the stream for household purposes. This year, Upton informed Downey that he was planning to build a small dam across the stream so that he would be able to pump water out of it more easily for irrigating his apple trees. Downey immediately instituted a proceeding to prevent Upton from constructing the dam.

The jurisdiction determines water rights by applying the common law.

15. If it were the only one true, which of the following additional facts or inferences would be most likely to cause a court to grant the relief requested by Downey?

    (A) Construction of a dam will increase Upton's consumption of water from the stream.
    (B) Construction of a dam will change the natural flow of the stream.
    (C) Construction of a dam will cause Upton to consume more water from the stream than is reasonably necessary for the enjoyment of Slopeacre.
    (D) Upton can continue to pump water from the stream without constructing a dam.

16. Assume for the purpose of this question only that because of a drought there is enough water in the stream to satisfy the needs of either Flatacre or Slopeacre, but not both, and that there are no other riparian owners. Who is entitled to use the water?

    (A) Upton, because he is the upstream owner.
    (B) Upton, because he needs the water for agricultural use.
    (C) Downey, because he needs the water for household use.
    (D) Downey, because he is the downstream owner.

17. When Fletcher died he left his farm to his son Sam for life with remainder to Unity Church. Because Fletcher had been a farmer, Sam tried farming the land for a while, but found the work unpleasant. Although gravel had never before been mined or removed from the land, Sam learned that he could derive a substantial income by doing so. He therefore dug a deep and extensive pit on the land from which he began removing gravel for sale to builders and other commercial purchasers.

    If Unity Church asserts a claim against Sam because of his removal of gravel the court should

    (A) grant Unity Church a proportionate share of any profits derived from the sale of gravel removed from the land.
    (B) issue an injunction against further removal of gravel and order Sam to account to Unity Church for profits already derived from the sale of gravel removed from the land.
    (C) deny relief to Unity Church, because no right of action will accrue until Unity Church's interest becomes possessory at the termination of Sam's estate.
    (D) deny relief to Unity Church, because a life tenant is entitled to remove minerals from an open pit.

18. Oscar, the owner of a summer beach cabin, conveyed it to his daughter Debra as a gift for her sixteenth birthday. Two years later, on her eighteenth birthday, Debra went to the cabin for the first time and found Adamo in possession of it. When she asked what he was doing there, Adamo said, "Anyone who lives around here can tell you that I've been coming here every summer." In fact, Adamo had occupied the beach cabin every summer for the past ten years, but had not occupied the cabin during other seasons.

Debra instituted a proceeding to evict Adamo. In defense, Adamo claimed that he had acquired title to the cabin by adverse possession. Statutes in the jurisdiction fix the period for acquiring title to realty by adverse possession at 10 years and the age of majority at 18 years.

Has Adamo acquired title by adverse possession.

(A) No, because computation of the period of adverse possession begins anew each time there is a change in ownership of the realty.

(B) No, because for the past two years the owner of the cabin was under a legal disability.

(C) Yes, if occupancy only during the summer was consistent with the appropriate use of the cabin.

(D) Yes, if Adamo had Oscar's permission to occupy the cabin during the summers.

19. Lenox was the owner of a commercial building which he leased to Ashdown for use as a retail shoe store for a period of five years. In the lease, Ashdown covenanted not to assign the premises without Lenox's written consent. A clause of the lease reserved Lenox's right to terminate the lease in the event of a breach of this covenant. Two years after Ashdown began occupancy, he sold the business to Boyer, his store manager. After obtaining Lenox's written consent, Ashdown assigned the balance of the lease to Boyer. Boyer operated the shoe store for several months and then sold it to Cole. As part of the sale, Boyer executed a document purporting to transfer to Cole all remaining rights under the lease. Boyer did not obtain Lenox's permission for this transfer. When Lenox learned of this transfer to Cole, he instituted a proceeding in which he sought Cole's eviction on the ground that the covenant not to assign had been violated.

Which of the following best states how the court will probably rule in Lenox's action?

(A) The covenant against assignment is void as a restraint against alienation.

(B) Lenox's only remedy is an action against Boyer for damages resulting from breach of the covenant.

(C) Lenox waived his rights under the covenant by consenting to the assignment by Ashdown to Boyerl.

(D) The transfer by Boyer to Cole was not an assignment but a sublease.

Questions 20-21 are based on the following fact situation.

Owsley was the owner of a large tract of realty with its southernmost boundary fronting on a public road. Owsley divided the tract into two parcels, one to the north of the other. Owsley named the southernmost parcel, which fronted on the public road, Southacre. He named the northernmost parcel Northacre, and sold it to Archer. Northacre did not have road frontage, and was accessible only by a visible dirt road which crossed Southacre. The deed by which Owsley conveyed Northacre to Archer contained language granting a right-of-way easement over the dirt road. Several years after purchasing Northacre, Archer purchased Southacre from Owsley. Archer never occupied Northacre and never used the dirt road which crossed Southacre.

20. Assume for the purposes of this question only that Archer subsequently sold Northacre to Barnhart by a deed which made no mention of a right-of-way easement across Southacre. If Barnhart claims that he received a right-of-way easement over Southacre, which of the following would be Barnhart's best argument in support of that claim?

    (A) The visible dirt road across Southacre which provided access to Northacre was a quasi-easement.
    (B) Since there was no other access to Northacre, Barnhart received an easement by implied reservation.
    (C) Since there was no other access to Northacre, Barnhart received an easement by necessity.
    (D) The grant of a right-of-way easement across Southacre contained in the deed by which Owsley conveyed Northacre to Archer benefits all subsequent purchasers of Northacre.

21. Assume for the purpose of this question only that Coates subsequently contracted to purchase Southacre from Archer, that Coates inspected Southacre and saw the dirt road which crossed it prior to contracting, and that the purchase contract made no mention of an easement or of the quality of title to be conveyed. Assume further that prior to closing of title, Coates refused to go through with the transaction on the ground that the existence of an easement across Southacre made Archer's title unmarketable. If Archer asserts a claim against Coates for breach of contract, which of the following would be Archer's most effective argument in support of his claim?

    (A) A contract to purchase real property merges with the deed by which the title is conveyed.
    (B) Coates had notice of the easement at the time he entered into the contract to purchase Southacre.
    (C) The existence of an easement does not make title unmarketable.
    (D) The purchase contract did not specify the quality of title to be conveyed.

Questions 22-24 are based on the following fact situation.

Zoning laws in Green City provided that all land on the north side of Main Street was restricted to residential use, and that commercial use was permitted on all land on the south side of Main Street. The zoning laws also provided that up two horses could be kept on any land zoned for residential use, but that no business could be operated on land zoned for residential use. Although all the other realty on the south side of Main Street was being put to commercial use, Homer owned and resided in a one story house located on the south side of Main Street.

Green Hills was a housing development located on the north side of Main Street. All deeds to realty in Green Hills contained language prohibiting the keeping of horses anywhere within the subdivision. The subdivision plan which had been filed when Green Hills was created provided that persons occupying realty in Green Hills were permitted to operate small businesses in their homes so long as such operation did not interfere with or annoy other residents in the subdivision.

22. Assume for the purposes of this question only that Typer operated a typing service from an office in her home in Green Hills, and that Foley entered into a contract to buy Typer's typing service and home. After entering into the contract of sale, however, Foley learned of the zoning law which prohibited the operation of any business in a residential zone. He immediately informed Typer that he would not go through with the purchase of Typer's home because of the zoning violation. If Typer asserts a claim against Foley for breach of contract, the court should find for

    (A) Foley, because the purchaser of realty cannot be forced to buy a potential litigation.
    (B) Foley, but only if he could not have discovered the zoning violation by reasonable inquiry prior to entering into the contract of sale.
    (C) Typer, because the zoning law which prohibited the operation of Typer's business existed before the contract of sale was formed.
    (D) Typer, because her business was permitted by provisions of the Green Hills subdivision plan.

23. Assume for the purpose of this question only that Graves purchased the land owned by Homer, tore down the existing house, and began construction of a three story office building. Kaham, who operated a business known as a water slide on the adjacent realty, objected on the ground that the building which Graves was constructing would block off Kaham's air and light, thus diminishing the value of his realty. If Kaham commences an appropriate proceeding against Graves seeking an order which would prohibit construction of the building, the court should find for

    (A) Graves if the construction of a three story office building is permitted by the zoning law.
    (B) Graves because commercial use of the realty is the highest and best use.
    (C) Kaham, because previous use by Homer created an implied easement for air, light, and view.
    (D) Kaham, if residential use by Homer was a continuing non-conforming use.

24. Assume for the purpose of this question only that Equis, a resident of Green Hills, began keeping horses in his yard. If his neighbor, Ralph, commences a proceeding in which he seeks an order preventing Equis from keeping horses, the court should find for

    (A) Equis because the zoning law permits the keeping of horses.

(B) Equis only if keeping horses is part of ordinary residential use.

(C) Ralph because of the language in Equis's deed which prohibits the keeping of horses.

(D) Ralph only if keeping horses is a nuisance.

Questions 25-26 are based on the following fact situation.

Olsen conveyed a parcel of realty "to Geller so long as liquor is not sold on the premises, but if liquor is sold on the premises, to the Foundation for Hereditary Diseases." Two years later, Geller began selling liquor on the premises.

25. Which of the following best describes Geller's interest in the realty on the day before he began selling liquor on the premises?

(A) void, since the interest of the Foundation for Hereditary Diseases could have vested more than 21 years after the death of all persons who were in being at the time of the conveyance.

(B) fee simple absolute.

(C) fee simple determinable on special limitation, since Geller's interest will terminate if liquor is ever sold on the premises.

(D) fee simple subject to a condition subsequent, which will ripen into a fee simple absolute if liquor is not sold during a period measured by a life or lives in being plus twenty-one years.

26. Which of the following best describes the interest of the Foundation for Hereditary Diseases in the realty on the day after Geller began selling liquor on the premises?

(A) fee simple absolute if the Foundation for Hereditary Diseases is a charity.

(B) right of re-entry.

(C) no interest, since at the time of the conveyance it was possible that the interest which the deed purported to grant to the Foundation for Hereditary Diseases would not vest within a period measured by a life or lives in being plus twenty-one years.

(D) shifting executory interest which will not become possessory until the Foundation for Hereditary Diseases takes some step to exercise its right.

ANSWERS TO MULTIPLE-CHOICE QUESTIONS

1. **B**   A reversion is a future interest of the grantor which will automatically follow a prior estate which will inevitably terminate (e.g., a life estate; a leasehold). A possibility of reverter is a future interest of the grantor which will automatically follow a prior estate which will not inevitably terminate (e.g., fee simple determinable). A right of re-entry is a future interest of the grantor which does not revert automatically, but which requires some act by the grantor in order for him/her to re-acquire a possessory right, and which follows an estate which will not inevitably terminate. Since the property was conveyed only for so long as it is used as a home for the elderly, it will automatically revert to the grantor if that use is ever discontinued. It is, thus, either a reversion or a possibility of reverter. Since it is not certain that it ever will cease to be used as a home for the elderly, however, the prior estate is not one which will inevitably terminate. For this reason, the grantor's interest is a possibility of reverter. **B** is, therefore, correct, and **A** is, therefore, incorrect. **C** is incorrect because if the property ever ceases to be used as a home for the elderly, no act of the grantor is necessary to make his interest possessory. **D** is incorrect because the Rule against Perpetuities does not apply to a grantor's interest.

2. **B**   A remainder is a future interest in a grantee which will automatically become possessory following a prior estate which will terminate inevitably (e.g., a life estate). An executory interest is a future interest in a grantee which will not automatically become possessory and which follows a prior estate which will not terminate inevitably. Since the interest of Senior Life will only become possessory if racial discrimination is practiced by Senior Center, and since this may never happen, the interest of Senior Life is best classified as a executory interest. **A** and **C** are, therefore, incorrect. Under the Rule Against Perpetuities, no interest is good unless it must vest, if at all, during a period measured by a life or lives in being plus 21 years. Since Senior Center might begin practicing racial discrimination after the period proscribed by the Rule, the interest of Senior Life seems to violate the Rule. Because of an exception, however, the Rule Against Perpetuities does not apply to the interest of a charity which follows the interest of a charity. Since Senior Center and

Senior Life are both charitable institutions, the Rule Against Perpetuities does not apply, and the interest of Senior Life is valid. **B** is, therefore, correct, and **D** is, therefore, incorrect.

3. **B** Under Statute I (a pure notice type statute), Parton's interest would be superior to Bessie's because while Bessie's interest was unrecorded, he purchased for value and without notice of the prior conveyance. Under Statute II (a race-notice type statute) Bessie's interest would be superior even though Parton purchased for value and in good faith (i.e., without notice of the prior conveyance), because Parton's interest was not recorded before Bessie's.

4. **A** Under this recording statute (a pure race type statute), the first interest recorded is superior. Bessie's interest derives from the deed which was recorded on April 3. Since Parton's deed was not recorded until April 5, Bessie's interest had priority.

    B is incorrect because under a race type statute, all that matters is the order in which the interests were recorded. **C** is incorrect because Bessie's interest derives from the deed which was recorded on April 3. The general warranty deed by which Marcel conveyed to Parton will determine Parton's rights against Marcel. But **D** is incorrect because the recording statute determines the rights of Marcel and Bessie as against each other.

5. **A** Whether they apply the doctrine of equitable conversion, the Uniform Vendor and Purchaser Risk Act, or some other system for apportioning the risk of loss under a real estate sales contract, all jurisdictions agree that the risk of loss from causes other than the fault of the vendor passes to the vendee when he takes possession of the realty prior to closing.

    B and **C** are incorrect because passage of the risk of loss does not depend on the purchase of fire insurance by either party. **D** is incorrect because the risk of loss passed to Bryant when he took possession of the realty.

6. **C** Some jurisdictions hold that an abstractor of title impliedly warrants the abstract to be accurate; all jurisdictions agree that there is at least an implied warranty that the service will be performed in a reasonable manner. Since the right-of-way deed was properly recorded, Titleco's failure to include it in the abstract which it furnished was a breach of either the promise to perform reasonably or the implied warranty of accuracy. In either event, since Belden was an intended creditor beneficiary of the contract between Sofield and Titleco, Belden can enforce it.

    If there was an implied warranty of accuracy **A** is incorrect because liability is imposed without fault for its breach. If there was no implied warranty of accuracy, **A** is incorrect because liability may be imposed if Titleco's lack of awareness of the right-of-way resulted from its failure to act reasonably. Since the right-of-way deed from the owner of Westacre to Johnson Chemical Company was properly recorded before any of the grants of Westacre took place, it was not outside the chain of title, and **B** is incorrect. **D** is incorrect because the liability of Titleco does not depend on covenants made by Sofield.

7.　**C**　The covenant against encumbrances is a representation that there are no easements or liens burdening the realty. If the realty is, in fact, burdened by such an encumbrance, the covenant is breached and liability is imposed on the covenantor.

This is so even though the purchaser relied on assurances in addition to the covenant, and even though the grantor was unaware of the existence of the encumbrance at the time he executed the covenant. **A** and **B** are, therefore, incorrect. **D** is incorrect because there is no indication that Sofield failed to act reasonably (i.e., was "negligent").

8.　**B**　The holder of an easement may not unreasonably burden the servient estate by using it in a way not contemplated when the easement was created. Since the dangers incident to the possible leakage of poisonous materials are much greater than those incident to the possible leakage of non-poisonous materials, the change in Johnson's intended use would unreasonably burden the estate of Belden.

Since most jurisdictions agree that commercial easements in gross may be freely alienated, **A** is incorrect. Non-use of an easement created by express grant is not sufficient to terminate it unless the holder of the easement was created by deed which was properly recorded, Belden had constructive notice of it when he purchased, and would not have been justified in relying on the absence of visible encumbrances. **D** is, therefore, incorrect.

9.　**B**　Ordinarily, a tenant who abandons the premises before the expiration of the lease is liable for rent for the balance of the term. If, however, the landlord *surrenders* its rights under the lease, the tenant will be free from liability for the balance of the term. A surrender generally takes place when the landlord occupies the premises for its own purposes.

Reletting the premises for the balance of the term might also result in a surrender, but this depends on the intent of the landlord. Here, there was much other vacant space in the building, and the landlord has relet the premises for rent lower than provided in the lease, and on a month-to-month basis. Therefore, it is not likely that Lance's intent was to surrender its rights, but rather, to relet for Tollup's account (as a mitigation of damages). **A** is, therefore, incorrect. The agreement between Lance and Tollup did not restrict use of the premises to any particular activity. For this reason, the fact that the premises are not well suited to the activity which Tollup had in mind, or that Tollup is no longer licensed in the practice for which he planned to use them, is irrelevant to his liability under the lease. **C** and **D** are, therefore, incorrect.

10. **A**   Ordinarily, a tenant who abandons the premises before the expiration of the lease is liable for rent for the balance of the term.

The lease may reserve to the landlord the right to terminate the tenancy and re-enter in the event of non-payment, but **B** is incorrect because this is alternative to the right to collect rent, not the source of it. A landlord who elects to terminate the tenancy, will not be entitled to collect rent for the balance of the term. **C** is incorrect, however, because a landlord may elect not to terminate, as did Lardner, and hold the tenant for rent. **D** is incorrect because neither party to a lease may avoid obligations under it merely by giving notice, unless the lease so provides.

11. **B**   Adpo has been in continuous possession for twenty years. His possession was hostile, because it was contrary to the rights of the City of Hampshire, the land's true owner. It was open and notorious because it was not hidden, and knowledge of his possession could have been obtained by anyone who looked. Having fulfilled all the statutory requirements, he would ordinarily be correct in his assertion that he has acquired title by adverse possession. Most jurisdictions, however, prohibit the acquisition of city or state property by adverse possession. This being the only legal obstacle to Adpo's assertion, the outcome will most likely depend on whether the jurisdiction permits the acquisition of city property by adverse possession.

A is incorrect because if the possession was open and notorious as described above, it does not matter whether the actual owner ever really knew of it. Some adverse possession statutes establish a condition that the adverse possessor pay taxes on the realty during the period of his adverse possession. **C** is incorrect, however, because this statute did not contain such a requirement. An adverse possessor who occupies land under color of title may become the owner of all the land which he believed he owned, including that which he did not actually occupy. Since Adpo asserts ownership only of the land which he occupied, however, color of title is irrelevant, and **D** is incorrect.

12. **B**   Joint tenancy is a form of co-ownership in which the joint tenants have the right of survival. This means that upon the death of one joint tenant, the others receive equal shares in her interest. When Marion died, Harold and Wilhemina received equal shares of her interest. The joint tenancy of Harold and Wilhemina continued, but each held a one-half interest in the whole instead of a one-third interest. Joint tenants may convey their interests inter vivos without each other's consent, but a joint tenant's grantee takes as a tenant in common with the remaining own-

ers. Thus, upon Wilhemina's conveyance to Bernard, Bernard became a tenant in common with a one-half interest; and upon Harold's conveyance to Charles, Charles became a tenant in common with a one-half interest.

A is incorrect because as a joint tenant, Marion could not effectively pass her interest by will. Since a conveyance by a joint tenant makes the grantee a tenant in common, neither Bernard nor Charles received a joint tenancy in any part of the estate. **C** is, therefore, incorrect. **D** is incorrect for this reason, and because Allan received no interest at all under Marion's will.

13. **D**   A person may acquire title to realty by adverse possession if she occupies it without its owner's permission openly, notoriously, and continuously for the statutory period of time. This occurs because the running of a statute of limitations then makes it impossible for the adverse possessor to be judicially ejected. Since a new owner acquires the old owner's right to eject an unlawful possessor, the statutory period of limitations continues to run in spite of changes in ownership. For this reason, the fact that Stephen became the owner in 1977 did not restart the period. If the owner of the realty is under a legal disability (e.g., infancy) at the time the adverse possession begins, commencement of the statutory period is delayed until the legal disability has terminated. If the owner is not under a legal disability at the time the possession begins, however, the fact that he subsequently suffers a legal disability, or the fact that title subsequently passes to a person who is under a legal disability will have no effect on the running of the statutory period. Since there is no fact indicating that Odette was under any legal disability in 1970 when Altman began her possession of the realty, the running of the statutory period commenced at that time, and continued without interruption upon the passage of title to Stephen. **D** is, therefore, correct and **A** is, therefore, incorrect. Since only a person with a right of possession can sue to eject an unlawful possessor, the statute of limitations cannot work against the holder of a future interest. Thus, an adverse possessor acquires only the possessory interest which existed at the time of her possession. If, for example, Odette had been the holder of a life estate with a remainder in Stephen, Altman's adverse possession during Odette's life could have led only to Altman's acquisition of a life estate by adverse possession. Then, upon Odette's death in 1977, a new period of possession would have begun against Stephen's fee interest. The will by which Stephen received title spoke only upon Odette's death, however. This means that when Altman began possession in 1970, Stephen had no future interest at all. Since there is no fact to the contrary, Odette's interest must have been a fee when Altman moved on, and it was this fee which Altman acquired by adverse possession. For this reason, **B** is incorrect. **C** is incorrect for the reasons given above, because at the time Altman's adverse possession began, the holder of the fee interest (Odette) was under no disability.

14. **D**   If leased realty is taken by eminent domain, the leasehold and the reversion merge in the taker, the leasehold is terminated, and the obligation to pay rent ceases. Since both the lessor and the lessee have had something of value taken for public use, each is entitled to receive just compensation for what s/he has lost. The lessor is entitled to receive the value of the leased premises (including the value of rent to be received) minus the value of the leasehold interest which he has already conveyed. The lessee is entitled to receive the value of the lease-hold. If not for the condemnation, however, the lessee would have been required to pay rent in order to enjoy the benefits of her leasehold. Since the condemna-tion terminates that obligation, the rent which the lessee otherwise would have been required to pay should be deducted from the value of her leasehold.

A is incorrect because the taking terminates the leasehold, and with it, the obli-gation to pay rent. The Rule Against Perpetuities provides that no interest is good unless it must vest if at all within a period of time measured by a life or lives in being plus twenty-one years. Since a lessee's interest in leased premises vests at the moment the lease is executed, the Rule Against Perpetuities is inap-plicable to it. **B** is, therefore, incorrect. Since the condemnation terminates Tee-ter's obligation to pay rent for the balance of the lease term, allowing her to keep the entire $30,000 would result in her receiving more than she has actually lost. For this reason, **C** is incorrect.

15. **C**   Those who own land adjacent to a flowing body of water (i.e., riparian owners) have some rights to use that water. Under modern common law, each riparian owner has the right to make reasonable use of the water. If construction of a dam would result in the consumption of more water than is reasonably necessary, a court might hold that Upton has no right to build the dam.

A is incorrect because Upton's increased use of the water might still be reason-able. At one time it was said that no riparian owner was permitted a use which altered the natural flow of the stream. If "natural flow" is given a literal mean-ing, this would make it virtually impossible for anyo ne but the furthest down-stream owner to use the water. For this reason, the natural flow rule has given way to a rule which bases riparian rights on reasonable use. Thus, even if the dam altered the natural flow, Upton would have a right to construct it so long as his use was reasonable. **B** is, therefore, incorrect. Under the reasonable use test, Upton may dam the stream so long as doing so would not make his water use unreasonable. **D** is incorrect because this would be so even if he could accom-plish the same without damming the stream.

16. **C**   Under the existing reasonable use doctrine, when it is necessary to determine which riparian owner is entitled to water which is in limited supply, the courts consider many factors. Most important, however, is the use to which each owner puts the water. Although agricultural use is considered "higher" than most other uses, domestic or household use is universally acknowledged to be the "highest"

use of all, entitling it to priority over all other uses. Since the choice to be made is between Upton's agricultural use and Downey's household use, Downey's rights will prevail.

A is incorrect because upstream owners do not ordinarily have greater rights than downstream owners. **B** is incorrect because household use is a higher use than agricultural use. **D** is incorrect because with the retreat from the natural flow doctrine, downstream owners do not have greater rights than upstream owners.

17. **B**   Voluntary waste consists of some act by a possessory tenant which diminishes the value of the realty or otherwise "injures the inheritance." One of the ways in which it is committed is by removing minerals from the land. Ordinarily, when a life tenant commits voluntary waste, the holder of a vested remainder is entitled to bring an immediate action at law for damages. In the alternative, the remainderman may be entitled to the equitable remedies of injunction and an accounting for profits already derived from the sale of such minerals.

Although it is understood that a possessory tenant may remove minerals from realty which is good for no other purpose, or may continue removing minerals from a mine which was open when his tenancy began, neither of these exceptions applies under the facts in this case. **B** is, therefore, correct. A possessory tenant who commits voluntary waste is not entitled to retain any of the profits from his activity. For this reason, Unity Church is entitled to all profits derived from the sale of gravel, rather than merely to a proportionate share. **A** is, therefore, incorrect. It is sometimes held that the holder of a contingent remainder or a remainder subject to defeasance has no right to sue for waste until its interest vests indefeasibly. Since the remainder interest held by Unity Church is already vested, however, **C** is incorrect. The rule which permits a possessory tenant to continue removing minerals from a mine which was open when he began his tenancy is sometimes known as the "open pit" doctrine. **D** is incorrect, however, because the facts indicate that gravel had never before been mined or removed from the land.

18. **C**   Title to property may be acquired by adverse possession if the person claiming such title occupies the realty openly, notoriously, hostilely, and continuously for the statutory period. Possession is "open and notorious" if the possessor has, in general, behaved as an owner. Since Adamo occupied the premises every summer, his possession was open and notorious. Possession is "hostile" if it is contrary to the rights of the owner. Since the facts do not indicate that Adamo had the owner's permission to occupy the cabin, his occupancy was hostile. Although possession must be "continuous," it is not necessary that it be without interruptions, so long as the interruptions are consistent with the appropriate use of the realty. Since this was a summer cabin, occupancy only during the summers might have been consistent with its appropriate use. If it was, Adamo has acquired title by adverse possession. **C** is, therefore, correct. Once the period of

possession has begun, it continues to run in spite of conveyances or other changes in ownership. Thus, **A** is an inaccurate statement and is, therefore, incorrect. If the owner of realty is under a legal disability at the time adverse possession begins, computation of the period of possession does not start until the disability ends. If, however, the owner is not under a legal disability at the time adverse possession begins, subsequent legal disability or legal disability of a subsequent owner does not interrupt the running of the period. **B** is, therefore, incorrect. Because of the requirement that adverse possession be hostile to the rights of the owner, one who occupies with permission of the owner cannot acquire title by adverse possession. **D** is, therefore, incorrect.

19. **C**   Under the "Rule in Dumpor's Case," many jurisdictions hold that if a landlord consents to an assignment by the tenant, the covenant against assignment is thereafter waived and the assignee may in turn assign to another without being bound by the covenant. Although it is not certain that the court in this jurisdiction would apply the rule, **C** is the only option listed which could possibly be effective in Cole's defense, and is, therefore, correct. Courts strictly construe restraints against the alienation of leasehold interests. This means that a covenant against assignments does not prevent subleases, and vice versa. **A** is incorrect, however, because although such covenants are strictly construed, they are not void. Ordinarily, an assignment made in violation of a covenant not to assign is valid, and the landlord has no remedy other than an action for damages resulting from the breach. Where, as here, however, the landlord reserves the right to terminate the lease in the event of a violation of the covenant, the assignment is voidable at the landlord's election. **B** is, therefore, incorrect. An assignment is a transfer of all remaining rights under a lease; a sublease is a transfer of less than all remaining rights. Since Boyer transferred all remaining rights to Cole, the transfer was an assignment, and **D** is incorrect.

20. **C**   An easement is a right to use the land of another. If the right benefits a parcel of realty, that parcel is known as the dominant estate. The parcel which is burdened by the easement is known as the servient estate. If the dominant estate and the servient estate were owned by the same person. and if a right-of-way easement across the servient estate is necessary to provide access to the dominant estate, the sale of either parcel results in an implied easement by necessity. Since Northacre and Southacre were both owned by Archer, and since the only access to Northacre was over the dirt road which crossed Southacre, Barnhart received an implied easement by necessity over Southacre when he purchased it. **C** is, therefore, correct. When the common owner of two parcels uses one of them for the benefit of the other, and when signs of that use are visible, a quasi-easement may exist which passes by implication to the buyer of the parcel which received the benefit of such use. **A** is incorrect, however, because Archer never actually used Northacre or the dirt road which crossed Southacre. A grantor of realty may reserve for himself an easement to use it, and under some circumstances (e.g.,

strict necessity), such a reservation may be implied. **B** is incorrect, however, because only a grantor can receive an easement by reservation. Ordinarily, an easement of record benefits subsequent owners of the dominant estate even if it is not mentioned in the deeds by which the dominant estate was conveyed to them. When the dominant estate and the servient estate merge (i.e., are owned by the same person), however, all existing easements terminate. **D** is, therefore, incorrect.

21. **B**   Although the existence of an easement may make title to realty unmarketable, most courts hold that this is not so where the buyer was aware of the easement at the time he contracted to purchase the realty. Since Coates saw the dirt road prior to contracting, it is likely that a court would hold that its existence does not prevent the title from being marketable. While it is not certain that a court would come to this conclusion, the argument in **B** is the only one listed which could possibly provide support for Archer's claim. **B** is, therefore, correct. If a buyer accepts a deed which does not conform to the requirements of the purchases contract, he has waived his rights under the contract because the contract is said to merge with the deed. **A** is incorrect, however, because Coates did not accept the deed and so is still protected by the terms of the contract. Marketable title means title that is reasonably secure against attack. Since the existence of an easement would provide the holder of a dominant estate with a ground to attack the rights of the holder of the servient estate, an undisclosed easement is usually sufficient to render title to the servient estate unmarketable. **C** is, therefore, incorrect. A covenant to deliver marketable title is implied in a contract for the sale of realty unless some other quality of title is specified. Since the contract between Archer and Coates did not specify the quality of title to be conveyed, Archer is required to convey marketable title. **D** is, therefore, incorrect.

22. **A**   Every contract for the sale of realty contains an implied covenant by the seller that he will deliver marketable title. Marketable title means title which is reasonably secure against attack. It is generally understood that title to property which is being used in violation of a zoning law is not marketable. If a seller is unable to deliver marketable title, the buyer is not required to complete the transaction because no person should be required to purchase potential litigation. Since Foley's agreement to purchase the house was connected with his purchase of the business, it is likely that a court would find that the zoning violation constitutes a defect which excuses Foley from going through with the purchase. Although it is not certain that a court would come to this conclusion, **A** is the only option which could possibly be correct. **B** and **C** are incorrect because the courts usually hold that an existing zoning violation makes title unmarketable. **D** is incorrect because a public law which prohibits a particular activity takes precedence over a private rule which permits it.

23. **A**   Ordinarily zoning laws determine the use to which land may be put. Thus, if the zoning law permits the construction of a three story office building, Graves may construct it. **A** is, therefore, correct. **B** is incorrect because there is no rule which requires a court to permit the highest and best use of realty. Although an easement for air, light, and view may be created by express grant, **C** is incorrect because courts do not recognize an implied easement for air, light, or view. If land was being used in a way which violates a zoning law passed after the use began, the non-conforming use is permitted to continue. **D** is incorrect, however, because the non-conforming use is never *required* to continue.

24. **C**   Developers are permitted to create conditions on the use of land in their subdivisions which are more restrictive than public laws. Thus, even where zoning law permits a particular activity, deed restrictions may validly prohibit it. Since restrictions contained in all the deeds to land in Green Hills prohibit the keeping of horses, a court will enforce these restrictions, and Ralph should receive the relief which he seeks. **C** is, therefore, correct, and **A** is, therefore, incorrect. Where a zoning law restricts land to residential use but does not define that use, the resolution of a dispute about whether that activity can be conducted there will depend on whether that activity is part of ordinary residential use. **B** is incorrect, however, because the deed restrictions in Green Hills clearly prohibit the keeping of horses. Although a court may enjoin a nuisance, **D** is incorrect because a court may enforce the deed restrictions without regard to whether keeping horses is a nuisance.

25. **C**   A fee simple determinable on special limitation is a fee interest which will terminate automatically upon the happening of a specified event. Courts almost always hold that a grant to a particular grantee "so long as" something does not happen creates this interest. **C** is, therefore, correct. Although an interest which might vest after a period measured by a life or lives in being plus twenty one years is void under the rule against perpetuities, this does not affect the validity of any prior estate. For this reason, even if the interest of the Foundation for Hereditary Diseases violates this rule against perpetuities, that has no effect on the validity of Geller's interest. **A** is, therefore, incorrect. A fee simple absolute is complete ownership which is not subject to defeasance. **B** is incorrect because of the special limitation created by the phrase "so long as." A fee simple subject to a condition subsequent is an interest which is subject to defeasance on the happening of a specified event, but which does not terminate until the holder of the future interest takes some step to make his/her interest possessory. **D** is incorrect because the phrase "so long as" results in an automatic termination upon the happening of the specified event and because the period described by the rule against perpetuities has no effect on an interest which is already possessory.

26. **C** Under the rule against perpetuities, no interest is good unless it must vest, if at all, during a period measured by a life or lives in being plus twenty one years. Since liquor might be sold on the premises after the expiration of this period, it is possible that the interest of the Foundation for Hereditary diseases would vest beyond the period of perpetuities. For this reason, its interest is void. **C** is, therefore, correct. The future interest of a charity is not subject to the rule against perpetuities if it follows the estate of another charity. Otherwise, the rule against perpetuities applies as it would to any other grantee. **A** is incorrect because there is no indication that Geller is a charity. **B** is incorrect because only a grantor can hold a right of re-entry. An executory interest is a future interest which follows an estate which is not certain to terminate. If it follows the estate of a grantor, it is a springing executory interest. **D** is incorrect, however, because the interest of the Foundation for Hereditary Diseases is void as explained above.

ESSAY EXAM QUESTIONS & ANSWERS

The following Essay Questions are taken from the *Real Property* volume of *Siegel's Essay & Multiple-Choice Questions and Answers*, a series written by Brian Siegel and published by us. The full volume contains 25 essays (with model answers), as well as 96 multiple choice questions (The essay questions were originally asked on the California Bar Exam, and are copyright the California Board of Bar Examiners, reprinted by permission.) The book is available from your bookstore, or directly from www.aspenpublishers.com.

QUESTION 1

Landlord rented a furnished apartment in his building to Tenant, a law student, for two years, beginning June 1. When Tenant arrived at the apartment on June 1, Ralph (the prior tenant) was still there. Tenant complained to Landlord and Landlord was able to evict Ralph on June 15. Tenant went into possession of the apartment on June 16. During early July, some children playing baseball broke a windowpane in Tenant's apartment. Tenant demanded that Landlord replace the windowpane, but Landlord refused. Rain, which subsequently came through the broken pane, caused damage to the living room floor, which began to warp.

The apartment above Tenant's was occupied by Charlie, a member of a famous rock group (The Charles River). The daily rehearsals (typically 2:00-6:00 p.m.) of this group interfered with Tenant's law studies so much that he complained repeatedly to Landlord. On July 15, three of Charlie's friends (the other members of Charlie's band) were arrested at Charlie's apartment and charged with possession of narcotics. The noise stopped immediately thereafter.

On August 30, Tenant discovered that the stove in his apartment was no longer functioning. On August 31, Tenant, disgusted with all these events, knocked on Landlord's door, tendered the key to Landlord, and said, "This place is a zoo; I wouldn't live here if you paid me!" Landlord took the key without saying a word. Landlord now comes to you wanting to sue Tenant for the accrued (Tenant has yet to pay any rent) and prospective rent. What would you advise Landlord? Discuss.

QUESTION 2

Alice has just shown you a deed which was recorded 40 years ago. This document reads as follows:

In consideration of love and affection, I hereby grant Sweetholm to my friend Josiah and the heirs of his body, this conveyance to take effect 10 years from the date hereof, provided that if Josiah dies without issue the estate is to go to my brother Ludwig and his heirs, and further provided that if animals, birds or children are ever kept on the property, the estate is to cease and determine.

[Signed] Vladimir

You ascertain from Alicia that her house, with its surrounding grounds of about 10 acres, is known as Sweetholm. Alicia tells you that she bought Sweetholm from Josiah's niece, Jennifer, 11 years ago. The deed transferred to Alicia "all my right, title and interest in Sweetholm." Alicia also tells you that when she bought the property the guest house near the southwest boundary of the estate was occupied by Danny, Jennifer's cousin. Danny had visited Jennifer 12 years ago and decided to stay to work on a novel. Jennifer had asked Alicia to let Danny stay there for awhile, "since he was finding himself." Alicia said it would probably be "all right, if Danny did not get in my way." Alicia thought it might be a good idea to have a male on the property to frighten away prospective thieves. Soon after Jennifer vacated Sweetholm, Danny built a separate mailbox outside the guest house and placed a doormat in front of the entrance, which read "Welcome to Danny's."

It seems that the estate bordering Sweetholm on the west, Laurel Hill, had been purchased 14 years ago by Wilson, a scientist doing research on the territorial habits of wild dogs, coyotes and wolves. Wilson had captured several wolves and brought them to Laurel Hill. When Alicia took over the property from Jennifer, Wilson talked to her about the wolves. Alicia promised him, in a valid writing, that she would allow the wolves to wander freely over Sweetholm. The wolves soon manifested their territorial behavior and took up residence on the southwest corner of Sweetholm.

Unfortunately, when Danny saw one of the animals wandering around near the guest house about 2 months ago, he suddenly took it into his head that it would make a nice pet. He enticed it into his enclosed patio and kept it there, even when it resisted his first efforts to make friends and bit his hand when he tried to feed it.

About a week ago Alicia received an unpleasant visit from Trivers, Wilson's co-experimenter, who had purchased Laurel Hill from Wilson last summer. Trivers threatened to sue Alicia because Danny had tampered with a subject involved in his experiment. Alicia became upset with the whole thing and evicted both Danny and the wolves from Sweetholm that very evening. Alicia hastily had a chicken wire fence constructed on the western boundary of Sweetholm so that the wolves could not get back in. Last night, (1) Danny called and claimed that he owned the guest house, and (2) Trivers called and threatened to obtain an injunction requiring Alicia to remove the chicken wire fence.

Alicia asks you whether Trivers and Danny really have any viable claims against her. She also wants to know whether there are any other people who might show up to claim an interest in Sweetholm.

In response to initial questioning from you, Alicia tells you that Vladimir is dead and Josef is his sole heir; that Ludwig is dead and Richard is his sole heir; and that Josiah is also dead, but Jennifer, his niece and only heir, is still alive. You have also learned that the Statute of Limitations for actions to recover real property is 10 years. Please evaluate the possible claims of Danny, Trivers, and any other person(s) you think might have a plausible claim to some interest in Sweetholm.

QUESTION 3

Art was the record owner of Greenacre, a vacant tract of land. Art and Bob discussed the sale of this land to Bob, and they orally agreed on a purchase price of $5,000 in cash. Art then typed up a statement setting forth all the terms that had been agreed upon, including the fact that Art would deliver to Carl, a real estate broker, a warranty deed conveying Greenacre to Bob and that Carl would hand deliver the deed to Bob if Bob gave Carl the purchase price within one month.

Art placed one copy of this statement, unsigned, unwitnessed and undated, in an envelope and mailed it to Bob. Upon receiving it, Bob telephoned Art and told him that the statement accurately reflected his understanding and that he would deliver $5,000 in cash to Carl within the month in accordance with their agreement.

Art then executed the warranty deed, complete in all respects, and gave it to Carl with a copy of his statement.

One week later, Art learned that a highway was to be built near Greenacre, greatly increasing its value. Art immediately wrote to Carl, telling Carl he had changed his mind and wanted the deed returned to him.

One day later and before Carl had received Art's last letter, Bob called Carl and said he had to show the deed to his bank to obtain a loan for the $5,000. Carl sent the deed to Bob, who promptly recorded it and immediately executed and delivered a warranty deed for Greenacre to Dale.

Bob has disappeared and has not paid the $5,000 to Art or Carl.

(1) In an action to quiet title between Art and Dale, who prevails? Discuss.

(2) What are the rights of Art and Dale against Carl? Discuss.

ANSWERS

ANSWER TO QUESTION 1

Assumptions: The lease was written and signed by Tenant (and so there is no Statute of Frauds problem even though the lease in question exceeded one year).

To advise Landlord ("LL") of his rights against Tenant ("T") it is initially necessary to determine if T can successfully assert any defenses against LL.

Duty to Deliver Possession: Under the English rule, a landlord has the obligation to assure his/her tenant that no other party will be in possession of the premises when the lease term commences. T might assert that LL breached his duty, since Ralph was in the apartment when T's lease term began. However, even assuming this jurisdiction adheres to this rule that the landlord must evict holdover tenants, T has probably waived (voluntarily relinquished a known right) this breach by going into possession of premises after Ralph moved out. At most, T can probably deduct the rent attributable to the period from June 1 through June 15. If the American view is followed, LL has the duty only to deliver *legal* possession, not actual possession, so the holdover (Ralph) would be T's problem.

Constructive Eviction ("CE"): A CE occurs where there is a substantial interference with a tenant's right of quiet enjoyment by reason of some cause for which the landlord is responsible, and the tenant vacates within a reasonable time thereafter. T might argue that a CE occurred by reason of (i) the noise caused by Charlie's friends, (ii) the broken window pane and warped floor, and (iii) the stove's malfunction.

In response, however, LL could assert the following arguments. With respect to the noises caused by Charlie's band, LL is not responsible for the activities of other tenants. In some states, where the lease contains a provision permitting the landlord to evict lessees who are disturbing other tenants, the landlord has been deemed responsible for the former. However, there is nothing in the given facts to indicate such a clause exists. Additionally, even assuming the band noise persisted from June 15th through July 15th (when 3 persons in the band were arrested), this probably did not constitute a substantial deprivation of T's right to the beneficial enjoyment of the premises since it occurred during daylight hours (rather than in the evening), when other tenants would be trying to sleep. Finally, LL could probably successfully argue that T waived the right to assert a CE by waiting 45 days after the noise had ceased to vacate the premises.

As to the broken window pane and consequent warped floor, LL could argue that, at common law, it is T's duty to make repairs, so T cannot complain about being deprived of the beneficial enjoyment of the premises when the condition which made them unsuitable was T's fault. As to the malfunctioning stove, LL could argue (1) again, this was T's responsibility, and (2) T apparently never even advised LL about this problem, and so he did not have the requisite opportunity to remedy this situation.

The Implied Warranty of Habitability: Many states recognize an implied warranty of habitability that leased premises will not become uninhabitable by reason of the landlord's failure to make repairs attributable to the natural deterioration of the premises. (A few jurisdictions limit this doctrine to situations involving housing code violations.) T might argue that defects vital to the use of the premises existed by reason of (i) the broken pane and consequent warping, and (ii) the malfunctioning stove.

The warping was the result of the failure to repair the window; so whoever had the responsibility for repairing would be liable for the warped floor. LL can argue that the widows should have been repaired by T since (1) the pane was broken by other persons (the children playing ball), as opposed to the natural deterioration of the premises, and (2) a broken window is not a defect which causes premises to become uninhabitable. As to the non-functioning stove, LL can argue that the stove would not cause premises to fall below the bar living requirements.

Finally, LL was (apparently) never even informed of this event.

LL should prevail against T on this issue too.

Surrender: T will also probably argue that LL's acceptance of the keys to the apartment constituted a surrender, so that therefore T is not liable for any rent accruing after August 31. However, the fact that LL merely permitted T to hand the keys to him probably does not, without more, demonstrate a willingness to permit T to avoid his prospective obligations under the lease.

Advice/Extent of LL's Recovery: (We'll assume that rent was payable monthly, and that the lease did ***not*** have an accelerated rent or liquidated damage clause.)

LL should be able to recover T's unpaid rent, and for the additional rentals as they become due. However, LL should probably attempt to locate a new tenant for the premises since (1) many states require a landlord to mitigate a tenant's liability, and (2) it may be difficult for LL to recover any judgment against T (even if one were obtained). Finally, LL should be advised to notify T that any subletting is being done for T's account. This precaution would preclude T from contending that a surrender of the premises had occurred via the subletting.

ANSWER TO QUESTION 2

Adverse Possession ("AP"): One obtains title to real property by AP where he/she, under a claim of right, enters upon and exclusively occupies another's land in an open, notorious and hostile manner throughout the requisite statutory period. Danny ("D") could claim that by remaining at Sweetholm after the sale to Alicia ("A") without the latter's explicit permission, the "claim of right" and "hostile" elements are satisfied. Additionally, creating a separate mailbox and putting out a welcome sign which bore his name met the "open" and "notorious" requisites. Finally, D's occupation of the guest house continued for a period of time in excess of the applicable Statute of Limitations. Thus, D could assert ownership to the guest house (along with an easement hereto and therefrom) under AP.

In some jurisdictions, the claim of right requirement is not satisfied unless the adverse claimant went upon the land with the belief that he/she was entitled to possess it. If this were such a jurisdiction, D's claim of AP would fail. In most states, however, the claim of right element is satisfied merely by the adverse possessor being aware that his/her habitation of the land in question was without the owner's permission. If this jurisdiction adhered to the latter view, A could contend that Jennifer ("J") had presumably advised D of her statement that it would be "all right" for D to remain on Sweetholm. If it could be shown that J had so informed D, A should prevail on this issue.

A could alternatively claim that D's occupation of the guest house was ***not*** "hostile." While this element is usually satisfied by the claimant's use of the land in an "open and notorious" manner, an exception to this rule exists where the rightful owner would not necessarily recognize that the adverse possessor's occupation of the land is hostile to his/her ownership interest (even though aware of it). In such situations the adverse claimant must communicate (via clear words or actions) that the land is being held in derogation of the legal owner's rights thereto. Holdover tenancies often constitute such a situation, since a holdover tenant is usually deemed to be occupying the premises with the landlord's implicit permission.

A could contend that D should be viewed as either having been her guest (i.e., a continuation of the relationship which D enjoyed with J) or a tenant at sufferance. In either event, D would have been obliged to either (1) inform A that his occupation of the guest house was hostile to A's claim of ownership thereto, or (2) have done acts which clearly communicated this view (i.e., prevented A from entering the structure, built a fence around it, etc.). The mailbox would not suffice, since A could have presumed that while D had felt comfortable in permitting J (his cousin) to receive his mail, he would not have the same trust in a stranger. Finally, A would assert that the doormat was not adequate to inform her that D was claiming superior title to the guest house.

A would probably prevail upon the "hostile" issue, and therefore it is unlikely that D would prevail upon his claim of AP.

If, however, D's claim of AP were successful, he would have a right of action against A for evicting him. D would probably be entitled to recover the reasonable rental value of the land during his eviction, as well as any other costs and expenses attendant upon the interference with his right to possession.

Injunction sought by Trivers ("T"): T might initially contend that A had granted an express easement to Wilson ("W") to permit animals involved in the experiment to roam throughout Sweetholm, and easements will automatically run with the benefitted estate.

A would initially argue that the right given to W was a license. An easement is ordinarily described as the right of one person to make a particular use of another's land. A license, however, is usually defined as the right to do a particular thing on another's land. A could assert that no right was granted to W to *use* her land. Rather, A merely indicated that W's wolves could randomly traverse Sweetholm. Thus, A would contend that the grant made to W was a license, and such interests are (1) ordinarily *not* assignable, and (2) revocable at any time by the licensor (subject to the licensee's right to recover for monetary damages resulting from the revocation). However, T could argue in rebuttal that since he was engaged in an experiment whereby the wolves wandered onto A's land, W (and now T) was actually *using* the land for a particular purpose (i.e., to record the results of an experiment).

Even assuming the grant to W was an easement, A could contend that it was an easement in gross (rather than an appurtenant easement). Such easements are ordinarily non-assignable. Easements in gross are those which *personally* benefit the holder thereof (as opposed to easements appurtenant, which primarily benefit the latter's *land*). The grant in question appears to have been made for the purpose of facilitating W's experiment (rather than enhancing the use or accessibility of Laurel Hill). While T could argue that the use of Laurel Hill is enhanced by having the right to permit animals involved in experimentation to cross into adjoining land, A's grant would probably be characterized as an easement in gross.

T might contend, however, even assuming the grant to W was deemed to be an easement in gross, it should be viewed as being "commercial" in nature. Such interests have been deemed to be irrevocable where, for example, a severe disruption to a utility (i.e., telephone and sewer lines) would occur. Although T could contend that maintenance of the fence by A would disrupt an experiment which has been carried on for a 14-year period, it is unlikely that T's easement in gross would be considered "commercial." Thus, A would probably prevail on this question.

Finally, T might argue that A's written statement to W, whereby A had agreed that she would take no action to prevent W's animals from coming upon Sweetholm, constituted a covenant which ran with the benefitted land. Since T is seeking an injunction, the covenant must be analyzed as an equitable servitude ("ES"). For the benefit of an ES to run against the covenantor: (1) the original parties must have intended it to run, and (2) it must touch and concern (affect the value or use) of the burdened land. Although there was no "successors, heirs and assigns" language, some courts take the view that where the promise touches and concerns the burdened parcel, the original parties probably intended for the covenantor's promise to run with the benefitted land. The value and use of Sweetholm is arguably diminished by the fact that wild animals could roam free on a portion of the land. However, A could probably successfully contend in rebuttal that there was no intent that the promise run with the land since it was given specifically to *W* for the purpose of permitting the latter to complete *his* experimentation.

Thus, T probably *cannot* obtain an injunction against A.

Ownership of Sweetholm: Richard (Ludwig's sole heir) could contend that the conveyance by Vladimir to Josiah was a fee tail (since the grant to Josiah is followed by the words "and the heirs of his body"). Therefore, when Josiah died without issue (J was merely his niece, rather than a lineal descendant), Sweetholm became the property of Ludwig (and his heirs).

A could argue in rebuttal that in many states the fee tail has been abolished entirely, and it is viewed as a fee simple absolute. In such case, Josiah would have been entitled to transfer the property to J. In other jurisdictions, however, the failure to have issue results in the estate terminating upon the death of the originally designated party. Under the latter view, Ludwig's heirs (Richard) would obtain title to Sweetholm upon Josiah's death. However, in such instance A could probably claim superior title to Sweetholm through AP. While it is not clear when Josiah died and J succeeded to possession of Sweetholm, the facts do indicate that A has apparently occupied the realty for 11 years and paid taxes on it. Having purchased the land from J, A presumably went into possession of Sweetholm under color of title. It therefore appears that A could defeat any claim of Richard to the property. Richard's remainder is vested, so it is not subject to the RAP.

Josef could, however, contend that J had a fee simple determinable or fee simple subject to a condition subsequent with respect to the provision pertaining to animals, and that the triggering event occurred when D retained one of the animals for a two-week period. However, A could contend in rebuttal that whichever future interest was held by Josef is unenforceable because implicit in the grant was that the **grantee** (rather than some other person who undertook such conduct without the owner's knowledge or consent) would not "keep" animals on Sweetholm. A should prevail on this argument, and therefore it is unlikely that Josef could presently claim paramount title to Sweetholm.

ANSWER TO QUESTION 3

(1) **Dale v. Art (quiet title action):** In an action by Dale ("D") to quiet title to Greenacre ("G/A") against Art ("A"), A can be expected to contend that Bob ("B") could not have conveyed G/A to D because no conveyance of G/A was made to B; and thus B had nothing to transfer to D. A transfer of land does not occur until there is delivery (completion of a valid deed by the grantor, with the intention that it be immediately operative) and acceptance of the deed by the grantee. Where an escrow has been established, there is usually a presumption that the grantor intended that the deed **not** be immediately operative until the conditions of the escrow are satisfied. Since the condition precedent to the deed being operative (the payment of $5,000 by B) never occurred, B never acquired title to G/A to transfer to D.

D, however, could contend that A should be equitably estopped from denying that the transfer to D was invalid. Some states have adopted the rule that where a grantee wrongfully acquires a deed from an escrow holder chosen by the grantor and then conveys the land to a bona fide purchaser ("BFP"), the grantor is estopped from denying the validity of the transfer against the latter. Assuming D parted with present consideration to acquire G/A (the facts are silent on this point), D would seem to be a BFP (since the land was vacant, a visit to G/A would not have put D upon inquiry notice of A's ownership interest). Also, since A had given B a warranty deed (as opposed to a quitclaim deed), D would have no reason to investigate B's title beyond a search of the grantor-grantee index.

Assuming D were a BFP, D would additionally contend that there is a maxim in the law that where one of two innocent parties must suffer, the loss should fall upon the more blameworthy person; and that such person is A since (1) A chose Carl, who incorrectly parted with possession of the deed, and (2) by giving Carl a "clean" deed (one with no conditions upon the face of it), A should have realized that it would be possible for B, if he ever obtained the deed from Carl, to "sell" G/A. While A might contend in rebuttal that escrows are a common device for transferring ownership of land and that Carl, as a real estate broker, should have been well aware of the potential for harm if the deed left his possession, D should prevail in his quiet title action against A (even though no actual conveyance took place).

(2a.) **Art v. Carl ("C"):** A would probably sue C for breach of contract and negligence. With respect to the former, C could contend that he has no liability because (1) no contract ever arose between him and A, since C (apparently) received no consideration, and (2) in any event, the Statute of Frauds (which pertains to the sale of land) was never satisfied, since C never signed the statement prepared by A. However, it would probably be implied into the A-C arrangement that the latter would receive a reasonable compensation for this efforts on behalf of A and B. Additionally, equitable estoppel could probably be successfully asserted to overcome these contentions, since A detrimentally relied upon C to act as escrow agent.

While C might next assert that A's damages are limited to $5,000 (the amount he would have received if the escrow had closed), rather than the enhanced value of the land, A should be able to successfully argue in rebuttal that since the conditions for the close of the escrow were never satisfied, he would have been able to recover the deed back. Therefore, he should be able to recover the present fair market value of G/A from C.

A would also contend that C, by agreeing to act as escrow agent, assumed a duty to A that he would not leave A in a worsened position; and so when C did, he became liable to A in negligence. While C might contend that he could only foresee damages of $5,000, A could probably successfully argue in rebuttal that C should have foreseen that (1) misdelivery of the deed could result in greater damages to A since A would have obtained the deed back at the conclusion of the escrow period, and (2) G/A might appreciate in value. Thus A's damages would again be the reasonable value of G/A.

(2b.) **D v. C:** If D paid consideration for the deed received from B and lost his quiet title action against A, he would probably sue C in negligence for permitting B to obtain control of A's deed; and thereby defraud D of whatever consideration he paid to B. While C might argue that he had no duty to D (who did not rely upon C) and that B's fraudulent actions were the actual cause of D's loss, D should be able to recover from C the consideration which was given to B (C should have reasonably foreseen that B might misuse A's deed, especially since it was absolute on its face).

SUBJECT MATTER INDEX

This index includes references to the Capsule Summary
and to the Exam Tips, but not to Q&A or Flow Charts

Rule of law, not construction, 43

SHIFTING INTERESTS
See EXECUTORY INTERESTS

SPRINGING INTERESTS
See EXECUTORY INTERESTS

STATUTE OF FRAUDS
Covenants, 72
Easements, 66
Land-sale contracts, 85

STATUTE OF USES
Generally, 44-45
Contingent remainder, destructibility of, 46
Conveyancing after, 44
Future interests after, 39
Present status of, 45
Unexecuted uses, 45

SUBDIVISION CONTROL
See ZONING, 82

TENANCY BY THE ENTIRETY
See ENTIRETY, TENANCY BY THE

TENANCY IN COMMON
See COMMON, TENANCY IN

TITLE ASSURANCE
Generally, 98-99
Covenants for title, 98
Lawyer, examination by, 98
Title insurance, 98
    Duty to make reasonable search, 96
    Scope of coverage, 99
    Zoning and building code violations, 58, 59,
        61, 80, 87

TITLE COVENANTS
Generally, 91-92, 148-149
Against encumbrances, 91, 92
Easement as breach of, 149
Further assurance, 91
Further covenants, 91, 92
How breached, 91
Measure of damages for breach, 92
Present covenants, 91-92
Prior knowledge of defect, 58, 92
Quiet enjoyment and warranty, 56, 91, 92
Right to convey, 91, 92
Running of, 92
Seisin, 91, 92
Statute of Limitations, 91
Types of, 89
When breached, 91, 92

TITLE REGISTRATION (THE TORRENS SYSTEM)
Generally, 98
Conclusiveness of certificate, 98

Fraud or forgery, 98
Insurance funds, 88, 94, 98
Involuntary liens and transfers, 86, 91
Mechanics of, 94
Nature of, 89-90
Tax liens, 94

TORRENS SYSTEMS
See TITLE REGISTRATION

TOTTEN TRUST, 32

USES
After Statute of Uses, 44, 45
Bargain and sale, 45
Prior to Statute of Uses, 68

WARRANTY OF HABITABILITY
See LANDLORD AND TENANT
    Sale of house, 58

WASTE
Generally, 38, 112-113
Acts constituting, 38, 112-113
Earth and minerals, mining of as, 113
Remedies for, 58
Timber, cutting of as, 112

WATER RIGHTS
Generally, 100-101, 153
Drainage, 82, 100
Ground water
    Subsidence of neighboring land, 101
Prior appropriation doctrine, 101
Riparian rights under common law, 101
    "Reasonable use", 101

WILD ANIMALS
Rights in, 29

WORTHIER TITLE, DOCTRINE OF
Generally, 44
Inter vivos branch, 31, 32, 39, 40, 43, 44
    Rule of Construction, 44

ZONING
Generally, 77-82
"Takings" clause
    Rough proportionality required for give-
        backs, 78
Abandonment of non-conforming use, 140
Aesthetic zoning, 80, 139
Conditional ("contract") zoning, 80
Density controls, 79
Due process limits on
    Procedural, 79
    Substantive, 79
Equal Protection Clause, 80, 81
Exclusionary zoning, 81-82

The Emanuel Law Outline Series

Each outline in the series is the work of Steven Emanuel. Each is packed with features that take you from next-day preparation to night-before-the-exam review. Outlines are available for all major law school subjects and many are revised annually. This year, Steve will prepare new editions of Evidence, Constitutional Law, Torts, Criminal Procedure and Property.

Available titles
Civil Procedure
Constitutional Law
Contracts
Corporations
Criminal Law
Criminal Procedure
Evidence
Property
Torts (General Edition)
Torts (Prosser Edition)

Law In A Flash Series

Flashcards add a dimension to law school study which cannot be matched by any other study aid, and these are the acknowledged leader in flashcards. They make legal issues and answers stick to your mind like glue. Each Law In a Flash card set contains 350-625 cards arranged to give you black-letter principles first. Then they teach you all the subtleties by taking you through a series of hypotheticals filled with mnemonics and checklists. Excellent for exam preparation.

Available titles
Civil Procedure 1
Civil Procedure 2
Constitutional Law
Contracts
Corporations
Criminal Law
Criminal Procedure
Evidence
Federal Income Taxation
Future Interests
Professional Responsibility
Real Property
Sales (UCC Article 2)
Torts
Wills & Trusts